SEVENTH EDITION

CONTEMPORARY ISSUES IN LEADERSHIP

SEVENTH EDITION

CONTEMPORARY ISSUES IN LEADERSHIP

Edited by

William E. Rosenbach,

Robert L. Taylor,

and

Mark A. Youndt

WESTVIEW PRESS

A MEMBER OF THE PERSEUS BOOKS GROUP

Westview Press was founded in 1975 in Boulder, Colorado, by notable publisher and intellectual Fred Praeger. Westview Press continues to publish scholarly titles and high-quality undergraduate- and graduate-level textbooks in core social science disciplines. With books developed, written, and edited with the needs of serious nonfiction readers, professors, and students in mind, Westview Press honors its long history of publishing books that matter.

Published by Westview Press,
A Member of the Perseus Books Group

Find us on the World Wide Web at www.westviewpress.com.

Every effort has been made to secure required permissions for all text, images, maps, and other art reprinted in this volume.

Westview Press books are available at special discounts for bulk purchases in the United States by corporations, institutions, and other organizations. For more information, please contact the Special Markets Department at the Perseus Books Group, 2300 Chestnut Street, Suite 200, Philadelphia, PA 19103, or call (800) 810-4145, ext. 5000, or e-mail special.markets@perseusbooks.com.

Library of Congress Cataloging-in-Publication Data

Contemporary issues in leadership / edited by William E. Rosenbach, Robert L. Taylor, and Mark A. Youndt. — 7th ed.
    p. cm.
Includes bibliographical references.
  ISBN 978-0-8133-4557-4 (pbk. : alk. paper) — ISBN 978-0-8133-4560-4 (e-book) 1. Leadership. I. Rosenbach, William E. II. Taylor, Robert L. (Robert Lewis), 1939– III. Youndt, Mark A.
  HM1261.C69 2012
  303.3'4—dc23
                              2011041417

Contents

— I —

HEART

— II —

RELATIONSHIPS

Exhibits, Tables, and Figures

FIGURES

Preface

The seventh edition is substantially different from previous editions. We include only five chapters from earlier editions. Two chapters that were original pieces written for the sixth edition have been revised and join the eighteen new chapters for a total of twenty-five chapters. You will find that the materials in this edition come from a variety of academic, professional, and practitioner-oriented publications from North America and abroad. Through electronic and manual searches, we initially identified more than 2,500 articles that dealt with some aspect of leadership and were published after the preparation of the last edition in 2005. We found that the majority of these did not warrant further consideration because they were too technical or narrow in scope or overly simple, "how-to" checklists. The present twenty-five chapters were selected from several hundred publications that crossed cultural, disciplinary, and organizational boundaries. The broad perspective of this edition provides a deeper appreciation and understanding of the ambiguity, dilemmas, and paradox associated with leadership. Some of the authors and the context in which they write provide interesting cultural perspectives on leadership.

Our search of the literature yielded a number of publications that deal with the concept of self-leadership, several of which are included in this book. We are pleased to find that followership continues to gain recognition as a legitimate and necessary component of leadership and that the reciprocal relationship between leader and followers is increasingly becoming the subject of study and research. In many ways, understanding the elements of effective followership provides important insights to leaders and how they lead. These articles should stimulate discussion and insight and for that reason, we have included five chapters on followers and followership in Part II.

We added a third editor for this edition to begin the transition to a new generation, ensuring that the title word, "contemporary," remains meaningful. Mark Youndt joins us to provide a contemporary perspective. His academic and professional experience yielded a new network for us that links us with current leadership issues, concerns, and perspectives. In addition, his experience working abroad increases our knowledge of international leadership issues and provides us with more breadth.

There are five parts to this edition. Part I focuses on the leader and the process of leadership. Five chapters describe concepts of leadership that range from self-leadership and transactional and transformational leadership to transcendental leadership and the intersection of self, group, and organizational leadership. We examine the heart of leadership. This leads to the realization that leadership development is an important piece in understanding character and context. Finally, we discuss the paradox of the dual role of leader and follower.

Part II extends the examination of the dynamic relationships between the leader and the followers. There are interesting variations to consider, and, as a result, we provide one model of follower styles along with a strategy for developing followers as partners and the implication of leader and follower switching roles.

In Part III we examine the leadership journey that starts with self-awareness and self-knowledge. Barriers to successful leadership development are discussed along with suggestions for avoiding or overcoming them. Two chapters describe the barriers women face on their leadership journey and how they can navigate the labyrinth of leadership and the choices they may have to make.

The hazards facing leaders are presented in Part IV. Success as a leadership trap is discussed along with emphasis on transparency and narcissism. How leaders become "bad" or toxic is discussed along with a description of how they got that way and how to avoid them. We also provide some insight as to how we often inhibit our opportunities to lead effectively.

Finally, in Part V we explore the soul of leadership with discussions of authenticity, morals, values, social responsibility, and organizational culture and the paradox and points of intersection associated with those leadership imperatives. In many ways, we believe this is the one area where we want readers to read, cogitate, and embrace. Leadership is not inherent or mechanical—it is a matter of who we are, what we believe, and the choices we make. We close with a bit of irony. Some seventy years ago, John Gardner wrote an essay called "The Antileadership Vaccine," which at the time stimulated a great deal of debate. It is a classic and, we believe, as relevant today as it was then. We trust you will appreciate his thoughts as well.

In this edition we recognize the critical need for effective leadership beyond the business environment. We provide leadership contexts in government, not-for-profit organizations, the military, education, and social movements. An exciting discovery was the increased resources from international journals on leadership and the realization that the issues in other places are not very different from the ones we have described in prior editions. We are grateful to the authors and publishers of the readings included in this edition as well as to our students and colleagues, who continue to ask questions about leadership that have no easy answers. We thank our colleagues from around the world who provided suggestions, meaningful feedback, and thoughtful criticism, which resulted in a much better book. Continuing support from our editors, Anthony Wahl and Michelle Welsh-Horst of Westview Press, inspired us to be thoughtful and thorough. Without the caring and professional support of Rosalyn Sterner, the manuscript would not have been completed—she really is the best. Finally, we treasure the support of Colleen, Linda, and Karen, particularly their understanding of our crazy way of working together.

WILLIAM E. ROSENBACH
ROBERT L. TAYLOR
MARK A. YOUNDT

PART I

HEART

Leaders are tested, again and again, throughout their careers, and the self-knowledge gained from these tests of character is the heart of leadership.

JOSEPH L. BADARACCO JR.

Leadership is widely discussed and studied but continues to remain an elusive and hazy concept. Although the study of leadership has emerged as a legitimate discipline, there is still little agreement about what leadership really is. Indeed, there are almost as many definitions of leadership as there are people attempting to define it. Yet we know good leadership when we experience it! Today, as in the past, the definitions are very often bounded by the academic discipline or the experience of those attempting definition. In 1978, Pulitzer Prize winner James McGregor Burns wrote that we know a lot about leaders but very little about leadership. However, Walter F. Ulmer Jr., former president and CEO of the Center for Creative Leadership, believes that we know more than we used to about leaders, but that much of our knowledge is superficial and fails to examine the deeper realms of character and motivation that drive leaders, particularly in difficult times.

If we are to begin to understand what leadership is, it is worthwhile to examine what leadership is not. Leadership is not hierarchical, top down, or based on positional power and authority. Although effective managers must practice good leadership and effective leaders must possess managerial skills, leadership is not management or some part or principle of it. To understand leadership, we must understand its essential nature, that is, the process of the leader and followers engaging in reciprocal influence to achieve a shared purpose. Leadership is all about getting people to work together to make things happen that might not otherwise occur or to prevent things from happening that would ordinarily take place.

Looking through the history of the study of leadership, we find that the earliest coherent thrust centered on an approach now referred to as the Great Man or Great Person theory. For a full generation, leadership scholars concentrated on identifying the traits associated with great leadership. At first it seemed obvious: are not great leaders exceptionally intelligent, unusually energetic, far above the norm in their ability to speak to followers, and so on? However, when these "obvious" propositions were subjected to test, they all proved false. Yes, leaders were found to be a bit more intelligent than the average, but not much more. And yes, they were more energetic and dynamic, but not significantly so. True, they were better-than-average public speakers with some charm, but again their overall advantage was not very great. And so it went: each of these and other leadership myths evaporated under the glare of scientific scrutiny.

What followed was a focus on the behavior of leaders. If the key was not *who* they were, perhaps the crux of leadership could be found in *what* they did. In fact, researchers were able to identify two crucial types of leader behavior: behavior centered on task accomplishments and behavior directed toward interpersonal relations. Their peers typically reported individuals who consistently exhibited high levels of both of these types of behavior as leaders. Those who engaged in a high level of task-related activity but only an average level of relationship-centered behavior were sometimes still designated leaders. But those who engaged only in a high level of relationship behavior were rarely designated leaders by their peers. And those who did little in the way of either task- or relationship-centered activity were never seen as leaders.

Perhaps, then, the essence of effective leadership was engaging in high levels of both task-oriented and relationship-centered activity. To test this possibility, researchers trained factory foremen in the two types of behavior and put them back on the job. For a while things did seem to improve, but the effects were short-lived. After only a few weeks the foremen went back to their old behaviors; performance and productivity also returned to their prior levels. Although further research showed that even sustained high levels of the new behaviors had limited long-term effects on employees' performance, productivity, or satisfaction, the task-oriented and relationship-centered leadership-training programs developed in the early 1960s were still popular. Serious students of leadership, however, soon recognized the need to look further for answers to the riddle of effective leadership.

Some took a new path, suggesting that leadership effectiveness might require different combinations of task and relationship behavior in different situations. Theoretically, the most effective combination would depend upon certain situational factors, such as the nature of the task or the ability level of employees reporting to a certain supervisor. Another somewhat different path was to combine the situational hypothesis with some variations of the personal characteristics approach. Like earlier attempts, however, these efforts to explain effective leadership met with limited results.

Interestingly, this focus on relationship and task behaviors was common to the many theories developed over the past decades. The attempts to develop predictive and prescriptive models led to serious research and popular fads as scholars worked to solve the leadership puzzle. As popular literature focused on leadership tools and techniques, most people remained skeptical about leaders and leadership. Thus, we must ask, what have we really learned?

In this book we distinguish between two basic types of leadership. *Transactional* leadership clarifies the role followers must play both to attain the organization's desired outcomes and to receive valued personal rewards for satisfactory performance, giving them the confidence necessary to achieve those outcomes and rewards. Transactional leadership is the equitable transaction or exchange between the leader and followers whereby the leader influences the followers by focusing on the self-interests of both. The self-interest of the leader is satisfactory performance, and the self-interests of the followers are the valued rewards gained in return for good performance. Used well, and in appropriate situations, transactional leadership will result in good performance. Transactional leadership is simply good management and might be considered managerial leadership.

Transformational or *transforming* leadership involves strong personal identification of followers with the leader. The transformational leader motivates followers to perform beyond expectations by creating an awareness of the importance of an organization's mission and vision in such a way that followers share beliefs and values and are able to transcend self-interests and tie the vision to the higher-order needs of self-esteem and self-actualization. Transformational leaders create a mental picture of the shared vision in the minds of the followers through the use of language that has deep meaning from shared experiences. In addition, they are role models: in their daily actions they set an example and give meaning to shared assumptions, beliefs, and values. Transformational leaders empower or, better yet, enable the followers to perform beyond expectations by sharing power and authority and ensuring that followers understand how to use them. These leaders are committed to developing the followers into partners. In the end, what transformational leaders do is to enable followers to transform purpose into action.

What we have learned from recent leadership research is that there is no one best way to lead—the most effective leadership style is dependent upon the organization's culture, the characteristics of the followers, the external environment, and the personal traits of the leader. Leadership is all about character, integrity, and competence. Effective leaders are confident, adaptable, and collaborative, and they take the initiative for their own self-development. They have a high degree of self-awareness resulting from introspection and proactive reflection, which leads to self-regulation and the ability to align their values with their intentions and behaviors.

Ultimately, leadership is always a personal choice.

LEADERSHIP PERSPECTIVES

In "Leadership" (Chapter 1), Marshall Sashkin proposes that there has been a paradigm shift in leadership theory and practice. He reviews the evolution of the concepts of transactional and transformational leadership and describes transformational leadership behaviors and characteristics as well as the social context of leadership. Sashkin also explains how The Leadership Profile (TLP) measures leadership effectiveness. Leadership matters, he writes, because it makes a difference.

In "What Makes a Leader?" (Chapter 2), Daniel Goleman, the premier expert on emotional intelligence, describes why emotional intelligence is the crucial component of leadership and how it is displayed in leaders. Superb leaders have very different ways of leading, and different situations call for different styles of leadership. Goleman has found, however, that effective leaders are alike in one crucial way: they all have a high degree of what has come to be known as emotional intelligence. He discusses each component of emotional intelligence and shows how to recognize it in potential leaders and how it can be learned.

Robert J. Allio, in "Leadership: The Five Big Ideas" (Chapter 3), argues that what we need to know about leadership springs from just five important research hypotheses. Those who aspire to become leaders or improve their performance as leaders must understand and incorporate these ideas into their personal leadership style.

In Chapter 4, "Transcendent Leadership," Mary Crossan and Daina Mazutis describe the key leadership challenges of leading across the levels of self, others, organizations, and society. They argue that most of the leadership discourse has focused almost exclusively on leadership of others and occasionally on the leadership of the organization as a whole, yet little has focused on the integral component of leadership of self. They provide evidence of the necessity of multiple levels of leadership, as well as some practical guidance, by drawing from in-depth interviews of six leaders in various contexts.

"Summit Leadership: Learn from Sir Edmund Hillary," by David Parmenter (Chapter 5), describes eleven lessons to be drawn from Sir Edmund Hillary's experience of climbing Mount Everest as a team member and later of working as a CEO.

1

❧

Leadership

Marshall Sashkin

THE PUZZLE OF LEADERSHIP

There have been almost as many leadership theories and models as authors who have written on the subject. This chapter is aimed at integrating as much as possible that is of value into an overall leadership approach.

The history of leadership thought and research is generally recognized as having followed a sequence of three primary areas of study. The first was the study of leadership traits. When this seemed to have been relatively unprofitable, as summarized in Ralph Stogdill's (1948) classic research review, the second area, the study of leader behavior, dominated research and theory for about twenty years. However, when this area, too, proved to provide a less comprehensive explanation to the puzzle of leadership than had been hoped, the third area of study came to the fore. This was, and is, the examination of leadership in the context of its setting. Even this approach failed to offer as powerful an answer to the question "What is leadership?" as had been hoped.

One way to resolve the puzzle of leadership is to simply insist that the way one has defined and measured leadership is the correct and only way to do so.

This chapter is based on and incorporates materials originally prepared by Marshall Sashkin and William E. Rosenbach.

Many writers on leadership have taken this approach and many continue to use simple, unsubstantiated assertion as their answer to the question of the nature of leadership. Some take a different approach and suggest that all three of the leadership aspects we have mentioned—personality, behavior, and the situational context—must be taken into consideration if we are to fully understand leadership. Although this makes sense, it still fails to provide a coherent answer.

We propose a somewhat different approach. Although accepting the premise that personality, behavior, and situation are all important, we take a step back. We start with a reexamination of the personal nature of leadership, not in terms of simple traits but in the sense of the basic element of human nature. This provides us with a central organizing framework for our concept of leadership.

LEADERSHIP CHARACTER

What is the nature of the leader's character? Is it simply a new set of traits? Though some had long dismissed traits as an adequate explanation for leadership, it is quite common for leadership scholars and practitioners to use trait-like models to assess individuals' "leadership competencies." Yet the approach we present here is as old as Stogdill and as current as the most recent "five-factor" personality theory (Costa and McCrae, 1992; Digman, 1990; McCrae and Costa, 1997; Wiggins, 1996).

Stogdill observed that although no single trait or set of independent traits seemed to be strongly associated with leadership, there were five *clusters* of traits that when taken together seemed to be linked to leadership. Taken together, Stogdill's cluster list and the five factors fit rather well with what we see as three elementary aspects of leader character.

Although these three basic aspects of leadership all concern the leader personally, it would be overly simplistic to call them *personality characteristics*. The three aspects we refer to are, nonetheless, the fundamental building blocks of personality. None are newly discovered; in fact, all have been recognized for several thousand years as aspects of human nature. Plato, for example, considered human nature as having three aspects. The first (and "highest" in his view) was reason. The second was courage—the potential for action consistent with what is "good" or "right." The third element Plato defined as "appetite," that is, emotional desire. A few thousand years later, the psychologist Ernest

Hilgard (1980) spoke of *cognition* (thought), *emotion* (feeling), and *conation* (action) as the three basic elements of the human psyche—thinking, feeling, and behaving.

Thus, ancient philosophy and modern psychology seem to agree on certain fundamental facts of human nature. However, unlike Plato or Hilgard, we see emotion as the centerpiece element, the lynchpin that ties thought to action. We believe that Freud, too, saw things this way. That is, it is the *feelings* of the infant that are at the core of early human awareness. Thought and action come to be enlisted in the service of satisfying emotional needs or what Plato dismissively called "appetites." What makes the difference in terms of what one might consider a "higher order" of functioning is, first, the way the relationships among the three elements actually play out. That is, the term *courage* links emotion to action in a positive sense and facilitates one's use of reason—thought—to act effectively. Second, the purpose or meaning of this process of emotion as guiding positive action through reason is, in the context of leadership, the achievement of common aims and mutual moral development. It is difficult not to see this as a "higher order" of things. We will briefly give our interpretation of the three basic elements of leadership character. We use the term *will* to introduce each, because we want to emphasize that these are not necessarily inborn or genetic traits. Rather, each can be—at least to some degree—developed and increased by almost anyone.

The Will to Act: Confident Leadership

One central element of human nature is the orientation toward action. Psychologist Julian Rotter (1966) observed that some people act as though what happens to them is a matter of chance or, at least, beyond their control. Such individuals are, he said, "externally controlled." Others appear to act in ways that show they personally feel in control of their lives—their actions and the consequences. These individuals are, Rotter says, "internally controlled." Stanford social psychologist Albert Bandura (1982) referred to the same dimension as "efficacy." He went beyond Rotter by pointing out that efficacy is learned through actions and outcomes in social contexts. Former president of the American Psychological Association Martin Seligman built his long research career around what he now calls "learned optimism." We prefer a label more simple than any of these: *self-confidence,* that is, the confidence to act.

This characteristic is also similar to the "big five" factor of conscientiousness. But however labeled or measured, this personal characteristic comes into operation by the will of the individual leader, who elects to act and to engage in goal-directed behavior, rather than to sit back and observe.

The Will to Use Power: Follower-Centered Leadership

This second element centers on feeling or affect. In our view it is power or control that is at the core of human affect. Harvard social psychologist David McClelland (1987) detailed how this central emotion and need develops over time, from birth and infancy through adulthood. Although the issue of using power to gain control over one's life is, then, a primary concern for all of us, it is also the foundation of leaders' *development* of the power need. That is, our instinctual need for power centers on personal survival, but for leaders a higher stage of development of this power need involves the ability to use power in positive, or what McClelland called "prosocial," ways. This benefits groups of others, not just oneself. Thus, what might otherwise be simple narcissism, or what former CIA personality analyst Jerald Post (1986) has, in referring to Saddam Hussein and some other leaders, called "malignant narcissism," can be turned into a more healthy orientation to the need for power.

The Will to Think Critically About Cause and Effect over Time: Visionary Leadership

The third and final element concerns cognition. Plato called it "reason," and learning theorist Hilgard labeled it "conation," but they were referring to the same thing. Reason is not simply intelligence. Our way of looking at reason is based on the work of Elliott Jaques (1986). In this view, reason, or what Jaques called (at different times) "cognitive complexity" and "cognitive capability," has three important aspects beyond generalized intelligence. First is the ability to think in terms of cause and effect, that is, to understand the "levers" that, by one's actions, determine whether or not one's goals are attained. Second is the ability to extend such thinking over time, into the relatively distant and not just the immediate future. Third is the ability to think critically, to make meaningful judgments about actions that involve use of power and influence in ways that produce positive outcomes.

CHARACTER DRIVES BEHAVIOR

Our earliest efforts to develop our approach to understanding leadership centered on the behaviors of leaders. The actions of effective leaders, who as Burns (1978) said transform followers into more self-directed leaders and transform social organizations into more productive and meaningful institutions, do seem to involve certain sorts of behaviors. These behaviors are more subtle than those that are at the center of older leadership behavior theories. Although there is no definitive list of the specific behaviors, it is still possible to identify some that are especially useful. Among the most important of the behaviors that transformational leaders rely on in order that their leadership might matter are the following four.

Communication Leadership

This first category of transformational leadership behavior involves focusing the attention of others on key ideas, the most important aspects of the leader's vision. In practice, this means using metaphors and analogies that make clear and vivid what might otherwise be abstract ideas. Of course, communication leadership does not neglect the basics of effective communication practices, skills such as active listening and giving and receiving feedback effectively. These actions contribute to effective communication between leaders and followers.

Credible Leadership

Leaders establish trust by taking actions that are consistent both over time and with what the leader has said. Leaders must also be sure to follow through on commitments, to do what they say they will do. Trust, of course, exists in the minds and hearts of followers and is not a directly observable leader behavior. But it is *consistency* over time and between words and actions and *credibility* in terms of fulfilling commitments that *produce* feelings of trust in followers.

Caring Leadership

This behavior involves showing respect and concern for people. Psychologist Carl Rogers called this behavior "unconditional positive regard." By this he meant caring about and respecting another person despite one's feelings or judgments about that person's actions. As religious leaders have said, one may hate the sin yet still love the sinner. Visionary leaders show that they care not just by "big" actions, such as ensuring employees' job security. They show it through everyday actions, such as remembering people's birthdays or even something as basic as learning and using their names.

Enabling Leadership

Transformational leaders enable followers by allowing them to accept challenges, such as taking on and "owning" a new project. But transformational leaders also are careful to plan for success. This means that leaders don't ask more of followers than they know the followers can accomplish. Followers might still feel a sense of risk in accepting what they see as a challenge. However, a transformational leader does what is necessary to ensure that real risk is low. The leader makes certain that empowered followers have the resources, skills, and knowledge they need to succeed.

Note that, unlike older behavioral theories of leadership, effective transformational leadership does not simply mean doing a lot of each of these four behaviors. It may be that one or another of them is most needed at a particular time or with regard to particular followers or groups of followers. Neither can the transformational leader simply follow some standard rule or prescription that calls for certain actions under certain conditions. Transformational leaders aim to define and construct those conditions by their actions. We can briefly consider just what organizational conditions—the *organizational culture*—transformational leaders want to create.

THE LEADER'S ROLE IN SHAPING THE ORGANIZATION'S CULTURE

Edgar H. Schein (1993) has said that the *only* important thing leaders do may well be constructing culture. They somehow help define and inculcate certain shared values and beliefs among organizational members. Values define what is right or wrong, good or bad; beliefs define what people expect to happen as a consequence of their actions. The values and beliefs shared by people in an organization are the essence of that organization's culture.

The elements of organizational culture are not a matter of random chance. They concern the most important and fundamental issues faced by people in organizations. These issues are *adaptation*, how people deal with external forces and the need to change; *goal achievement*, the nature of organizational goals, how they are defined, and their importance; *coordination*, how people work together to get the job done; and *the strength of shared values and beliefs*, that is, the degree to which people in the organization generally agree that these values and beliefs are important and should guide their actions. We will briefly consider each issue and the values and beliefs relevant to it.

Adaptation

Consider two specific beliefs about change and adaptation. The first goes like this: "We really just have to go along with outside forces; what we do can't make much of a difference." Such a belief has some clear implications for action—or inaction. After all, why bother? Contrast this outlook with the belief, "We can control our own destiny." The former belief may be more accurate in an objective sense. However, it also pretty much ensures that nothing will be done and that what is done will not make a difference. After all, no one expects it to. Even if the second belief is not as accurate, it makes it more likely that people will take actions to affect short-range outcomes as well as their long-range destiny. Perhaps their actions will have positive effects. What people expect becomes more likely. This is called a *self-fulfilling prophecy.*

Beliefs concerning change and adaptation are the organizational analog of self-confidence, the belief that one's destiny is a matter of internal control. It is especially important that leaders teach followers self-confidence, since only then is it likely that the organization will develop the sort of culture that results in successful adaptation to change.

Goal Achievement

"Every person, every department, has its own goals; the organization is best served by competition among them." Does that sound like a typical organizational value? Unfortunately it is; it's unfortunate because such values don't serve the organization well. Contrast it with this one: "We are all here to serve our customer by identifying and meeting the customer's needs, whatever they may be." That value says a lot about how goals are defined and what goal achievement is all about. And unlike the first value, this one does benefit the organization.

The issue of goals relates to the leader's need for power and what attempts are made to satisfy that need. The leader may benefit the organization by empowering others. Or the leader may benefit only himself or herself, through narcissistic self-aggrandizement. Leaders' empowerment of others is important because it places the value of goal achievement in a larger, organizational context. Achievement of goals becomes important not just in a personal, or even a group, sense, but as an organizational value.

Coordinated Teamwork

Many organizations seem to operate on the maxim "Every person for himself or herself; we all compete to be best." But this is not a very functional value when the very essence of organization is to perform tasks that require the coordinated work of several individuals and groups. In contrast, the value "We all must work together" is a much better expression of the reality of organization. Only when people work together effectively can an organization prosper.

We spoke of vision or cognitive power as the means by which leaders think through complicated chains of cause and effect and decide how to create desirable outcomes. This means looking at the organization as a system and thinking about how it fits together, which happens, of course, through the coordinated efforts of organization members. This is one reason leaders must help followers develop their cognitive power, their own vision. Then followers will be better able to coordinate their efforts effectively.

Shared Values and Beliefs

In some organizations one hears people say, "Everyone has the right to his or her own philosophy." Although that might seem to be a sound democratic ideal, it makes poor organizational sense. Such a value destroys the potentially positive effect of the three beliefs and values just identified. If everyone can buy into or reject them at will, how can these values and beliefs have a consistent impact on people's behavior?

Contrast this with a very different value: "Everyone here is expected to adhere to a common core of values and beliefs." This value supports and strengthens positive values related to adapting ("We can control our world"), achieving goals ("Results for our customers are what counts"), and coordinating efforts through teamwork ("Cooperative teamwork is what counts around here"). Of course, such a value would make values and beliefs that lead to *ineffective* adaptation, goal achievement, or teamwork even more dysfunctional. That's why cultural strength alone, the degree to which the members of the organization share a common set of values and beliefs, is a poor predictor of organizational effectiveness. Shared values and beliefs can support increased organizational effectiveness. They can also impair effectiveness. When all hold to the same flawed beliefs, their combined efforts may lead to total disaster! Thus, the results of a strong organizational culture depend on the specific values and beliefs that culture is built on.

HOW LEADERS CONSTRUCT CULTURE

It is relatively easy to see how the personal characteristics required for transformational leadership relate to the fundamental aspects of organizational culture. It is another thing, however, to ask how leaders actually construct cultures. How do they go about defining and inculcating values and beliefs? There are three general approaches that are especially important.

First, leaders develop a clear, value-based *philosophy*, a statement of organizational purpose or mission that everyone understands. This task is anything but simple. A philosophy does not spring fully formed from the brow of the leader. Leaders must use their cognitive power to assess the organization's context, its environment, and the key factors in that environment. Then, they must solicit and incorporate into the vision the thoughts, values, and beliefs of others: executives, managers, and front-line employees.

Second, leaders empower others to define organizational *policies* and develop *programs* based on the values and beliefs contained in the philosophy. It is programs and policies that put values and beliefs into organizational action. For example, hiring and promotion policies should take into account values consistent with those in the organization's philosophy, as well as applicants' knowledge and skill. Reward systems and bonus programs should be based on the values of cooperation and innovative action, not on competition over a limited pool of resources.

Finally, leaders inculcate values and beliefs through their own individual behaviors, their *personal practices*. Leaders model organizational values and beliefs by living them constantly and consistently. This is why the leadership behaviors we described earlier are so important. Many people think of these behaviors as tools with which leaders explain their vision to followers and convince them to carry out that vision. There is some truth to this. However, these behaviors are most important because leaders use them to demonstrate and illustrate the values and beliefs on which organizational visions are founded. That's why transformational leadership takes so much time and effort—and why transformational leaders must be good managers with strong management skills.

Leaders use everyday managerial activities—a committee meeting, for example—as opportunities to inculcate values. In such a meeting the leader may guide a decision making process while making it clear that final authority and responsibility rest with the group. By doing this a leader takes what might otherwise be a bureaucratic process and instills the value of empowerment into that process. Whenever possible, leaders overlay value-inculcating actions on ordinary bureaucratic management activities. It's now clear why, without a sound base of management skills on the part of leaders, transformational leadership is not possible.

We have also, now, come full circle in that we can see how culture is constructed by the behavioral actions of transformational leaders. We see how the leader's character drives those behaviors. Character also enables transformational leaders to see what actions are needed to establish within an organization's culture the values and beliefs that transform followers into self-directed leaders and create high-performing transformational cultures.

SOUNDS GOOD: DOES IT REALLY WORK?

The test of any theory is, of course, the degree to which it helps one predict future results on the basis of current information and the extent to which it proves useful for designing actions that produce desired results. A great social scientist said, "There is nothing as practical as a good theory!" From the initial development of transformational leadership we have placed a strong emphasis on measuring the concepts being defined and linking those measures to practical outcomes.

The most current version of these measures is called The Leadership Profile (TLP). It is a fifty-item assessment questionnaire completed by a leader and by several of the leader's associates, to give a comprehensive measure of the leader's behavior, character, and culture-building actions. The TLP consists of ten "scales," each one measuring a specific aspect of leadership behavior or character. The scales are briefly defined in Table 1.1. Note that the first two scales measure the essence of good management. That's because good management is an important foundation for effective leadership. Repeated refinement of the TLP has produced an assessment tool that has been demonstrated to yield a reliable and valid measure of leadership that matters.

Dozens of research studies have been conducted since the early 1980s to test the theory described in this chapter. Details of some of these studies can be found in the book *Leadership That Matters* (2003), by Marshall and Molly Sashkin. Overall, it has been demonstrated that leadership that matters is strongly and consistently associated with sound measures of effective organizational culture. Most important of all, it has been repeatedly shown that in banks, schools, manufacturing facilities, and a wide range of other organizations there is a strong and significant relationship between leaders' TLP assessments, which measure the degree to which a leader exhibits leadership that matters, and measures of organizational performance.

IN SUM

Leadership involves the will to act, to use power in a positive or prosocial manner, and to think through the consequences of actions, over time. Leaders who

TABLE I.I—THE LEADERSHIP PROFILE

Scale	What Scale Measures
I: Capable Management	Measures how well a leader accomplishes day-to-day basic administrative or managerial tasks. Capable managers make sure that people have the knowledge, skills and resources they need to get the job done right and know what is expected of them.
II: Reward Equity	Effective leaders promise followers what followers value in exchange for good performance, and they deliver on their promises.
III: Communication Leadership	Assesses the ability to manage and direct the attention of others through especially clear and focused interpersonal communication, by using metaphors and analogies that make abstract ideas clear and vivid.
IV: Credible Leadership	Measures whether a leader "walks the talk" by engaging in behavior that is consistent both over time and with what the leader has said.
V: Caring Leadership	Measures the degree to which a leader demonstrates respect and concern for others.
VI: Enabling Leadership	Effective leaders create opportunities for followers to be empowered, to "own" the actions that yield successful results.
VII: Confident Leadership	Effective leaders believe they control their own fate. This scale measures the extent to which the leader possesses and displays this sort of self-confidence.
VIII: Follower-Centered Leadership	Measures the degree to which a leader sees followers as empowered partners rather than as subordinates to be manipulated.
IX: Visionary Leadership	Assesses the extent to which a leader sees and takes actions that will produce successful outcomes over the long term.
X: Culture-Building Leadership	Measures the extent to which a leader builds a culture based on shared values and beliefs that facilitate effective performance.

possess these characteristics are able to determine and to carry out the specific actions needed to transform followers into more capable self-leaders and to construct the sort of transformational organizational culture we have described.

Simple as this prescription may sound, it is far from simple in action. Understanding of the real, underlying nature of leadership, as described here, is sorely lacking both in organizations and among leadership experts. And the development of leaders who are capable of leadership that will truly make a difference and matter to people and organizations remains an abiding challenge.

But it is crucial to remember that it is character that is at the heart of transformational leadership, that drives transformational leadership behavior, and that enables such leaders to construct transformational organizational cultures. This is why we close by returning, briefly, to the essential nature of leadership. The three personal characteristics, based in the underlying aspects of human nature, seem to be at the heart of everything we do to develop and improve leadership. They are so important that they deserve a final emphasis, by means of a true anecdote.

Some years ago dancer Ray Bolger, the scarecrow in *The Wizard of Oz* movie, was asked what he thought was the underlying lesson or theme of the story. He replied that a person who saw *The Wizard of Oz* should leave with the understanding that *every* person has a heart, a mind, and the potential for courageous action. These are, of course, the three personal characteristics at the core of this presentation and of our understanding of the nature of leadership. They are, Bolger also observed, the essential gifts that make us human.

Leadership matters because it makes a difference. This difference occurs in the lives of followers, in a group or organization. There's also a difference in group or organizational performance. And there is an important difference in the organization itself as a result of leadership that matters. Thus, our approach to leadership differs from others most basically in our view of the *purpose* of leadership. The English author and essayist Samuel Johnson said, "The only aim of writing is to enable the readers better to enjoy life or better to endure it." This happens, we think, because great authors lead readers to find or make meaning in their own lives. The same can be said of good leaders in general.

References

Axelrod, R. H., & Sashkin, M. (2000). Outcome measurement in a leadership development program. Paper presented at the annual meeting of the Academy of Management, Toronto, August.

Bandura, A. (1982). Self-efficacy mechanism in human agency. *American Psychologist, 37,* 122–147.

Burns, J. M. (1978). *Leadership.* New York: Free Press.

Costa, P. T., Jr., & McCrae, R. R. (1992). Normal personality assessment in clinical practice: The NEO Personality Inventory. *Psychological Assessment, 4,* 5–13.

Digman, J. M. (1990). Higher-order factors of the Big Five. *Journal of Personality and Social Psychology, 73,* 1246–1256.

Hilgard, E. R. (1980). The trilogy of mind: Cognition, affection, and conation. *Journal of the History of the Behavioral Sciences, 16*, 107–117.

Jaques, E. (1986). The development of intellectual capability. *Journal of Applied Behavioral Science, 22*, 361–383.

McClelland, D. C. (1987). *Human motivation.* Cambridge, UK: Cambridge University Press.

McCrae, R. R., & Costa, P. T., Jr. (1997). Personality trait structure as a human universal. *American Psychologist, 52*, 509–516.

Post, J. M. (1986). Narcissism and the charismatic leader-follower relationship. *Political Psychology, 7*(4), 675–687.

Rotter, J. (1966). Generalized expectancies for internal versus external control of reinforcement. *Psychological Monographs, 80* (Whole No. 609).

Sashkin, M., & Sashkin, M. G. (2003). *Leadership that matters.* San Francisco: Berrett-Koehler.

Schein, E. H. (1993). *Organizational culture and leadership.* San Francisco: Jossey-Bass (2nd ed., 1993).

Stogdill, R. M. (1948). Personal factors associated with leadership. *Journal of Psychology, 25*, 37–71.

Wiggins, J. S. (Ed.) (1996). *The five-factor model of personality: Theoretical perspectives.* New York: Guilford.

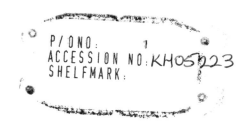
2

ℰℐ

What Makes a Leader?

Daniel Goleman

All businesspeople know a story about a highly intelligent, highly skilled executive who was promoted into a leadership position only to fail at the job. And they also know a story about someone with solid—but not extraordinary—intellectual abilities and technical skills who was promoted into a similar position and then soared.

Such anecdotes support the widespread belief that identifying individuals with the "right stuff" to be leaders is more art than science. After all, the personal styles of superb leaders vary: Some leaders are subdued and analytical; others shout their manifestos from the mountaintops. And just as important, different situations call for different types of leadership. Most mergers need a sensitive negotiator at the helm, whereas many turnarounds require a more forceful authority.

I have found, however, that the most effective leaders are alike in one crucial way: They all have a high degree of what has come to be known as *emotional intelligence*. It's not that IQ and technical skills are irrelevant. They do matter, but mainly as "threshold capabilities"; that is, they are the entry-level requirements for executive positions. But my research, along with other recent studies, clearly shows that emotional intelligence is the sine qua non of leadership. Without it, a person can have the best training in the world, an incisive,

Reprinted by permission of *Harvard Business Review* (November-December 1999). Copyright 1999 by the Harvard Business School Publishing Corporation. All rights reserved.

analytical mind, and an endless supply of smart ideas, but he still won't make a great leader.

In the course of the past year, my colleagues and I have focused on how emotional intelligence operates at work. We have examined the relationship between emotional intelligence and effective performance, especially in leaders. And we have observed how emotional intelligence shows itself on the job. How can you tell if someone has high emotional intelligence, for example, and how can you recognize it in yourself? In the following pages, we'll explore these questions, taking each of the components of emotional intelligence— self-awareness, self-regulation, motivation, empathy, and social skill—in turn (see Table 2.1).

EVALUATING EMOTIONAL INTELLIGENCE

Most large companies today have employed trained psychologists to develop what are known as *competency models* to aid them in identifying, training, and promoting likely stars in the leadership firmament. These psychologists have also developed such models for lower-level positions. And in recent years, I have analyzed competency models from eighty-eight companies, most of which were large and global and included the likes of Lucent Technologies, British Airways, and Credit Suisse.

In carrying out this work, my objective was to determine which personal capabilities drove outstanding performance within these organizations, and to what degree they did so. I grouped capabilities into three categories: purely technical skills like accounting and business planning; cognitive abilities like analytical reasoning; and competencies demonstrating emotional intelligence such as the ability to work with others and effectiveness in leading change.

To create some of the competency models, psychologists asked senior managers at the companies to identify the capabilities that typified the organization's most outstanding leaders. To create other models, the psychologists used objective criteria such as a division's profitability to differentiate the star performers at senior levels within their organizations from the average ones. Those individuals were then extensively interviewed and tested, and their capabilities were compared. This process resulted in the creation of lists of ingredients for highly effective leaders. The lists ranged in length from seven to fifteen items and included such ingredients as initiative and strategic vision.

When I analyzed all these data, I found dramatic results. To be sure, intellect was a driver of outstanding performance. Cognitive skills such as big-picture

TABLE 2.1—FIVE COMPONENTS OF EMOTIONAL INTELLIGENCE AT WORK

	Definition	*Hallmarks*
Self-Awareness	The ability to recognize and understand your moods, emotions and drives, as well as their effect on others	• Self-confidence • Realistic self-assessment • Self-deprecating sense of humor
Self-Regulation	The ability to control or redirect disruptive impulses and moods	• The propensity to suspend judgment—to think before acting • Trustworthiness and integrity • Comfort with ambiguity • Openness to change
Motivation	A passion to work for reasons that go beyond money or status	• A propensity to pursue goals with energy and persistence • Strong drive to achieve • Optimism, even in the face of failure • Organizational commitment
Empathy	The ability to understand the emotional makeup of other people	• Skill in treating people according to their emotional reactions • Expertise in building and retaining talent • Cross-cultural sensitivity • Service to clients and customers
Social Skills	Proficiency in managing relationships and building networks	• An ability to find common ground and build rapport • Effectiveness in leading change • Persuasiveness • Expertise in building and leading teams

thinking and long-term vision were particularly important. But when I calculated the ratio of technical skills, IQ, and emotional intelligence as ingredients of excellent performance, emotional intelligence proved to be twice as important as the others for jobs at all levels.

Moreover, my analysis showed that emotional intelligence played an increasingly important role at the highest levels of the company, where differences in technical skills are of negligible importance. In other words, the higher the rank of a person considered a star performer, the more emotional intelligence capabilities showed up as the reason for his or her effectiveness. When I compared star performers with average ones in senior leadership positions, nearly 90 percent of the difference in their profiles was attributable to emotional intelligence factors rather than cognitive abilities.

Other researchers have confirmed that emotional intelligence not only distinguishes outstanding leaders but can also be linked to strong performance. The findings of the late David McClelland, the renowned researcher in human and organizational behavior, are a good example. In a 1996 study of a global food and beverage company, McClelland found that when senior managers had a critical mass of emotional intelligence capabilities, their divisions outperformed yearly earnings goals by 20 percent. Meanwhile, division leaders without that critical mass underperformed by almost the same amount. McClelland's findings, interestingly, held as true in the company's U.S. divisions as in its divisions in Asia and Europe.

In short, the numbers are beginning to tell us a persuasive story about the link between a company's success and the emotional intelligence of its leaders. And just as important, research is also demonstrating that people can, if they take the right approach, develop their emotional intelligence (see Exhibit 2.1).

EXHIBIT 2.1—CAN EMOTIONAL INTELLIGENCE BE LEARNED?

For ages, people have debated whether leaders are born or made. So, too, goes the debate about emotional intelligence. Are people born with certain levels of empathy, for example, or do they acquire empathy as a result of life's experiences? The answer is both. Scientific inquiry strongly suggests that there is a genetic component to emotional intelligence. Psychological and developmental research indicates that nurture plays a role as well. How much of each perhaps will never be known, but research and practice clearly demonstrate that emotional intelligence can be learned.

One thing is certain: Emotional intelligence increases with age. There is an old-fashioned word for the phenomenon: maturity. Yet even with maturity, some people still need training to enhance their emotional intelligence. Unfortunately, far too many training programs that intend to build leadership skills—including emotional intelligence—are a waste of time and money. The problem is simple: They focus on the wrong part of the brain.

Emotional intelligence is born largely in the neurotransmitters of the brain's limbic system, which governs feelings, impulses and drives. Research indicates that the limbic system learns best through motivation, extended practice and feedback. Compare this with the kind of learning that goes on in the neocortex, which governs analytical and technical ability. The neocortex grasps concepts and logic. It is the part of the brain that figures out how to use a computer or make a sales call by reading a book. Not surprisingly—but mistakenly—it is also the part of the brain targeted by most training programs aimed at enhancing emotional intelligence. When such programs take, in effect, a neocortical approach, my research with the consortium for Research on Emotional Intelligence in Organizations has shown they can even have a *negative* impact on people's job performance.

To enhance emotional intelligence, organizations must refocus their training to include the limbic system. They must help people break old behavioral habits and establish new ones. That not only takes much more time than conventional training programs, but it also requires an individualized approach.

Imagine an executive who is thought to be low on empathy by her colleagues. Part of that deficit shows itself as an inability to listen; she interrupts people and doesn't pay close attention to what they're saying. To fix the problem, the executive needs to be motivated to change, and

SELF-AWARENESS

Self-awareness is the first component of emotional intelligence—which makes sense when one considers that the Delphic oracle gave the advice to "know thyself" thousands of years ago. Self-awareness means having a deep understanding of one's emotions, strengths, weaknesses, needs, and drives. People with strong self-awareness are neither overly critical nor unrealistically hopeful. Rather, they are honest—with themselves and with others.

People who have a high degree of self-awareness recognize how their feelings affect them, other people, and their job performance. Thus a self-aware person who knows that tight deadlines bring out the worst in him plans his time carefully and gets his work done well in advance. Another person with high self-awareness will be able to work with a demanding client. She will understand the client's impact on her moods and the deeper reasons for her frustration.

Exhibit 2.1 (Continued)

then she needs practice and feedback from others in the company. A colleague or coach could be tapped to let the executive know when she has been observed failing to listen. She would then have to replay what others are saying. And the executive could be directed to observe certain executives who listen well and to mimic their behavior.

With persistence and practice, such a process can lead to lasting results. I know one Wall Street executive who sought to improve his empathy—specifically his ability to read people's reactions and see their perspectives. Before beginning his quest, the executive's subordinates were terrified of working with him. People even went so far as to hide bad news from him. Naturally, he was shocked when finally confronted with these facts. He went home and told his family—but they only confirmed what he had heard at work. When their opinions on any given subject did not mesh with his, they, too, were frightened of him.

Enlisting the help of a coach, the executive went to work to heighten his empathy through practice and feedback. His first step was to take a vacation to a foreign country where he did not speak the language. While there, he monitored his reactions to the unfamiliar and his openness to people who were different from him. When he returned home, humbled by his week abroad, the executive asked his coach to shadow him for parts of the day, several times a week, in order to critique how he treated people with new or different perspectives. At the same time, he consciously used on-the-job interactions as opportunities to practice "hearing" ideas that differed from his. Finally, the executive had himself videotaped in meetings and asked those who worked for and with him to critique his ability to acknowledge and understand the feelings of others. It took several months, but the executive's emotional intelligence did ultimately rise, and the improvement was reflected in his overall performance on the job.

It's important to emphasize that building one's emotional intelligence cannot—will not—happen without sincere desire and concerted effort. A brief seminar won't help; nor can one buy a how-to manual. It is much harder to learn to empathize—to internalize empathy as a natural response to people—than it is to become adept at regression analysis. But it can be done. "Nothing great was ever achieved without enthusiasm," wrote Ralph Waldo Emerson. If your goal is to become a real leader, these words can serve as a guidepost in your efforts to develop high emotional intelligence.

"Their trivial demands take us away from the real work that needs to be done," she might explain. And she will go one step further and turn her anger into something constructive.

Self-awareness extends to a person's understanding of his or her values and goals. Someone who is highly self-aware knows where he is headed and why; so, for example, he will be able to be firm in turning down a job offer that is tempting financially but does not fit with his principles or long-term goals. A person who lacks self-awareness is apt to make decisions that bring on inner turmoil by treading on buried values. "The money looked good so I signed on," someone might say two years into a job, "but the work means so little to me that I'm constantly bored." The decisions of self-aware people mesh with their values; consequently, they often find work to be energizing.

How can one recognize self-awareness? First and foremost, it shows itself as candor and an ability to assess oneself realistically. People with high self-awareness are able to speak accurately and openly—although not necessarily effusively or confessionally—about their emotions and the impact they have on their work. For instance, one manager I know of was skeptical about a new personal-shopper service that her company, a major department-store chain, was about to introduce. Without prompting from her team or her boss, she offered them an explanation. "It's hard for me to get behind the rollout of this service," she admitted, "because I really wanted to run the project but I wasn't selected. Bear with me while I deal with that." The manager did indeed examine her feelings; a week later, she was supporting the project fully.

Such self-knowledge often shows itself in the hiring process. Ask a candidate to describe a time he got carried away by his feelings and did something he later regretted. Self-aware candidates will be frank in admitting to failure—and will often tell their tales with a smile. One of the hallmarks of self-awareness is a self-deprecating sense of humor.

Self-awareness can also be identified during performance reviews. Self-aware people know—and are comfortable talking about—their limitations and strengths, and they often demonstrate a thirst for constructive criticism. By contrast, people with low self-awareness interpret the message that they need to improve as a threat or a sign of failure.

Self-aware people can also be recognized by their self-confidence. They have a firm grasp of their capabilities and are less likely to set themselves up to fail by, for example, overstretching on assignments. They know, too, when to ask for help. And the risks they take on the job are calculated. They won't ask for a challenge that they know they can't handle alone. They'll play to their strengths.

Consider the actions of a mid-level employee who was invited to sit in on a strategy meeting with her company's top executives. Although she was the most junior person in the room, she did not sit there quietly, listening in awestruck or fearful silence. She knew she had a head for clear logic and the skill to present ideas persuasively, and she offered cogent suggestions about the company's strategy. At the same time, her self-awareness stopped her from wandering into territory where she knew she was weak.

Despite the value of having self-aware people in the workplace, my research indicates that senior executives don't often give self-awareness the credit it deserves when they look for potential leaders. Many executives mistake candor about feelings for "wimpiness" and fail to give due respect to employees who openly acknowledge their shortcomings. Such people are too readily dismissed as "not tough enough" to lead others.

In fact, the opposite is true. In the first place, people generally admire and respect candor. Further, leaders are constantly required to make judgment calls that require a candid assessment of capabilities—their own and those of others. Do we have the management expertise to acquire a competitor? Can we launch a new product within six months? People who assess themselves honestly— that is, self-aware people—are well suited to do the same for the organizations they run.

SELF-REGULATION

Biological impulses drive our emotions. We cannot do away with them—but we do much to manage them. Self-regulation, which is like an ongoing inner conversation, is the component of emotional intelligence that frees us from being prisoners of our feelings. People engaged in such a conversation feel bad moods and emotional impulses just as everyone else does, but they find ways to control them and even to channel them in useful ways.

Imagine an executive who has just watched a team of his employees present a botched analysis to the company's board of directors. In the gloom that follows, the executive might find himself tempted to pound on the table in anger or kick over a chair. He could leap up and scream at the group. Or he might maintain a grim silence, glaring at everyone before stalking off.

But if he had a gift for self-regulation, he would choose a different approach. He would pick his words carefully, acknowledging the team's poor performance without rushing to any hasty judgment. He would then step back to consider the reasons for the failure. Are they personal—a lack of effort? Are there any mitigating factors? What was his role in the debacle? After considering these questions, he would call the team together, lay out the incident's consequences, and offer his feelings about it. He would then present his analysis of the problem and a well-considered solution.

Why does self-regulation matter so much for leaders? First of all, people who are in control of their feelings and impulses—that is, people who are reasonable—are able to create an environment of trust and fairness. In such an environment, politics and infighting are sharply reduced and productivity is high. Talented people flock to the organization and aren't tempted to leave. And self-regulation has a trickle-down effect. No one wants to be known as a hothead when the boss is known for her calm approach. Fewer bad moods at the top mean fewer throughout the organization.

Second, self-regulation is important for competitive reasons. Everyone knows that business today is rife with ambiguity and change. Companies merge and break apart regularly. Technology transforms work at a dizzying pace. People who have mastered their emotions are able to roll with the changes. When a new change program is announced, they don't panic; instead, they are able to suspend judgment, seek out information, and listen to executives explain the new program. As the initiative moves forward, they are able to move with it.

Sometimes they even lead the way. Consider the case of a manager at a large manufacturing company. Like her colleagues, she had used a certain software program for five years. The program drove how she collected and reported data and how she thought about the company's strategy. One day, senior executives announced that a new program was to be installed that would radically change how information was gathered and assessed within the organization. While many people in the company complained bitterly about how disruptive the change would be, the manager mulled over the reasons for the new program and was convinced of its potential to improve performance. She eagerly attended training sessions—some of her colleagues refused to do so—and was eventually promoted to run several divisions, in part because she used the new technology so effectively.

I want to push the importance of self-regulation to leadership even further and make the case that it enhances integrity, which is not only a personal virtue but also an organizational strength. Many of the bad things that happen in companies are a function of impulsive behavior. People rarely plan to exaggerate profits, pad expense accounts, dip into the till, or abuse power for selfish ends. Instead, an opportunity presents itself, and people with low impulse control just say yes.

By contrast, consider the behavior of the senior executive at a large food company. The executive was scrupulously honest in his negotiations with local distributors. He would routinely lay out his cost structure in detail, thereby giving the distributors a realistic understanding of the company's pricing. This approach meant the executive couldn't always drive a hard bargain. Now, on occasion, he felt the urge to increase profits by withholding information about the company's costs. But he challenged that impulse—he saw that it made more sense in the long run to counteract it. His emotional self-regulation paid off in strong, lasting relationships with distributors that benefited the company more than any short-term financial gains would have.

The signs of emotional self-regulation, therefore, are not hard to miss: a propensity for reflection and thoughtfulness, comfort with ambiguity and change, and integrity—an ability to say no to impulsive urges.

Like self-awareness, self-regulation often does not get its due. People who can master their emotions are sometimes seen as cold fish—their considered responses are taken as a lack of passion. People with fiery temperaments are frequently thought of as "classic" leaders—their outbursts are considered hallmarks of charisma and power. But when such people make it to the top, their impulsiveness often works against them. In my research, extreme displays of negative emotion have never emerged as a driver of good leadership.

MOTIVATION

If there is one trait that virtually all effective leaders have, it is motivation. They are driven to achieve beyond expectations—their own and everyone else's. The key word here is *achieve*. Plenty of people are motivated by external factors such as a big salary or the status that comes from having an impressive title or being part of a prestigious company. By contrast, those with leadership potential are motivated by a deeply embedded desire to achieve for the sake of achievement.

If you are looking for leaders, how can you identify people who are motivated by the drive to achieve rather than by external rewards? The first sign is a passion for the work itself—such people seek out creative challenges, love to learn, and take great pride in a job well done. They also display an unflagging energy to do things better. People with such energy often seem restless with the status quo. They are persistent with their questions about why things are done one way rather than another; they are eager to explore new approaches to their work.

A cosmetics company manager, for example, was frustrated that he had to wait two weeks to get sales results from people in the field. He finally tracked down an automated phone system that would beep each of his salespeople at 5 P.M. every day. An automated message then prompted them to punch in their numbers—how many calls and sales they had made that day. The system shortened the feedback time on sales results from weeks to hours.

That story illustrates two other common traits of people who are driven to achieve. They are forever raising the performance bar, and they like to keep score. Take the performance bar first. During performance reviews, people with high levels of motivation might ask to be "stretched" by their supervisors. Of course, an employee who combines self-awareness with internal motivation will recognize her limits—but she won't settle for objectives that seem too easy to fulfill.

And it follows naturally that people who are driven to do better also want a way of tracking progress—their own, their team's, and their company's. Whereas people with low achievement motivation are often fuzzy about results, those with high achievement motivation often keep score by tracking such hard measures as profitability or market share. I know of a money manager who starts and ends his day on the Internet, gauging the performance of his stock fund against four industry-set benchmarks.

Interestingly, people with high motivation remain optimistic even when the score is against them. In such cases, self-regulation combines with achievement motivation to overcome the frustration and depression that come after a setback or failure. Take the case of another portfolio manager at a large investment company. After several successful years, her fund tumbled for three consecutive quarters, leading three large institutional clients to shift their business elsewhere.

Some executives would have blamed the nosedive on circumstances outside their control; others might have seen the setback as evidence of personal failure. This portfolio manager, however, saw an opportunity to prove she could lead a turnaround. Two years later, when she was promoted to a very senior level in the company, she described the experience as "the best thing that ever happened to me; I learned so much from it."

Executives trying to recognize high levels of achievement motivation in their people can look for one last piece of evidence: commitment to the organization. When people love their job for the work itself, they often feel committed to the organization that makes that work possible. Committed employees are likely to stay with an organization even when they are pursued by headhunters waving money.

It's not difficult to understand how and why a motivation to achieve translates into strong leadership. If you set the performance bar high for yourself, you will do the same for the organization when you are in a position to do so. Likewise, a drive to surpass goals and an interest in keeping score can be contagious. Leaders with these traits can often build a team of managers around them with the same traits. And of course, optimism and organizational commitment are fundamental to leadership—just try to imagine running a company without them.

EMPATHY

Of all the dimensions of emotional intelligence, empathy is the most easily recognized. We have all felt the empathy of a sensitive teacher or friend; we have all been struck by its absence in an unfeeling coach or boss. But when it comes to business, we rarely hear people praised, let alone rewarded, for their empathy. The very word seems unbusinesslike, out of place amid the tough realities of the marketplace.

But empathy doesn't mean a kind of "I'm okay, you're okay" mushiness. For a leader, that is, it doesn't mean adopting other people's emotions as one's own and trying to please everybody. That would be a nightmare—it would make action impossible. Rather, empathy means thoughtfully considering employees' feelings—along with other factors—in the process of making intelligent decisions.

For an example of empathy in action, consider what happened when two giant brokerage companies merged, creating redundant jobs in all their divisions. One division manager called his people together and gave a gloomy speech that emphasized the number of people who would soon be fired. The manager of another division gave his people a different kind of speech. He was up front about his own worry and confusion, and he promised to keep people informed and to treat everyone fairly.

The difference between these two managers was empathy. The first manager was too worried about his own fate to consider the feelings of his anxiety-stricken colleagues. The second knew intuitively what his people were feeling, and he acknowledged their fears with his words. Is it any surprise that the first manager saw his division sink as many demoralized people, especially the most talented, departed? By contrast, the second manager continued to be a strong leader, his best people stayed, and his division remained as productive as ever.

Empathy is particularly important today as a component of leadership for at least three reasons: the increasing use of teams, the rapid pace of globalization, and the growing need to retain talent.

Consider the challenge of leading a team. As anyone who has even been a part of one can attest, teams are cauldrons of bubbling emotions. They are often charged with reaching a consensus—hard enough with two people and much more difficult as the numbers increase. Even in groups with as few as four or five members, alliances form and clashing agendas get set. A team's leader must be able to sense and understand the viewpoints of everyone around the table.

That's exactly what a marketing manager at a large information technology company was able to do when she was appointed to lead a troubled team. The group was in turmoil, overloaded by work and missing deadlines. Tensions were high among the members. Tinkering with procedures was not enough to bring the group together and make it an effective part of the company.

So the manager took several steps. In a series of one-on-one sessions, she took the time to listen to everyone in the group—what was frustrating them, how they rated their colleagues, whether they felt they had been ignored. And then she directed the team in a way that brought it together: She encouraged people to speak more openly about their frustrations, and she helped people raise constructive complaints during meetings. In short, her empathy allowed her to understand her team's emotional makeup. The result was not just heightened collaboration among the members but also added business, as the team was called on for help by a wider range of internal clients.

Globalization is another reason for the rising importance of empathy for business leaders. Cross-cultural dialogue can easily lead to miscues and misunderstandings. Empathy is an antidote. People who have it are attuned to subtleties in body language; they can hear the message beneath the words being spoken. Beyond that, they have a deep understanding of the existence and importance of cultural and ethnic differences.

Consider the case of an American consultant whose team had just pitched a project to a potential Japanese client. In its dealings with Americans, the team was accustomed to being bombarded with questions after such a proposal, but this time it was greeted with a long silence. Other members of the team, taking the silence as disapproval, were ready to pack up and leave. The lead consultant gestured them to stop. Although he was not particularly familiar with Japanese culture, he read the client's face and posture and sensed not rejection but interest—even deep consideration. He was right: When the client finally spoke, it was to give the consulting firm the job.

Finally, empathy plays a key role in the retention of talent, particularly in today's information economy. Leaders have always needed empathy to develop and keep good people, but today the stakes are higher. When good people leave, they take the company's knowledge with them.

That's where coaching and mentoring come in. It has repeatedly been shown that coaching and mentoring pay off not just in better performance but also in increased job satisfaction and decreased turnover. But what makes coaching and mentoring work best is the nature of the relationship. Outstanding coaches and mentors get inside the heads of the people they are helping. They sense how to give effective feedback. They know when to push for better performance and when to hold back. In the way they motivate their protégés, they demonstrate empathy in action.

In what is probably sounding like a refrain, let me repeat that empathy doesn't get much respect in business. People wonder how leaders can make hard decisions if they are "feeling" for all the people who will be affected. But leaders with empathy do more than sympathize with the people around them: They use their knowledge to improve their companies in subtle but important ways.

SOCIAL SKILL

The first three components of emotional intelligence are all self-management skills. The last two, empathy and social skill, concern a person's ability to manage relationships with others. As a component of emotional intelligence, social skill is not as simple as it sounds. It's not just a matter of friendliness, although people with high levels of social skill are rarely mean-spirited. Social skill, rather, is friendliness with a purpose: moving people in the direction you desire, whether that's agreement on a new marketing strategy or enthusiasm about a new product.

Socially skilled people tend to have a wide circle of acquaintances, and they have a knack for finding common ground with people of all kinds—a knack for building rapport. That doesn't mean they socialize continually; it means they work according to the assumption that nothing important gets done alone. Such people have a network in place when the time for action comes.

Social skill is the culmination of the other dimensions of emotional intelligence. People tend to be very effective at managing relationships when they can understand and control their own emotions and can empathize with the feelings of others. Even motivation contributes to social skill. Remember that people who are driven to achieve tend to be optimistic, even in the face of setbacks or failure. When people are upbeat, their "glow" is cast upon conversations and other social encounters. They are popular, and for good reason.

Because it is the outcome of the other dimensions of emotional intelligence, social skill is recognizable on the job in many ways that will by now sound familiar. Socially skilled people, for instance, are adept at managing teams—that's their empathy at work. Likewise, they are expert persuaders—a manifestation of self-awareness, self-regulation, and empathy combined. Given those skills, good persuaders know when to make an emotional plea, for instance, and when an appeal to reason will work better. And motivation, when publicly visible, makes such people excellent collaborators; their passion for the work spreads to others, and they are driven to find solutions.

But sometimes social skill shows itself in ways the other emotional intelligence components do not. For instance, socially skilled people may at times appear not to be working while at work. They seem to be idly schmoozing—chatting in the hallways with colleagues or joking around with people who are not even connected to their "real" jobs. Socially skilled people, however, don't think it makes sense to arbitrarily limit the scope of their relationships. They build bonds widely because they know that in these fluid times, they may need help someday from people they are just getting to know today.

For example, consider the case of an executive in the strategy department of a global computer manufacturer. By 1993, he was convinced that the company's future lay with the Internet. Over the course of the next year, he found kindred spirits and used his social skill to stitch together a virtual community that cut across levels, divisions, and nations. He then used this de facto team to put up a corporate Web site, among the first by a major company. And on his own initiative, with no budget or formal status, he signed up the company to participate in an annual Internet industry convention. Calling on his allies and persuading various divisions to donate funds, he recruited more than fifty people from a dozen different units to represent the company at the convention.

Management took notice: Within a year of the conference, the executive's team formed the basis for the company's first Internet division, and he was formally put in charge of it. To get there, the executive had ignored conventional boundaries, forging and maintaining connections with people in every corner of the organization.

Is social skill considered a key leadership capability in most companies? The answer is yes, especially when compared with the other components of emotional intelligence. People seem to know intuitively that leaders need to manage relationships effectively; no leader is an island. After all, the leader's task is to get work done through other people, and social skill makes that possible. A leader who cannot express her empathy may as well not have it at all. And a leader's motivation will be useless if he cannot communicate his passion to the organization. Social skill allows leaders to put their emotional intelligence to work.

It would be foolish to assert that good old-fashioned IQ and technical ability are not important ingredients in strong leadership. But the recipe would not be complete without emotional intelligence. It was once thought that the components of emotional intelligence were "nice to have" in business leaders. But now we know that, for the sake of performance, these are ingredients that leaders "need to have."

It is fortunate, then, that emotional intelligence can be learned. The process is not easy. It takes time and, most of all, commitment. But the benefits that come from having a well-developed emotional intelligence, both for the individual and for the organization, make it worth the effort.

3

❧

Leadership

The Five Big Ideas

Robert J. Allio

All rising to a great place is by a winding stair.

FRANCIS BACON

Years of research and analysis by biographers, historians, and management scholars have produced an enormous library of books that the authors claim offer important findings and insights on leaders and leadership. But how useful in practice are all these creatively marketed advice books? And how can managers distinguish between books that are merely faddish and those that offer genuine insight? My analysis shows that, when the marketing hype is discounted, the seemingly nonstop stream of leadership books springs from just five important research hypotheses that are endlessly debated and recycled:

- Good leaders have good character.
- There's no best way to lead.
- Leaders must collaborate.
- Adaptability makes longevity possible.
- Leaders are self-made.

Reprinted by permission of *Strategy and Leadership* (Vol. 37, No. 2, 2009). Copyright 2009 Emerald Group Publishing Limited.

Those who aspire to become leaders or improve their performance as leaders need to understand the issues in the debate and use their own judgment to select best practices they can incorporate into their personal leadership style.

I. GOOD LEADERS HAVE GOOD CHARACTER

Ultimately we can reduce the idea of character in action to a leader's mandate to "do the right thing" as compared to the bureaucratic, and sometimes ethically questionable, process of merely "doing things right." Implicit in this dichotomy is the recognition that good leaders are both competent—they get the right job done—and ethical—they act with integrity. In contrast to these effective leaders, we characterize individuals who have high integrity but few skills as ineffectual idealists; we label those skillful individuals who lack integrity as scoundrels; and we indict those careerists who lack both genuine competence and integrity as the impostors of our society (see Figure 3.1).[1]

The specification for competence encompasses all the important leadership tasks: establishing purpose and clarifying the values of the organization, developing a vision, articulating a strategy, adapting to change, creating a community that is committed to the enterprise and its strategy, monitoring strategy implementation and developing future leaders.

The leadership mandate for integrity and character is less obvious. But clearly, competence alone does not suffice, as witness recent history's pantheon of corrupt CEOs. Recent egregious exemplars of this behavior trajectory include Dennis Kozlowski at Tyco, Jeffrey Skilling at Enron, and Bernie Ebbers at WorldCom. When the leadership path gets rocky, there's also a risk that idealistic and ethical leaders who are on the cusp of failure will evolve into corrupt tyrants—or sacrifice their principles on the altar of pragmatism and expediency.

In the past twenty years or so, perhaps motivated by the Enron scandal and other examples of unbridled selfish behavior, we have searched for explanations of why apparently competent men and women abandon their visions and lose their moral compass, perhaps succumbing to self-entitlement or weakness of will (ancient Greek philosophers called this akrasia). From news reports we can conclude that sometimes would-be visionaries, seduced by power and a growing sense of certitude, first become isolated and then lose their way. When plans fail to deliver wins, they grow tyrannical, wield power wrongly, and devolve into fallen stars and self-serving deciders, surrounded by fawning acolytes. And such leaders and their followers often share a collective cultish-

FIGURE 3.1—PERSONAL BEHAVIOR

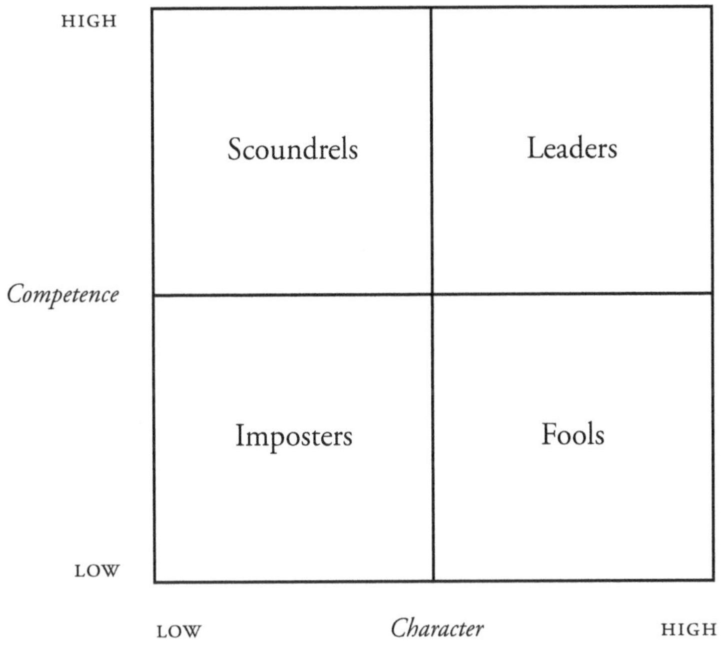

HIGH

Scoundrels	Leaders
Imposters	Fools

Competence

LOW

LOW   *Character*   HIGH

ness that allows each side to accept inappropriate and flawed common goals and behavior.[2]

Whether this sorrowful scenario is the consequence of flawed leadership character or a misguided group response to a situation is debatable. Some critics have suggested that the untrammeled competition of free markets may corrode character and expose the basest elements of human nature. On the one hand, many analysts today still succumb to the fundamental attribution error: they overemphasize the personality basis for behavior and underemphasize the role of the situation. Social psychologist Phillip Zimbardo underscores this conclusion in his recent study of the Abu Ghraib prisoner abuse incident.[3] He explains "evil" behavior as more the consequence of the situation and system (the Lucifer effect) rather than the character of the individuals. On the other hand, many good leaders guide their organizations successfully past a foolish but tempting risk, yet never get full credit because they prevented a potential future crisis.

We often accuse heads of organizations of failing to lead, but they are equally guilty of failing to manage. Leaders conceive of strategy as the link between the

TABLE 3.1—ROLES OF LEADERS AND MANAGERS

Leader	*Manager*
Takes the long view	Takes the short view
Formulates visions	Makes plans and budgets
Takes risks	Avoids risks
Explores new territory	Maintains existing patterns
Initiates change	Stabilizes
Transforms	Transacts
Empowers	Controls
Encourages diversity	Enforces uniformity
Invokes passion	Invokes rationality
Acts morally	Acts amorally

firm's values and purpose and its vision, while managers accept strategy as simply the precursor to implementation. Yet leaders must always monitor implementation of the strategy, a task that they too often delegate to their managers. I would argue that a leader's true mastery shows itself in the delicate balance he or she achieves between managing and leading—neither micromanaging nor becoming infatuated with strategy in the abstract.

Although the dichotomy between the two is somewhat artificial, some writers differentiate more extensively the role of a leader from the role of a manager. Table 3.1 summarizes the consensus about how their roles and perspectives differ.

2. THERE'S NO BEST WAY TO LEAD

What guides leaders when they act to achieve their goals? A lot of authors are tempted to sell books by offering a universal leadership approach. But no single model fits all situations. The evidence now is overwhelming: how to lead effectively will depend on the organization's culture and values, the behavior of the followers, the personal traits of the leader, the strategy to be implemented, the resources available for the task, the urgency of the challenge, and the externalities facing the organization.

Leaders do make choices of style. The many style paradigms have included servant leadership (Robert Greenleaf), transforming leadership (James MacGregor Burns), and leadership as an art form (Max DePree).[4–6] Yet the ideal leader—one who endures to satisfy the needs of all the stakeholders—is a mythical invention promoted by many leadership books. The reality is that our standards for identifying effective leaders change as business history is written in newspaper headlines and our perspective alters. Paradigms for leadership evolve as organizations rise and fall. Thus, in each era we exalt a particular class of individuals as the ideal leader.

In the early 1900s, pioneers like Thomas Edison, William Durant, and Andrew Carnegie were treated as heroes of capitalism. Later the fledging business press canonized leaders of family dynasties (duPont, Ford) in the early 20th century. After their successful military campaigns of WWII, generals like George Patton and Douglas MacArthur were seen by many as prototypical leaders—strong-willed individuals who could bring order and efficiency to the organization. However, some successful generals—such as Dwight Eisenhower, first as president of Columbia University and then of the United States—had a less glorious career as civilian leaders. For a time in the 1960s and 1970s, when commercial litigation was battering a number of industries, quite a few enterprises selected lawyers as the model leader to rein in risky practices and pursue legal strategies. A few decades later we embraced and then rejected the "corporate saviors" who were specifically recruited to be turnaround leaders because of their ruthlessness ("Chainsaw" Al Dunlap of Sunbeam). And in recent years the whole world has been infatuated with a long reign of technology wizards as leaders—a group that included Andrew Grove at Intel, Bill Gates at Microsoft, and Steve Jobs at Apple. And the next paragon for leadership may well be the post-bankruptcy reorganization specialist.

Most North American theorists have underestimated the critical importance of social norms in setting behavior paradigms for leaders. For example, Alexis de Tocqueville concluded from his study of the US in the 19th century that the American stress on individualism produces rancor and tension that can isolate us and undermine our freedom, devaluing our belief in the ideal of community and society.[7] Individualism and self-reliance remain core US values, although today we reject the extreme self-centeredness and narcissism manifested by celebrity CEOs such as Jack Welch (formerly of GE) and Carly Fiorina (formerly of Hewlett-Packard).

Over the past 50 years, we have obtained rapid access to unparalleled amounts of information—we are no longer ignorant of how the organization works. As a result, we are no longer willing to abdicate total responsibility for running the ship of state to our leaders. It's no surprise, then, that today's favored model for leadership is the self-effacing, humanistic individual; co-creation of unique customer value is today's mantra for enlightened leaders.

3. LEADERS MUST COLLABORATE

Leaders must exercise power, but tyranny, autocracy, and coercion in today's egalitarian society will only alienate their followers. Good leaders must collaborate with employees, customers, suppliers, and all the other stakeholders, and at the same time manage their conflicting interests so that no one set of stakeholders has been paid more than enough to secure their willing and active participation (an approach that Jim Sinegal, CEO of Costco, has been credited for performing with exceptional skill).[8]

Power has always been a critical resource in the leader's armamentarium. The archetypal advocate for the utility of power was 15th Century statesman Niccolò Machiavelli. In his magnum opus The Prince, Machiavelli advised his client, Cesare Borgia, to use power as a tool, noting that the cultivation of fear is more important for leaders than the cultivation of love.[9] Conquer by force, he tells him. Commit all your crimes against the people at the start of the regime. Be both a lion—strong and ruthless—and a fox—sly and duplicitous. Recent treatments of the role of power include David McClelland's examination of social motivation; his taxonomy includes the drives for affiliation, achievement, and power.[10] Leaders, in McClelland's view, have strong needs to exercise power.

Whether the leader wields power subtly or blatantly, however, will likely determine success or failure. History shows us that influence is more effective than coercion. Perhaps the original spokesman for the importance of a gentle style was Lao Tzu, the great Taoist sage. In his Tao Te Ching, we find the image of a self-effacing leader who is effective despite (or because of!) his low profile.[11] German novelist Hermann Hesse repeats this point in his story of Leo, a self-effacing factotum who guides a group of travelers.[12] (Hesse's hero is the model for the 20th century embrace of servant leadership.)

In contemporary management theory, the Theory X/Theory Y dichotomy proposed by Douglas McGregor represented an important landmark in the turning away from earlier autocratic models toward a participative approach.[13] Allan Cohen and David Bradford, among others, have written at length on the exercise of influence without authority, while author Jim Collins now promotes "Level 5" leadership, with its emphasis on humility.[14, 15] J. Sterling Livingston identified empathy as critical to management success, and Daniel Goleman's broader concept of the need for emotional intelligence has influenced many prescriptions for how to be an effective leader.[16, 17]

The central point is that good leaders design and manage a collaborative process of decision-making and conflict resolution to which all the stakeholders subscribe. In the absence of such a process, implementation of strategy falters or fails.

4. ADAPTABILITY IS THE KEY TO LONGEVITY

Leaders come and go, their demise usually hastened by futile attempts to maintain stability and retain the existing order. Indeed, helping organizations adapt to change is perhaps the single most important leadership competency.

Strategies that worked last year may serve us poorly if economic, social, or technological forces undergo change—or if a competitor seizes an opportunity to innovate or serve an emerging market. And as an industry matures, the leadership imperatives of the firm shift from entrepreneurial fervor to marketing to cost control and ultimately to management of cash flow.

Furthermore, even skilled leaders frequently forecast the wrong discontinuities. Firms that cling to old missions or old values are particularly vulnerable to Darwinian extinction. The alternative is to abandon commitment to the status quo with all its apparent stability and consider a policy of resilience and adaptability. Stable systems are seductive, however, and organizations everywhere enjoy the feeling of safety that develops when change is slow. They subscribe to what James O'Toole characterized aptly as the "ideology of comfort and the tyranny of custom."[18]

Big change is hard; constant change is harder still. This is because organizations initially prosper by selecting a strategy that works, and then investing more and more resources in established internal systems to support it. When returns eventually diminish, the classic response is to invest even more resources in the failing strategy. As a result, long-established firms build up a powerful legacy of management strategies and systems, supported by a staff that cannot imagine any alternatives. In sociological terms, described by psychologist Kurt Lewin and others, a given system is frozen in a particular state.[19] To move to a new state, leaders must first unfreeze the system, move it to a new position, and then apply appropriate forces to stabilize it. Sometimes an entirely new business model is needed. Yet the process of managing change is one that few have mastered. John Kotter has proposed one helpful eight-step process that includes establishing a sense of urgency, achieving short-term wins, and consolidating the improvements.[20]

5. LEADERS ARE SELF-MADE

Where do great leaders come from? William Shakespeare offered his complete list ("Some are born great, some achieve greatness, and some have greatness thrust upon them").[21] Yet we still debate with fervor the answer to this query: is a leader's success or failure a manifestation of character, genes, or the underlying business or economic conditions?

The first exponent of the thesis that leaders are born was Thomas Carlyle, who in 1841 tells us, "The history of what man has accomplished in this world is at bottom the history of the great men who have worked here."[22] Most contemporary writers disagree with Carlyle; Ralph Stodgill's classic study failed to show any significant correlation between a leader's personality traits and his effectiveness.[23]

In contrast, philosopher Georg Wilhelm Friedrich Hegel was convinced that leaders emerge as history unfolded; the leader is but a pawn in the script that has already been written.[24] Russian novelist Leo Tolstoi, using Napoleon as his case history, similarly asserted with assurance that "a king is history's slave."[25]

Today's popular view is that all men and women can make themselves into leaders, escaping the handicaps of their own personal history and the constraints of their environment. This is the "everyman theory" of leadership—based on the dubious thesis that any manager can and should become a leader.[26]

The corollary to this thesis is that leadership can be taught. This belief underpins the curricula of most business schools and their executive training programs. Regrettably, we lack any hard evidence that a didactic approach to leadership development produces superior leaders. But even more dismaying is that some of the students are unfit (or unwilling) to act with the courage and wisdom that good leadership demands, or may even use their training program credentials to gain access to power, which they then misuse.

On the other hand, there's no doubt that leadership can improve with practice. In Aristotle's model of virtue, men become just by performing just acts. They become brave by performing acts of bravery, and so on. Some recent views on leadership echo this Aristotelian philosophy: men make themselves leaders by performing acts of leadership. Robert Thomas (the crucible model) and others have argued for this pragmatic approach to developing leaders: careful selection, followed by on the job training, complemented with careful mentoring.[27, 28]

The reality is that leadership theory and principles can be taught, but leadership behavior must be learned. Individuals evolve into leaders as they experiment with alternative approaches to new challenges and slowly integrate the successful approaches into a personal leadership style and strategy.

FOUR RESEARCH CHALLENGES

Notwithstanding the occasional success of "leaderless groups," it seems axiomatic that organizations perform better when an effective leader is at the helm. If we accept this premise, we can identify four aspects of leadership that demand more study and understanding:

Selection. Organizations seem to perversely select and retain leaders who are not up to the task. They lack either competence or character or both.

Boards need to learn to make better succession decisions. Too often they take the easy way out, selecting the next man or woman in line as the heir to the throne. More and more often today, however, they seek saviors from outside the firm, a tacit admission of a failed development program. Delegation of the search process to outside firms also reduces board responsibility and accountability for the final selection.

Of course, not all of us even aspire to leadership, preferring to accept roles as loyal followers, a choice that backfires when managers allow themselves to become enablers of flawed leaders. So we need research into how to pick the right leader for a specific job.

The guidelines for selecting leaders should be self-evident: potential leaders must have integrity, be motivated to excel, exhibit high skills in learning, adapting and communicating, and be able to work with their followers to accomplish the right jobs. Yet we lack a tool that enables us to screen with full confidence those fit candidates from the flawed (or worse, the clever dissemblers). Skilled human resource practitioners have developed many instruments that offer some measure [of] managerial competence or performance—my favorite being the process of carefully interviewing a candidate's current and past subordinates, superiors and peers. The critical problem, however, is that seldom is HR capable of doing an effective job of matching the firm's situation and culture with the attributes of its next potential leader.

What we need: a simple diagnostic that increases the probability that our candidates for leadership will succeed.

Training. We have accepted as an act of faith that we can train men and women to be leaders. As a result, organizations invest millions of dollars and thousands of hours in leadership development. But the returns on these investments are meager.

We also admire particular corporate development processes as an efficient producer of good leaders. GE is the current cynosure, although not all of its alumni have distinguished themselves (witness Robert Nardelli at Home Depot and Gary Wendt at Conseco). Indeed, researchers Groysberg, McLean, and Nohria postulate that leaders are not likely to be successfully transferred from one corporation to another.[29]

What are the alternatives? Teaching leadership competence by simulation of leadership situations continues to attract apostles. Students can also find a variety of experiential programs at Outward Bound and similar organizations. But there is little evidence that decisions taken on a mountain wilderness trip inform leadership behavior in the office. Moreover, any new behavior adopted during these programs usually regresses to old behavior when participants return home. Finally, attempts to create classroom simulations that reproduce the reality of actual leadership challenges haven't clearly succeeded either.[30]

What we need: a syllabus for learning that actually does enable men and women to improve their leadership capabilities.

Followership. The key insight today is that leaders and followers constitute part of a system. They are linked symbiotically, with each having the ability to support or degrade the performance of the other. Although by definition, leaders have followers, much of management research has concentrated on formulating behavior recommendations for leaders.

But blame for organizational underperformance appears recently to have shifted from leaders to their followers. Barbara Kellerman indicts followers as seekers after safety, security, and self-preservation, while Mark Slouka observes caustically that power and fame still impress the majority of us today ("The race of man loves a lord!"). And this subservience by followers enables malfeasance and misbehavior on the part of our leaders.[31, 32]

Since followers often have a vested interest in the status quo that blinds them to its risks, the leader who would make change must inspire them to support his or her vision. Unfortunately, as Fyodor Dostoevsky's Grand Inquisitor observes, the populace may prefer a leader who tells them what to believe to a leader who shows them the hard path to self-determination.[33]

Psychologist Erich Fromm expounds on this same theme in his classic treatise on man's attempt to escape from freedom.[34]

How followers support or ignore the initiatives of their leaders is critical. (And all of us, leaders included, periodically find ourselves in the role of followers.) What must we do to enhance the effectiveness of the leader-follower system?

What we need: Training programs for followers, as well as leaders. Guidance on how followers can find meaning and purpose in their work and avoid either disengagement or arrant rebellion.

Metrics. If only we knew how to measure leadership effectiveness! Short-term results can be cruelly deceiving. But increase in shareholder value is a flawed measure for long-term performance, and improvements in revenue, earnings per share, or stakeholder value are not perfect metrics either. Author Michael Raynor argues that the continuance of corporation is an end in itself; management's sole purpose is to ensure corporate survival.[35] In this view, a leader's long-term contribution to that survival is a legitimate measure of effectiveness, which in practice keeps historians in business, but it doesn't offer operational guidance to managers!

Of course, recognizing an effective leader is not always easy, for leaders do not necessarily reveal themselves by the force of their personality or the acclaim of a multitude of followers. It is especially difficult to identify good leadership in the short run. Even conjuring up lists of historical leaders is risky business. When Winston Churchill, the man who shepherded Britain through its great WWII crisis, campaigned [to become Prime Minister of Britain] a few years later in 1945, voters rejected him. The point is that leadership appraisals appear to wax and wane.

What we need: robust grading systems and clear measures for leadership effectiveness as a function of short-term and long-term results, success in balancing the needs of multiple stakeholders, and skill in helping the organization survive the inevitable periodic crises.

FIVE PRESCRIPTIONS FOR
IMPROVING LEADERSHIP QUALITY

In sum, though there are still many components of leadership that we don't understand, we can make five generalizations about how to negotiate the winding stair to become an effective leader:

- Integrity is an essential leadership virtue.
- Leaders develop a personal style that balances managing with leading.
- Leaders win when they commit to collaboration.
- Leadership entails adroit adaptation.
- Good leadership requires constant practice!

Notes

1. GE adopted a similar creed in its stress in the 1990s on nurturing Type I managers—those who met commitments while adhering to the values of the corporation (see General Electric 1995 Annual Report).

2. Bert Spector and Henry Lane, "Exploring the distinctions between a high performance culture and a cult," *Strategy & Leadership*, Vol. 35, No. 3, 2007.

3. Phillip Zimbardo, *The Lucifer Effect*, Random House, 2007.

4. Robert K. Greenleaf, *Servant Leadership*, Perennial Press, 1971.

5. James MacGregor Burns, *Leadership*, Harper & Row, 1978.

6. Max DePree, *Leadership Is an Art*, Dell, 1989.

7. Alexis de Tocqueville, *Democracy in America*, New American Library, 1991.

8. Michael E. Raynor, "End shareholder value tyranny: Put the corporation first," *Strategy & Leadership*, Vol. 37, No. 1, January/February, 2009.

9. Niccolò Machiavelli, *The Prince*, Modern Library, 2008.

10. David McClelland, *Human Motivation*, Cambridge University Press, 1987.

11. Lao Tzu, *Tao Te Ching* (Stephen Mitchell translation), Harper Perennial, 1991.

12. Hermann Hesse, *Journey to the East*, Picador, 1956.

13. Douglas McGregor, *The Human Side of Enterprise*, McGraw-Hill, 1960.

14. Allan Cohen and David Bradford, *Influence Without Authority*, Wiley, 1990.

15. Jim Collins, "Level 5 leadership," *Harvard Business Review*, January, 2001.

16. J. Sterling Livingston, "The myth of the well-educated manager," *Harvard Business Review*, January, 1971.

17. Daniel Goleman, *Emotional Intelligence*, Bantam, 1995.

18. James O'Toole, *Leading Change*, Jossey-Bass, 1995.

19. Kurt Lewin and Martin Gold, *The Complete Social Scientist: A Kurt Lewin Review*, American Psychological Association, 1999.

20. John Kotter, *Leading Change*, Harvard Business Press, 1996.

21. William Shakespeare, *Twelfth Night*, Act II.

22. Thomas Carlyle, *On Heroes, Hero-Worship, and the Heroic in History*, University of California Press, 1993.

23. Ralph Stodgill, "Personal factors associated with leadership," *Journal of Psychology*, Vol. 25, 1948.

24. Georg Wilhelm Friedrich Hegel, *Lectures on the Philosophy of History*, J. Sibree, 1956.

25. Leo Tolstoi, *War and Peace*, The Heritage Press, 1938.

26. Ram Charan, *Leaders at All Levels*, Jossey-Bass, 2008.

27. Robert J. Thomas, *Crucibles of Leadership*, Harvard Business School Press, 2008.

28. Robert J. Allio, "Leadership development: Teaching vs. learning," *Management Decision*, Vol. 43, No. 7/8, 2005.

29. Boris Groysberg, Andrew McLean, and Nitin Nohria, "Are leaders portable?" *Harvard Business Review*, May, 2006.

30. Recent developments in virtual reality—most notably with programs such as Second Life—offer more exciting possibilities for leadership development. Second Life is the 3D virtual world hosted by Linden Lab on the Second Life Grid. Any organization can create its own virtual world experience using the Second Life Grid development platform and toolset. See www.Secondlife.com.

31. Mark Slouka, "Democracy and deference," *Harpers Magazine*, January, 2000.

32. Barbara Kellerman, *Bad Leadership*, Harvard Business School Press, 2004.

33. Fyodor Dostoevsky, *The Brothers Karamazov*, Farrar, Straus, Giroux, 2002.

34. Erich Fromm, *Escape from Freedom*, Avon, 1965.

35. Raynor, "End shareholder value tyranny."

4

❧

Transcendent Leadership

Mary Crossan and Daina Mazutis

Mastering others is strength. Mastering yourself is true power.

LAO TZU

WILL THE REAL LEADER PLEASE STAND UP?

The publishing industry in the United States produces over 5,000 new business titles every year, selling billions of dollars worth of business advice for managers and would-be corporate leaders.[1] Of these five thousand titles, a large number are on leadership specifically. To make matters worse, leadership advice is not restricted to the business shelves; recommendations can also be found in other sections: self-help, finance, home, career, and even religion. In their sincere efforts to lead effectively, managers may therefore become understandably confused by the plethora of new and fashionable leadership theories from which to choose the strategies that promise to make them successful.

Unfortunately, the discourse on leadership in academia is not much different. A recent review by Yammarino, Dionne, Chun, and Dansereau (2005) found at minimum 17 different leadership theories, ranging from the classical

---

approaches (such as path-goal theory and Ohio State) to more contemporary forms (such as charismatic and transformational leadership). However, this study did not include other dominant streams of leadership such as upper echelon/strategic leadership or shared leadership perspectives. In addition, the field has also recently seen an upsurge of research into new positive forms of leadership (authentic, spiritual, servant, moral, ethical, prosocial, responsible, Level 5, primal, etc.) which were not included in this discussion. This begs the question: How many different "effective" leadership theories are there? And could the real leader please stand up?

We argue, as well, that much of the discourse on leadership has focused almost exclusively on leadership of others and occasionally on the leadership of the organization as a whole, yet little has focused specifically on perhaps the most integral component of leadership: leadership of self. Managing in increasingly complex and dynamic environments, today's strategic leaders can benefit greatly from learning how to "master themselves" (in addition to others and the organization) by developing self-awareness and self-regulatory capabilities. By doing so, they would be less susceptible to following the latest management fads and fashions as propagated by the 5,000-plus new business books and 17-plus leadership theories, through a better alignment of their internal values and beliefs with their strategic decisions and actions.

Our knowledge of how successful leaders master this level of leadership is virtually non-existent, however. The extant literature has focused instead on how these leaders have either transformed their organizations or their employees. There has been a notable absence in linking success at the organizational level to success in leadership of self. We concur with Crossan, Vera, and Nanjad [2008] that in order for long term sustained firm performance to materialize in today's dynamic business environment, today's leader needs to master leadership at all three levels—self, others, and the organization—a concept the previously-cited authors refer to as transcendent leadership. In fact, leadership at the societal level is also a likely requirement of transcendent leadership.

Crossan et al.'s use of "transcendent" is consistent with that of Aldon (1998) and Gardiner (2006), among others. Gardiner, for example, focused on the transcendent qualities of self and the transcending of the organization to the societal level. Aldon focused on the levels of self and others to bridge spirituality and science. As such, the term transcendent is ideally suited to a model holding that leaders need to transcend the levels, as it captures the quality of going above and beyond, within and between levels.

Building on the work of Crossan et al., we provide practitioners with some evidence of the necessity of multiple levels of leadership, as well as some practical guidance, by drawing from in-depth interviews of six North American business leaders in various contexts, both profit and not-for-profit. We begin by reviewing what we know about leadership and what has changed in the business landscape of the 21st century that necessitates a different approach. We conclude by giving some practical advice on leadership at all three levels—self, others, and the organization—to help leaders ensure long term, sustainable firm performance in today's dynamic environments. Leadership at the societal level is also discussed.

WHAT WE KNOW FOR SURE

Many authors have put forth lists of "must-dos" for successful strategic leadership in and of the organization (Boal & Hooijberg, 2000). With regards to leadership in organizations, much work has been done on understanding dyadic and small-group level leadership, anchored heavily in a supervisor's transactional and/or transformational leadership roles. Transformational leadership is described as the ability to induce immediate followers to deliver performance beyond expectations through inspirational motivation, individualized consideration, intellectual stimulation, and idealized influence (Bass, 1985). Transactional leadership focuses more on the exchange between managers and subordinates through constructive and corrective behaviors (Avolio & Bass, 2004). Both types of leadership, however, focus on the leader's immediate followers and define success in terms of positive follower outcomes such as increased employee commitment, job satisfaction, empowerment, task engagement, job performance, and extra effort (Avolio, Gardner, Walumbwa, Luthans, & May, 2004).

With regards to leadership of the organization, or strategic leadership, even more lists of required activities exist. For example, Ireland and Hitt (2005) state that strategic leadership in the 21st century is based on determining the firm's purpose and vision, exploiting and maintaining core competences, developing human capital, sustaining an effective organizational culture, emphasizing ethical practices, and establishing balanced organizational controls. In his competing values model, Quinn (1988) argues that executives must play eight competing leadership roles simultaneously: innovator, broker, facilitator, mentor, coordinator, monitor, producer, and director. Similarly, Hart and Quinn (1993) assert that CEOs play four roles—vision setter, motivator, analyzer, and taskmaster—to affect firm performance. House and Aditya (1997, p. 445) describe the main tasks of strategic leadership in both transactional (e.g., implementation of compensation and control systems) and transformational terminology (e.g., formulation of organizational goals and strategy).

Nonetheless, very little is said in these models about the critical component of leadership of self. In fact, the original model of strategic leadership (or, upper echelon theory) specifically highlights that strategic decisions taken by members of the top management team or dominant coalition are bound by cognitive processes of which they are likely unaware (Hambrick & Mason, 1984). A leader's values and beliefs are said to affect the selective perception of information on which decisions are made, as well as the final strategic decisions taken. Furthermore, one of the major causes of CEO failure has specifically been identified as "mindset failure," whereby leaders are either blind to the changes that need to be made or too arrogant to admit they are on the wrong path (Finkelstein, 2003). As such, executive cognitions can and do play a critical role in the success, or failure, of the organization.

In the end, while the individual tasks and roles of strategic leaders are clearly very important to firm performance, ensuring that any competitive advantage is sustained will also depend on a leader's ability to manage oneself in addition to others and the organization. The ability to recognize your own internal biases, to be aware of the mental maps that are causing your selective perception, and to self-regulate your actions to be consistent with internal standards will be crucial to navigating the complex changes in today's business environment.

WHAT HAS CHANGED

Today's business climate has been described as fast changing and disruptive, hostile and turbulent (Bettis & Hitt, 1995; Brown & Eisenhardt, 1998; D'Aveni, 1994; Hambrick, 1988). The era of globalization, of the knowledge worker, and of relentless technological innovation has given rise to unprecedented complexity, uncertainty, and dynamism in today's business environment (Hitt, Keats, & DeMarie, 1998; Ireland & Hitt, 2005; Nadler & Tushman, 1999). This hyper-competition, characterized by intense and rapid competitive moves, makes sustainable competitive advantage extremely difficult to achieve and leads to environments where discontinuous change occurs more rapidly (D'Aveni, 1994; Hambrick, 1988). The accompanying increased risk and uncertainty has rendered a firm's strategic response capabilities a key source of competitive advantage (Bettis & Hitt, 1995), thereby placing particular demands on today's strategic leaders with respect to interpreting the environment, crafting the appropriate strategy, and building an organization that thrives in such contexts.

There has also been a shift in the moral and ethical climate of business, particularly since the very well-publicized failures of WorldCom, Enron, and Tyco. In a post 9/11 world plagued by compromised Western ideals of security and prosperity, corporate scandals that recount individual greed and rampant materialism have led to an increased distrust of, if not disdain for, corporate leaders. It has also brought to the forefront a more public discourse on issues of trust, honesty, integrity, and morality. Today's leaders are therefore exposed to a much higher level of public scrutiny in an environment where most corporate actions must be completely transparent, given that global information dissemination is almost instantaneous. Given the increasing complexity of today's business context, what actions can leaders take to secure long term sustained performance?

WHAT NEEDS TO BE DONE

As discussed, skill sets including leadership of others and leadership of the organization are critical in today's dynamic environments. In addition to these very well documented roles and functions of strategic leaders, however, today's leaders must also learn and master leadership of self. Leadership of self includes the responsibility of being self-aware and proactive in developing personal strengths. Building on the work of Crossan et al. [2008], a strategic leader who leads within and amongst the levels of self, others, and the organization is defined as a transcendent leader and will be better positioned to rise to the challenge of leading in a complex, turbulent, and highly transparent environment.

To demonstrate, a leader who excels at only one level of leadership cannot realize sustained performance benefits for the organization. For example, despite being adept at leading your team and instilling motivation, commitment, and loyalty in your immediate followers (leadership of others), leadership in today's dynamic environment necessitates a coherent alignment of your actions with the strategy of the organization as a whole (leadership of the organization), as well as strong self-leadership to effectively navigate the difficult trade-offs in complex decisions (leadership of self). Even leadership at two levels will not lead to long term performance, for the leader who is able to turn a

FIGURE 4.1—TRANSCENDENT LEADERSHIP: STRATEGIC LEADERSHIP
WITHIN AND AMONGST THREE LEVELS

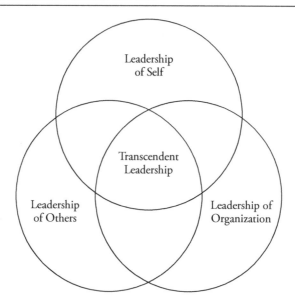

SOURCE: Crossan, Vera, and Nanjad [2008].

company around and motivate employees to follow is still very susceptible to
falter without a strong sense of self, a moral or ethical compass, or the character
strengths to help them face inevitably difficult decisions. Leadership at all three
levels, or transcendent leadership, is therefore key to effective strategic leadership in today's dynamic environments (see Figure 4.1).

LEADERSHIP OF SELF

In order to lead in today's turbulent times, during which both competitive
and ethical stakes have been raised, strategic leaders must actively develop personal strengths such as self-awareness and self-regulation. Self-awareness "refers
to one's awareness of, and trust in, one's own personal characteristics, values,
motives, feelings, and cognitions" (Ilies, Morgeson, & Nahrgang, 2005, p.
377). Only by being aware of one's limited field of vision, which is influenced
by one's values and cognitive base, can a leader understand his/her own selective perceptions and interpretations, and the manner in which these influence
the strategic decisions they make (Hambrick & Mason, 1984). Today's leaders
must be aware of their own weaknesses and cognitive biases, and acknowledge

the role their perceptions may have on their thoughts, feelings, actions, and strategic decisions. Self-awareness does not refer only to recognizing one's shortcomings; it can also be key to understanding your own unique capabilities and in leveraging that knowledge and experience to make smarter decisions. As such, self-reflection and introspection are key mechanisms through which leaders can achieve clarity with regard to their core values and mental models, and how these shape the decisions they make (Gardner, Avolio, Luthans, May, & Walumbwa, 2005).

Coupled with the ability to be self-aware, the capability of self-regulation is also critical to leadership of self and is the process whereby a leader aligns his/her values with intentions and actions (Avolio & Gardner, 2005). This process includes making one's motives, goals, and values completely transparent to followers, leading by example, and demonstrating consistency between what one says and what one does. Today's strategic leaders cannot get by with deliberately manipulating their image, falsely portraying their intentions, or engaging in impression management. Rather, they must ensure that they self-regulate their behaviors so that the outcomes they anticipate from their actions are congruent with their internal standards (Gardner et al., 2005). By doing so, they effectively manage internal tensions and avoid conflicts between their personal values and organizational responsibilities, allowing for more honest and transparent interactions with multiple constituents.

In our interviews with corporate leaders, leadership at this level was readily apparent in only about half the subjects. For example, the President and CEO of a major metropolitan hospital exhibited significant leadership of self; she regularly engages in self-assessment exercises to better understand her leadership and communication styles and their impact not only on her top management team, but also on the organization as a whole. Furthermore, she has made self-awareness a mandatory practice throughout the organization via the implementation of self-diagnosis tools that have allowed all management and staff to engage in more open and efficient communications. Approximately 70% of her staff has also engaged in Koestenbaum's Leadership Diamond analysis, a systems tool which allows one to discuss his/her strengths and weaknesses with their immediate subordinate(s) and supervisor(s), particularly as they relate to their leadership style and perceptions of their leadership style. This CEO is also attempting to implement the practice of developing and sharing personal vision statements to better align individual, group, and organizational objectives. Leading by example, she was the first to complete her personal vision statement and share it with her entire management staff, calling the self-reflective and self-disclosure exercise "one of the hardest things I have ever done."

Other leaders interviewed also indicated that they were highly self-aware and engaged in self-regulatory behaviors. The president and owner of a direct marketing company, for example, acknowledged that in addition to setting the strategic vision for her firm, she also sets out every year a personal strategic plan whereby she outlines what she wants to accomplish in her own life (e.g., establishing an African outreach program). The president and owner of a multi-million dollar retail operation also demonstrated that she was highly self-reflective, stating that one of the issues that regularly 'kept her up at night' is "yesterday . . . you always question; did I do yesterday as good as I could have?"

In contrast, other leaders could not provide any examples of self-reflective behavior—even upon direct questioning—and seemed to lack self-awareness and self-regulatory capabilities, in general. When asked what he would do differently from a leadership perspective if he were to run the same event over again, the chairperson of a national sporting event, for instance, replied that he would take more time to select a better top management team. When asked if any of the negative reactions to his hands-on leadership style prompted him to reconsider his leadership approach, he said: "No. It is just part of the job," which was to articulate the vision and ensure buy-in. If there was dissension, his job was to rein people in. In the end, although the event was successful, his impact on the organization appears to have been somewhat different from the other leaders interviewed. Had this been a recurring event, we doubt that his leadership style would have been conducive to long term sustained performance.

Leadership of self may also extend beyond self-awareness and self-regulation to developing a particular set of character strengths that can help guide leaders through the dynamic competitive, and challenging ethical, climate of our time. The extensive research of Peterson and Seligman (2004) on character strengths and virtues, for example, can be employed to describe leadership of self. They identify "six core moral virtues that emerge consensually across cultures and throughout time" and which are associated with a set of character strengths, as follows:

(1) Wisdom and knowledge—Creativity, curiosity, open-mindedness, love of learning, perspective;
(2) Courage—Bravery, persistence, integrity, vitality;
(3) Humanity—Love, kindness, social intelligence;

(4) Justice—Citizenship, fairness, leadership;
(5) Temperance—Forgiveness and mercy, humility or modesty, prudence, self-regulation; and
(6) Transcendence—Appreciation of beauty and excellence, gratitude, hope, humor, spirituality.

Although some of these character strengths may seem at odds with the commonly held view of strategic leaders, personal attributes such as humility, modesty, and persistence have been empirically linked to Level 5 Leaders, or those leaders who have led companies that have gone from Good to Great (Collins, 2001). Positive moral and psychological capital are also theorized to be core strengths in authentic, spiritual, servant, and ethical leadership models (Fry, 2003; Greenleaf, 1977; Kanungo & Mendonca, 1996; Luthans & Avolio, 2003).

Dynamic environments will therefore place a premium on leadership of the self. When facing the many tradeoffs that arise in complex and changing environments, the leader will need a high level of self-awareness and deep judgment. A strong individual compass will prevent today's leader from simply drifting or responding to the environment and ensure that the strategic decisions made on behalf of the firm are not simple enactments of their cognitive biases, but rather self-aware, self-regulated actions rooted in introspection and self-reflection.

LEADERSHIP OF SELF AND OTHERS

Unlike leadership of self, much has been written on leadership of others, ranging from the behavioral theories and the effect of leaders on followers to the interaction of the leader and follower relationship with the organizational context (Vera & Crossan, 2004). Most of the research in leadership, in fact, has focused on the dyadic or small-group interface at various managerial levels throughout the organization. However, our focus herein is the strategic leader at the top of the organization and we add only that in today's dynamic environments, leaders must have a portfolio of both transformational and authentic leadership behaviors to effectively lead others. The integration of leadership of self with leadership of others is therefore just one necessary component of transcendent leadership.

For example, in addition to crafting a compelling vision, transformational leaders are said to move followers beyond self-interest to self-actualization through charisma, inspiration, intellectual stimula, and individual consideration (Bass, 1985). We argue, however, that in order to do so effectively in the challenging ethical climate of our time, these transformational leadership behaviors must also be married with deep introspection and leadership of self. Authentic leaders are said to be "those who are deeply aware of how they think and behave and are perceived by others as being aware of their own and others' values/moral perspectives, knowledge, and strengths; aware of the context in which they operate; and who are confident, hopeful, optimistic, resilient, and of high moral character" (Avolio, Luthans, & Walumbwa, 2004, p. 4, as cited by Avolio et al., 2004).

These character strengths are embodied in the self-awareness and internalized regulatory processes described above, as well as in the framework presented by Peterson and Seligman (2004), and are considered essential in developing similar strengths in one's followers.

The interviewed hospital president and CEO specifically noted how important it was, in setting the strategic plan for the hospital, to be aware of others' values and perspectives, including all levels of the organization in drafting the vision for the next five years: "We talk about that a lot, about being self aware. . . . In order for an organization to change, each individual has to change. And you don't change unless you are very aware of how you need to change, and are willing to do that."

Furthermore, she incorporates different learning styles into her communications, noting if others are more visual, oral, or sensory learners and then modifying her approach. This awareness is also used in generative coaching sessions with her top management team and has cascaded down in dyadic sessions throughout the organization. The aim is to engage the staff, energize them, and encourage them not only to learn about their own strengths and weaknesses, but also to feel safe in expressing their ideas. These generative coaching sessions build relationships and understanding between the two team members to support self-awareness and facilitate the capacity of all members of the organization to be more resourceful, flexible, and creative in the achievement of the strategy.

This CEO claims that the process of building self-awareness and self-regulatory leadership capabilities in her management team is a process built on trust. Importantly, she notes that "trust is not just about having good characteristics, such as integrity. It is about being consistent. If you say you are going to do something, you do something." With regards to valuing her people, she emphasizes that "it is all about the workplace. We don't get a part of a person;

we get the whole person. So, what goes on here affects your family. . . . Happy staff members are more likely to provide better care." By modeling positive leader behaviors in dyadic and small group situations, this leader is able to shape the self-awareness and self-regulatory processes of her followers, helping them develop clarity about their values, identity, and emotions (Gardner et al., 2005). These skills have been formalized in the institute's shared values of:

- Listening to appreciate diversity;
- Learning through dialogue and reflection;
- Leading with courage, transparency, and forgiveness; and
- Serving patients, families, and others with kindness.

In contrast, a recent study on managerial failure highlighted personality-based factors as one of the causal variables resulting in a leader's inability to obtain results during times of change. Specifically, managers believed that only those leaders who apply themselves to breaking bad habits and personally adhere to the highest standards of integrity, consciously expressing humility and genuine concern, were likely to achieve the results desired (Longenecker, Neubert, & Fink, 2007). Thus, integrating leadership of self with leadership of others can be said to be a key requirement of today's strategic leaders.

LEADERSHIP OF SELF AND OF ORGANIZATIONS

Crossan et al. [2008] state that leadership of self and others must also be integrated with leadership of organizations, which includes setting strategy, managing the non-human elements of the firm such as structures, rules, and procedures, and ensuring fit with the external context. Today's leaders are not just passive recipients of the rapid and turbulent changes in their environments, but rather can be dominant forces in affecting change both in their own strategies and organizations, as well as in how they interact with the overall external context.

Strategy. In setting the firm's strategy, today's leader understands the organization as a dynamic system of forces and actors that cannot be completely controlled, and therefore provides minimal constraints and simple rules within which strategy can emerge (Brown & Eisenhardt, 1998; Eisenhardt & Sull, 2001). Because the transcendent leader understands that he/she is simply part of this system, rather than setting tightly configured plans which are equally tightly controlled, he/she establishes performance aspirations within which individuals feel free to experiment and execute. The key skill is to balance stability and innovation, creatively disturbing the status quo of the organization but also enabling the firm to work at dynamic equilibrium by developing in the firm both planning and improvisational capabilities. The strategic leader who has mastered the level of self should be able to communicate value-based visions, not of a specific future, but of a set of processes and principles that will lead to a higher state of capability. The hospital CEO, for example, has implemented the following guiding principles for strategic renewal, stating that the organization is aspiring to move from a culture of "blaming to accountability; from 'command and control' to stewardship; from bosses to coaches; and from silos to systems."

Organization. In managing the non-human elements of the firm, it is the responsibility of today's leader to ensure that the organization operates adaptively by designing fluid structures, modularity of function, and easy recombination. Today's dynamic environment requires flexible, innovative, and responsive organizational structures and systems. Having provided a deep structure of values and vision, therefore, the transcendent leader can encourage initiative, ownership, and flexible career paths for organizational members, combining entrepreneurship, self-organization, and member ownership in mutually reinforcing ways (Miles, Snow, Mathews, Miles, & Coleman, 1997). This type of structure supports meritocracy and considers leadership roles to be the domain of all organizational members, depending on their ability to best lead in a given context. The president of the direct marketing firm, for example, acknowledges that her organization has moved to this more organic level. While there is a formal structure in place, she says: "It is turning into fun, and it is turning into opportunities. The people that are here, now more than ever, are picking up the reins where I don't have to. . . . I am able to trust them. They are bringing in more technology, they are bringing in more ideas and concepts, and reaching out to new clients and acquiring different kinds of contracts. . . . It is really exciting."

Environment. In managing the organization's fit with the external context, today's leader ensures that individuals, groups, and the organization have a high capacity to learn from their external and internal environments. The transcendent leader promotes learning through experimentation, experience, diversity of opinion, and collaboration. He/she understands the competitive challenges of the industry and ensures that the firm's systems, structure, and strategy are aligned to support the flow of ideas from individuals to the team and the organization and the flow of learning from the organization back to teams and individuals, managing the tension between exploitation and exploration (Crossan & Hulland, 2002; Vera & Crossan, 2004).

The CEO and President of the metropolitan hospital clearly embodies this learning orientation, building the organization's strategic map on learning and growth enablers, first asking: "What are the key strengths we need in structure, culture, and skills to excel at our desired customer and financial outcomes?" This is then manifest in the organization, not only in the processes and procedures outlined previously in the sections on leadership of self and others, but also in the implementation of formal programs such as Kaizen analysis of work-flow bottlenecks and Nine Sigma review of operating procedures. Best practices and benchmarks are therefore sought not only from within the healthcare field, but from manufacturing and other external "high consequence" industries, as well. This leader has a clear vision that more change, risk, and complexity is on the horizon and is ensuring that the internal processes are in place at the hospital to support the dynamic environment: "The problems we are solving are no different [than the airline or chemical manufacturing industry]. It is a cultural leadership backdrop: the engagement, and the empowerment, and that you can make your own changes and make them work. That is what will sustain change. It is all about change."

In fact, almost all of the executives interviewed explicitly or implicitly supported a learning organization by regularly attending and sending their staff to seminars, conferences, or other learning opportunities. For example, the owner of a retail operation believes strongly that her employees' willingness to learn is a key contributing factor to her company's continued growth and success, and regularly pays for staff to attend brand "universities," an irregular practice in the competitive retail industry. The owner of a small electrical service business has also joined a community of best practices in his industry and takes his staff on learning expeditions at host businesses throughout North America, in addition to receiving guests himself.

In short, the responsibilities of crafting strategy, establishing the structure of the organization, and making sense of the environment are key to leading in today's dynamic context. Only through deep self-awareness and the aligning of internal values and beliefs with strategic actions, will leadership of others and the organization intersect to ensure transcendent leadership and sustained, long term firm performance.

BEYOND THE ORGANIZATION

Although not explicitly included in the original model of transcendent leadership, Crossan et al. [2008] suggest that, given today's complex and uncertain yet increasingly transparent environment, today's leaders are likely to have to transcend the organizational level and master leadership at the societal level, as well. Consistent with the growing literature on corporate social responsibility and performance, we agree with the contention that the responsibilities of today's strategic leaders have moved beyond making a profit and obeying the law, to include being ethical and a good corporate citizen (Carroll, 1999). In fact, doing so is unequivocally aligned with leadership of self and displaying enduring character strengths such as courage, humanity, and justice (Peterson & Seligman, 2004).

Most leaders interviewed did extend their leadership beyond the immediate organization and into the community, serving on boards, getting involved in local causes, and organizing charity fundraisers. Explaining why he funds a yearly event for over 600 people (this year, to salute the military), the president of the small electrical services company claimed that one reason he likes to get involved is because "it sets an example in the community and maybe somebody else will do something like that . . . maybe not for that same cause. . . . I'm not looking for it to happen, but I know that it does. If I do something nice, somebody else will do something nice, as well."

The president of the direct marketing firm looks forward to the opportunity to partner with local not-for-profit organizations as a way of giving back to the community, and states this as part of her leadership philosophy: "I volunteer in a variety of areas, and so do most of my management team. . . . It is something that is encouraged at every level, being involved in the community . . . because we are very blessed by this community."

Yet, simply focusing on the societal level without regard for the organization has been referred to by some as self-serving at best and corporate theft at worst. Transcendent leaders need to understand the inter-relationship of leadership across levels and have the capacity to do so.

TRANSCENDENT LEADERSHIP: LEADING WITHIN AND ACROSS (AND BEYOND) LEVELS

In today's dynamic and ethically challenging environment, strategic leaders must be able to lead within and amongst the levels of self, others, and the organization, and likely beyond to even the societal level. Leadership at one level will no longer be sufficient to guarantee high firm performance in the long run. The era of the turnaround CEO, for example, is over. Although highly adept at leadership of the organization, this singular focus on restructuring or cost-cutting has proven to lead mostly to short term financial gains, but not to long term sustainable performance. Similarly, firm performance will also suffer if the strategic leader is focused only on transformational leadership, instilling followers with high levels of motivation, commitment, and loyalty. Without leadership of self, employees may be motivated and committed to the wrong projects; without leadership of the organization in its changing and dynamic environment, the potential for failure is magnified.

As such, only the transcendent leader (who possesses high levels of leadership of self, others, and the organization) can deliver higher sustained firm performance in today's dynamic environments. If you haven't stopped to reflect on your own leadership style, now is the time to become more self aware of your own cognitive biases and capabilities, and to understand how these may have shaped or continue to shape your strategic decisions. One former CEO of a large consumer foods company emphasized that major strategy change must begin with yourself. He remarked: "How do you expect the organization to change if you don't?" One of his more difficult experiences included confronting what he referred to as his "rackets": the excuses individuals build up in advance to explain any possible failing. He suggests they are our personal safety valve to avoid holding ourselves accountable. It is imperative, therefore, that you ask yourself if the direction your firm is headed is aligned with your internal values and beliefs. Then, look to see if this self-regulated behavior is reflected in your interactions with others and the systems and procedures you have put in place in your organization.

If you've read just a couple of last year's leadership best sellers, you have likely received only a third of this advice. Most contemporary books on the subject, and in fact much of the academic discourse as well, has focused on one level of leadership only: either leadership of the organization or leadership of others and, less frequently, leadership of self. Nonetheless, in order to navigate today's dynamic environments and the heightened moral and ethical climate of our time, developing the skills of a transcendent leader will be key to ensuring sustained long term performance for your firm. Learning to lead within and amongst the levels of self, others, and the organization—and beyond—will be associated with the highest level of firm performance in today's continually changing business landscape.

References

Aldon, L. J. (1998). Transcendent leadership and the evolution of consciousness. Unpublished doctoral dissertation, University of San Diego, CA.

Avolio, B. J., & Bass, B. (2004). *Multifactor leadership questionnaire–5X* (3rd ed.). Menlo Park, CA: MindGarden, Inc.

Avolio, B. J., & Gardner, W. L. (2005). Authentic leadership development: Getting to the root of positive forms of leadership. *The Leadership Quarterly, 16*(3), 315–338.

Avolio, B. J., Gardner, W. L., Walumbwa, F. O., Luthans, F., & May, D. R. (2004). Unlocking the mask: A look at the process by which authentic leaders impact follower attitudes and behavior. *The Leadership Quarterly, 15*(6), 801–823.

Avolio, B. J., Luthans, F., & Walumbwa, F. O. (2004). Authentic leadership: Theory-building for veritable sustained performance (Working Paper). Lincoln, NE: Gallup Leadership Institute.

Bass, B. M. (1985). *Leadership and performance beyond expectations.* New York: The Free Press.

Bettis, R. A., & Hitt, M. A. (1995, Summer). The new competitive landscape. *Strategic Management Journal, 16*(special issue), 7–19.

Boal, K. B., & Hooijberg, R. (2000). Strategic leadership research: Moving on. *The Leadership Quarterly, 11*(4), 515–549.

Brown, S. L., & Eisenhardt, K. (1998). *Competing on the edge: Strategy as structured chaos.* Boston: Harvard Business School Press.

Carroll, A. B. (1999). Corporate social responsibility: Evolution of a definitional construct. *Business and Society, 38*(3), 268–295.

Collins, J. (2001). *Good to great.* New York: Harper Business.

Crossan, M., & Hulland, J. (2002). Leveraging knowledge through leadership of organizational learning. In C. Choo & N. Bontis (Eds.), *Strategic management of intellectual capital and organizational knowledge: A collection of readings* (pp. 711–723). New York: Oxford University.

Crossan, M., Vera, D., & Nanjad, L. [2008]. Transcendent leadership: Strategic leadership in dynamic environments. *The Leadership Quarterly.*

D'Aveni, R. (1994). *Hypercompetition: Managing the dynamics of strategic maneuvering.* New York: The Free Press.

Eisenhardt, K. M., & Sull, D. N. (2001). Strategy as simple rules. *Harvard Business Review, 7*(1), 107–116.

Finkelstein, S. (2003). *Why smart executives fail and what you can learn from their mistakes.* New York: Portfolio.

Fry, L. (2003). Toward a theory of spiritual leadership. *The Leadership Quarterly,* 14(6), 693–727.

Gardiner, J. J. (2006). Transactional, transformational, and transcendent leadership: Metaphors mapping the evolution of the theory and practice of governance. *Leadership Review,* 6, 62–76.

Gardner, W. L., Avolio, B. J., Luthans, F., May, D. R., & Walumbwa, F. O. (2005). Can you see the real me? A self-based model of authentic leader and follower development. *The Leadership Quarterly,* 16(3), 343–372.

Greenleaf, R. K. (1977). *Servant leadership.* New York: Paulist Press.

Hambrick, D. C. (1988). *Navigating change.* Boston: Harvard Business School Press.

Hambrick, D. C., & Mason, P. (1984). Upper echelons: The organization as a reflection of its top managers. *Academy of Management Review,* 9(2), 193–206.

Hart, S. L., & Quinn, R. E. (1993). Roles executives play: CEOs, behavioral complexity, and firm performance. *Human Relations,* 46(5), 543–574.

Hitt, M. A., Keats, B. W., & DeMarie, S. M. (1998). Navigating in the new competitive landscape: Building strategic flexibility and competitive advantage in the 21st century. *Academy of Management Executive,* 12(4), 22–42.

House, R. J., & Aditya, R. N. (1997). The social scientific study of leadership: Quo vadis? *Journal of Management,* 2(23), 409–473.

Ilies, R., Morgeson, F., & Nahrgang, J. (2005). Authentic leadership and eudaemonic well-being: Understanding leader-follower outcomes. *The Leadership Quarterly,* 16(3), 373–394.

Ireland, R. D., & Hitt, M. A. (2005). Achieving and maintaining strategic competitiveness in the 21st century: The role of strategic leadership. *Academy of Management Executive,* 19(4), 63–77.

Kanungo, R., & Mendonca, M. (1996). *Ethical dimensions of leadership.* Thousand Oaks, CA: Sage Publications.

Longenecker, C. O., Neubert, M., & Fink, L. (2007). Causes and consequences of managerial failure in rapidly changing organizations. *Business Horizons,* 50(2), 145–155.

Luthans, F., & Avolio, B. (2003). Authentic leadership development. In K. S. Cameron, J. E. Dutton, & R. E. Quinn (Eds.), *Positive organizational scholarship.* San Francisco: Berrett-Koehler Publishers, Inc.

Miles, R., Snow, C., Mathews, J., Miles, G., & Coleman, H. (1997). Organizing in the knowledge age: Anticipating the cellular form. *Academy of Management Executive,* 11(4), 7–20.

Nadler, D. A., & Tushman, M. L. (1999). The organization of the future: Strategic imperatives and core competencies for the 21st century. *Organizational Dynamics,* 28(1), 45–60.

Peterson, C., & Seligman, M. (2004). Strengths of character and well-being. *Journal of Social and Clinical Psychology,* 23(5), 603.

Quinn, R. E. (1988). *Beyond rational management: Mastering the paradoxes and competing demands of high performance.* San Francisco: Jossey-Bass.

Vera, D., & Crossan, M. (2004). Strategic leadership and organizational learning. *The Academy of Management Review,* 29(2), 222–240.

Yammarino, F., Dionne, S., Chun, J., & Dansereau, F. (2005). Leadership and levels of analysis: A state-of-the-science review. *The Leadership Quarterly,* 16(3), 79–919.

5

⌘

Summit Leadership
Learn from Sir Edmund Hillary

David Parmenter

Sir Edmund Hillary has been credited with many things, yet few people realize what a great leader he was. After climbing Mount Everest as a team member, he achieved everything else as a CEO. Having read the book *View from the Summit* and *Hellbent or the Pole* by Geoffrey Lee Martin, I extract eleven lessons that we can apply.

Lesson 1: Properly set up your base camp. Many projects fail because of lack of planning and failure to get the infrastructure, resources, and training in place at the outset. Aspiring leaders tend to be more interested in measuring the speed of early progress than ensuring that the campaign will be completed on time and on budget. If meticulous planning and testing of gear on the glaciers in South Island before the Antarctic Expedition worked for Hillary, you should invest more time, energy, and money in setting up a base camp from which a successful summit attempt is possible.

Lesson 2: If you hope to be picked for the summit team, don't rely on reputation alone. How often are you surprised when you're *not chosen* to lead a special

Reprinted by permission of *Leadership Excellence* (February 2011). Copyright 2011 Executive Excellence.

project or *passed over* for a management or leadership position? Hillary knew there were at least three pairs of climbers capable of making the summit in Sir John Hunt's expedition. He wanted to ensure that Sir John would not overlook his team (Hillary and Tenzing), so he devised a test of stamina to show they were the fittest team. Hillary and Tenzing ascended from base camp to advanced base and back in one day—a task previously done in two days. In business, you have *endless opportunities* to highlight your strengths and show that *you are the best candidate.*

Lesson 3: Having the best team does not mean you'll be selected and succeed if you ignore the politics. Hillary had climbed endless peaks with *George Lowe* in 1952–1953. They were clearly the best Himalayan climbing team *based on experience.* Having joined the Hunt expedition, and halfway to Everest, Hillary realized that Lowe and himself, two *New Zealanders,* would not be allowed to the summit first. A takeover by two Kiwis would *never be allowed* on a British-sponsored expedition. Hillary changed his climbing partner, teaming with Sherpa *Tenzing Norgay,* and they became the first to ascend to the summit of Everest. You may have the best team, but if you don't have the support of the top team, you may need to make alternative selections to satisfy certain stakeholders. *You need to be flexible and aware of stakeholders' needs and perceptions, and the politics they answer to.*

Lesson 4: When selecting a team, ensure they are multi-skilled and have a sense of humor. Hillary was careful in his selection of staff. He recognized that in times of difficulty you want to have someone who can laugh at adversity. The last thing Hillary wanted was a team member going into a panic, or worse, a person who would rather look for a scapegoat. In addition Hillary looked for *the right mix of skills.* He recognized that having more staff does not necessarily make the team stronger. The expedition's reporter also doubled as a tractor driver; the doctor took a dentistry training course; and the cook learned extra skills, and the geologist was a mountaineer. Why would a CEO appoint people who are one-dimensional? They may be excellent when the going is easy, but the first to give up when stormy weather arrives.

Lesson 5: Do small deeds of kindness. Hillary is legendary for his small acts of kindness. For example, on hearing that a two-year-old child was seriously ill in a hospital, he immediately wrote an inspirational note to him. Naturally it was inspirational both to the parents and to their now-teenage son. *Aspiring leaders should seek to perform small acts of kindness and consideration daily*— those small acts will build a *leadership legacy.*

Lesson 6: Humility and drive are good bedfellows. Sir Edmund Hillary's obituaries mention how little he sought for himself. He achieved at everything he did, yet he never sought the limelight. His legacy is one of contribution to Mother Earth. Many Sherpa pilots, doctors, nurses, and lawyers were taught to read and write through his schools. My daughter, with a tear in her eye, once said, "He has taught me that anything is achievable."

Bill Gates is another great leader who is humble. While the press follows his every move, he seldom seeks the limelight. In a recent trip to New Zealand he was asked by a Kiwi who did not recognize him, "What do you do?" He replied, "I am in computers." The understatement of the year!

Warren Buffett, the greatest investor alive today, always looks for a CEO who is a quiet achiever rather than a flash-in-the-pan "show pony."

As a leader, remind yourself that *humility is a strength,* not a weakness. Mount a picture of Hillary on your wall as a reminder. Strive to make the world a better place. The meaning of life can be summed up in one word: *legacy.* Some of us leave a legacy through our children, some through inspiration of others, and some through deeds.

Lesson 7: Dream of (visualize) your eventual goal. Hillary was an avid comic book reader in his youth, and on long walks would *imagine himself as a hero.* He read about and idolized Shackleton and later dreamed of being the first to climb Everest. Why was the first British team unsuccessful in 1953? Was equipment failure the excuse? Yet, could they have invented a new way of climbing with oxygen bottles when they came up against *the Hillary step?* Hillary improvised a shuffle, using the oxygen bottles on the back pack and his feet as a pair of wedges, and inch by inch, in the thin air, using all of his legendary strength made it up the tight shaft. This route, now roped, is followed by thousands. The *drive to succeed* pushed Hillary to "*knock the bugger off.*" As a leader, you need to *dream of your eventual goal*—to smell, see, feel, touch, and hear what it would be like to succeed. You need to use *neuro-linguistic programming* to make your dreams your reality.

Lesson 8: Giving it a go when your instincts say no is not a great idea. Do you continue on a path when everything around you is sending signals to stop or change course? Are you compelled to complete the task rather than listen and change tactics? Hillary suffered a similar fate on his Antarctic Expedition. Twice he tried to cross over, with his Fergusson tractors, ice bridges that he felt uneasy about. These failed attempts could have proved deadly. In each case, he later found a safer route (a better option). Before you say, "Let's give it a go," look for an alternative route; you may well find the *safe bridge*.

Lesson 9: Seek help when you need it. For some aspiring leaders, seeking help is a sign of failure or weakness. In reality, seeking help can provide you with a leap up the ladder of success. Hillary sought the help of Admiral George Dufek often during his expedition to the South Pole. That help proved vital to Hillary—and rewarding for Admiral Dufek. He helped Hillary choose the site of Scott Base, which has been used ever since. And he helped Hillary at other critical stages of the expedition. What's remembered is that that expedition was successful and the gratitude Hillary had for Admiral George Dufek is clearly stated. You'll avert many costly failures if you seek advice from a trusted and wise mentor/advisor.

Lesson 10: In all projects, you can achieve other goals if you provision for them. Halfway through a project, you may realize that *higher goals could have been achieved if you'd done some planning and provisioning for them in the first place.* When asked by Vivian Fuchs to provide a Kiwi support expedition to his grand traverse of the Antarctic, Hillary had in mind the possibility of Kiwis also getting to the South Pole, and so he planned and provisioned for this possibility, even though it was never on the official agenda. His successful expedition was a triumph of Kiwi ingenuity (getting three converted tractors to the South Pole), and of his great vision. Look for *other possibilities* when planning your next expedition; you may achieve *more important goals.*

Lesson 11: Don't start a project if you can't see it through to the end. Whether ascending Mount Everest, driving tractors through the South Pole, jet boating up the Ganges, or building schools in Nepal, Hillary had a unique cluster of skills: he was a great planner, a person who is focused, and one who completes tasks. Often aspiring leaders start projects with little planning and commit only until the next interesting project comes up or when tying up the loose ends gets too boring. Hence, organizations are littered with projects *in limbo.* These projects are of *no value* until you refocus on completing them.

− PART II −

RELATIONSHIPS

> *All over this country, corporations and government agencies, there are millions of executives who imagine that their place on the organization chart has given them a body of followers. And of course it hasn't. It has given them subordinates. Whether subordinates become followers depends on whether the executives act like leaders.*
>
> JOHN GARDNER

Whether we ask successful leaders to describe the relationship they want with their followers or ask successful followers to describe the relationship they want with their leaders, we get essentially the same description. Our experience is that when followers are asked what attributes they want most from a leader, the response is, most often, honesty, respect, and a sense of belonging. Each understands the perspective of the other, and both recognize that they can be successful in the long term only if they share success. However, leadership theory and practical applications derived from theory focus, all too often, on the role of the leader in creating success, thereby undervaluing the role of the follower. In far too many organizations, the leadership role is seen as the only avenue to personal success, and therefore it is developed, encouraged, appreciated, and rewarded, whereas followership often is not.

Contemporary organizations can no longer depend upon the leader alone. The trend to form work teams so that a diversity of knowledge and skills is used to confront complex situations characterizes the environment today. We must study and appreciate the role of the follower in the dynamics of group and organizational success and recognize that all of us occupy the dual role of follower and leader. Most of us are followers more often than we are leaders, and nearly every leader also serves as a follower. Followership dominates our lives and our organizations, and leaders come from the ranks of the followers. In fact, few leaders can be successful without first having learned the skills of following. Aristotle's *Politics,* Plato's *Republic,* Homer's *Odyssey,* and Hegel's *Phenomenology of Mind* affirm the mastery of followership as the sine qua non of leadership: qualities that we associate with effective followers are the same qualities that we find in effective leaders. The experience of following also gives leaders perspective and enables them to share vision, communicate with empathy, treat people as individuals, and empower followers to achieve shared goals and objectives. Effective leaders realize that they are also followers and purposefully set the example when performing that role. Thus, a major tenet of developing effective leadership is understanding, experiencing, and modeling effective followership.

In organizations where good followership is appreciated, effective followers and leaders are very comfortable moving from one role to the other. Fortunately, more and more organizations are recognizing that good followership leads to a strategic advantage and have begun to develop and reward effective followers.

In an attempt to get around the stereotypes associated with followership, many organizations refer to their followers with terms such as *constituents, associates, members,* or *colleagues.* The term *subordinate* has begun to fade from the vocabularies. However, what we call people in our organizations matters much less than how we treat them. No matter what they are called, followers who are treated with disdain by those in charge are clearly regarded as subordinates.

Followers want to feel a sense of partnership with the leader in accomplishing goals and defining a path to the future. Social, economic, and technological conditions have encouraged a better-educated and more sophisticated constituency; superior education, skills, and access to information are no longer the sole purview of leaders. As a result of the blurred differences between followers' abilities and their own, leaders must more actively involve followers in organizational processes.

If leaders are to develop good followers, they must encourage participation in the creation of the vision, mission, and goals for the organization while allowing their ideas to be modified and "owned" by everyone. Separating the individual from leadership creates "we," building a true sense of involvement and empowerment among followers. Hence a requisite leadership communication skill is listening, and the necessary followership communication skill is courageously speaking up.

Failure to recognize interdependencies between leader and follower can have serious consequences for both. These interdependencies are critical to a leader's success and ensure an ongoing pattern of leadership development. In many ways, leaders serve followers—certainly a reversal of traditional perceptions. But effective leaders create opportunities, help provide necessary resources, delegate authority, and vigorously support the decisions made and actions taken. Often, leaders must watch while others do things differently than they would have. Helping people learn by allowing them to make mistakes takes true courage and results in organizational learning. This is how leaders develop effective followers, who, in turn, are learning the elements of effective leadership.

Many leaders thrive on having followers revere them. Unfortunately, the organization becomes completely dependent upon that leader—everything happens because of her or him. Truly effective leaders have people around them who are bright, critical, courageous, and independent. Decisions are made at the organizational level having the most information. Followers are given the means and responsibility to do the job; creativity and innovation are prized. Thus, leaders are best evaluated on the basis of organizational success and how well they develop their followers.

LEADERSHIP PERSPECTIVES

In Chapter 6, William E. Rosenbach, Thane S. Pittman, and Earl H. Potter III present their conceptual model of followership in "What Makes a Follower?" They describe effective followers as partners who are committed to taking the initiative for high performance and healthy relationships with their leaders. The authors argue that leaders who encourage partnerships and followers who seek to be partners characterize organizations that thrive in the rapidly changing global environment.

In "Courageous Followers, Courageous Leaders: New Relationships for Learning and Performance" (Chapter 7), Ira Chaleff posits that courage is required of both leaders and followers if they expect their dynamic reciprocal relationships to lead to high performance.

Craig Pearce, in "Follow the Leaders," Chapter 8, suggests that teams of experts can be a lot more effective if they practice shared leadership. He discusses benefits and limitations of shared leadership in teams.

In Chapter 9, "Turbo-Charge Your Leadership Through Mentoring," Lois J. Zachary proposes that it is the leader's responsibility to serve as a role model, to mentor the next generation of leaders, and to ensure continual learning. When leaders strengthen others through mentoring, she says, they strengthen themselves.

In "When Mentoring Goes Bad" (Chapter 10), Dawn E. Chandler, Lillian Eby, and Stacy E. McManus describe how and why mentoring can go "bad." They explain how to manage mentoring relationships and how to recognize early stages of potential problems.

6

❧

What Makes a Follower?

William E. Rosenbach, Thane S. Pittman,
and Earl H. Potter III

Much about the nature of leadership has changed over the years, as many of the chapters of this book describe. And while we have seen minor changes in the content of leadership, most of this change has occurred in the context of leadership which is undergoing rapid and turbulent transformational change. The dynamic global economic and political environment, scarcity of resources, market place competition, instantaneous communications, new technologies and a rapidly changing workforce make effective leadership essential in these ambiguous, complex and uncertain times. The people in our workforces are more diverse, multicultural and heterogeneous, more dispersed, demand more collaboration than competition, insist on better interpersonal relationships with their leaders and they have high expectations for what their organizations will do to support them. We have traditionally looked to our leaders to create the plan, define the path and encourage the heart. In times such as these, more thought should be given to involving followers in these critical components of leadership.

More thought should be given to the follower—what good followers might be, what good followers must be, and how to develop good followers. An organization that can succeed with followers who simply do what they are told

Reprinted with permission of the authors.

Dr. Robert Ginnett has studied airline crews in order to describe the behavior of the most effective pilots in command. Ginnett found that the most effective leaders were those who engaged the entire crew as partners, with the result that each was fully involved in and attentive to the ongoing mission. Moreover, the leader had created an environment in which crew members were enabled to behave as partners, sharing information as they got it, offering alternative perspectives without fear, and actively seeking ways to improve operations at all times.

poses leadership challenges that are different from the challenges of leading a team of creative, engaged followers. Conditions that call for proactive followers call for a particular approach to human capital development and leadership.

Leadership experts have long argued for consultation among leaders and followers when conditions permit, usually when the problem is complex, expertise is widely distributed among the members of a group, and there is time for deliberation. Then, there are the times when the pace of action is fast and orders are called for. The challenge these days is that the tempo of operations has increased in general. It is too easy to believe that every situation is one in which there is no time for consultation and no place for alternative ideas. Yet, the evidence is clear that followers often have information and ideas that are essential to the success of operations. In fact, the failure to bring all perspectives to bear on an operation can have disastrous consequences.

FOLLOWER STYLES

The most effective followers know that they cannot be fully effective unless they work with both a commitment to high performance and a commitment to developing effective relationships with colleagues (including their supervisor), whose collaboration is essential to success in their own work. These followers are intent on high performance and recognize that they share the responsibility for the quality of the relationship they have with their leaders. Two dimensions (performance initiative and relationship initiative) describe four follower roles that are familiar to organizational leaders: the subordinate, the contributor, the politician, and the partner.

Types of Followers

Subordinate. The subordinate is a follower who does what he or she is told—competent at a satisfactory level but not one to whom the organization looks for leadership or to whom challenging assignments are given. We have seen this follower in traditional assembly line operations. The subordinate keeps a job and may rise in a seniority-driven organization but demonstrates neither an interest in relationships nor a commitment to high performance. The subordinate is the only kind of valued follower in hierarchical organizations that operates only with orders from the top and obedience from the bottom. In organizational settings where this is desired behavior, "good" followers will exhibit these characteristics even when they are fully capable of and even desirous of behaving like individuals described in other quadrants of this analysis. It is also the likely style of a somewhat or completely disaffected follower who is not interested in giving anything extra, believes that high performance will not be recognized and rewarded, or whose job is not one of his or her primary concerns. New followers in an organization may also temporarily adopt this style while they attempt to discover "which way the wind is blowing" in terms of organization culture and expected follower behavior.

Contributor. This type of follower behaves in an exemplary way, works hard and is known for the quality of his or her work. This person rarely seeks to understand the perspective of the boss, however, and generally waits for direction before turning to new challenges. Although this person is thorough and creative in obtaining the resources, information, and skills that are needed to do the job, the interpersonal dynamics of the workplace are not of particular concern. As a result, the contributor rarely shares her or his expertise and knowledge. These individuals can develop into full partners by gaining skills and perspectives on the relationship initiative dimension. Alternatively, their valued inclinations can be accommodated and their work value maximized by allowing them to focus on where they excel and what they feel comfortable doing, and by removing or minimizing aspects of the job that call for interpersonal relationships with the supervisor and others. Contributors pose a leadership challenge to develop them into contributing and engaged organization citizens.

Politician. The politician gives more attention to managing relationships than to maximizing performance. This person possesses valuable interpersonal qualities that are often misdirected or misunderstood. Followers such as these are unusually sensitive to interpersonal dynamics and are valuable for their ability to contribute when interpersonal difficulties have arisen or might arise. They can provide valuable assistance to the leader because they are willing and able to give insights into group relationships. However, often these followers neglect the defined aspects of their jobs in favor of the more relationship-oriented or political aspects of their relationship with the supervisor and others. This is a particular problem when others rely on them for job performance. Politicians can become full partners by focusing on job performance and learning how to balance these two concerns, or they can be accepted as they are and given responsibilities that call primarily for the skills and inclinations they possess. Since politicians often have well developed networks, they can be valuable during times of rapid change, threatening competition and organizational vulnerabilities. Jobs characterized by the dual role of follower and leader often are ideal for the politician.

Partner. Partners are those who have the competence and energy to do the job that they are assigned but who are also attentive to the purpose of the organization. At any time partners understand and share the goals of their leader and use this understanding to focus their own efforts. Such followers seek to master the skills required for their job and maximize their own accomplishments while seeking also to understand their boss's agenda and the strategy for accomplishing that agenda. Partners understand how to get ideas into play when the tempo of operations is high and when it is time to do what they are asked.

The most effective leaders develop their followers as partners by teaching them how to play this role. But not all organizational members are, or need to be, partners. The role of partner is reserved for mature team members who are high performers with the experience and commitment to understand the big picture. It is a role to which all followers can aspire and is not dependent upon rank or position. Leaders and followers who behave as partners make modern organizations work at all times and under all conditions.

The partner is committed to high performance and effective relationships. The energy given to the development of relationships serves the purpose of gaining the kind of understanding that leads to plans and actions that anticipate new directions and contributions that serve unmet needs. Organizations that anticipate and keep pace with change in the global environment are characterized by leaders who encourage partnership and followers who seek to be partners.

Sometimes the best way to staff an organization that will rely on its members' behaving as partners is to hire them. At other times, leaders will need to develop partners from those assigned to the organization. In either case, leaders who have to hire or develop partners need a model to guide their efforts. What follows is such a model (Figure 6.1).

FIGURE 6.1—FOLLOWER STYLES

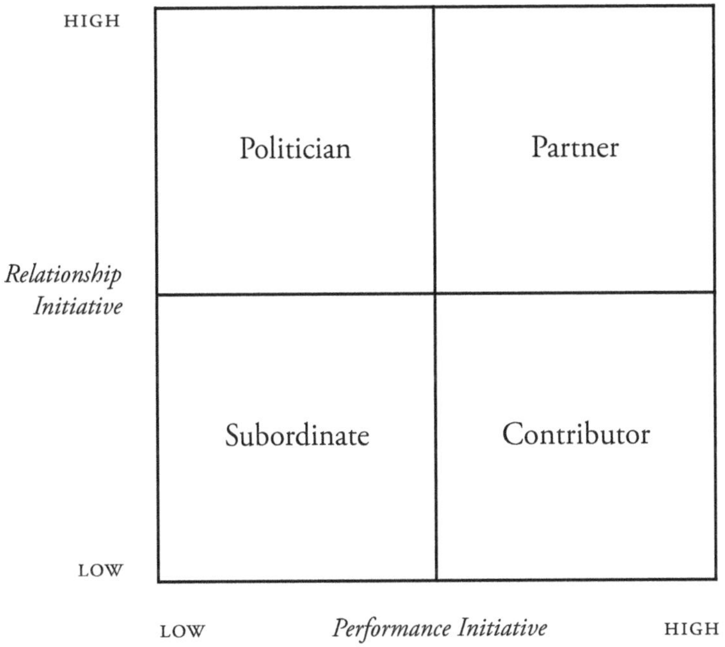

FOLLOWER BEHAVIORS

The four types of followers can be identified by their behavior on the performance initiative dimension and the relationship initiative dimension.

Performance Initiative

Performance initiative refers to the follower's active efforts to do a good job. A person who demonstrates a great deal of performance initiative finds ways to improve his or her own performance in the organization, which might include improving skills, sharing resources with team members and trying new strategies. The people at the high end of this scale understand that their future depends on the future of the organization and are not content to simply do what they were asked to do yesterday. At the low end of this scale one finds satisfactory performers, whereas at the high end one finds experts who lead in their fields and whose contributions strengthen the performance of the organization.

To assess this dimension of follower initiative, we need to consider the extent to which the follower thinks of ways to get his or her assigned job done, the extent to which the follower treats himself or herself as a valuable resource, how well the follower works with coworkers, and what view the follower takes toward organizational and environmental change. Followers differ in the extent to which they take positive initiatives in each of the four domains described below:

Doing the Job. Followers vary in the extent to which they strive to be as good as they can be at what they do. At one end of this continuum are the followers who go through the motions, performing the tasks that are assigned to them up to the minimum standards required to keep their jobs, and doing little or no more. At the other end of this continuum, some followers care deeply about the quality of their performance. They set standards for themselves and others that are higher than the minimum prescribed by the organization, and that are focused on effective performance rather than on merely meeting defined standards. For these followers, work is an important and integral part of their lives. They take pride in what they do and apply high personal standards for performance from which they can derive personal satisfaction. They usually have leaders who model behaviors that lead to high commitment to superior job performance and who inspire followers to emulate them.

Working with Others. Another important dimension of follower performance is working with others in the organization. At one extreme is the follower who cannot work well with others and therefore is continually involved in arguments and disputes, irritating everyone in the process. These followers actually interfere with the performance of others in the organization. In contrast, some followers work alone. They do not have difficulties with others, but they do not really work with them either. Their performance is solely dependent on what they themselves do (or so they think). But many followers do take advantage of working with others, to varying degrees. When followers work effectively with others, they are able to balance their own personal interests with the interests of others, discovering a common purpose and working to achieve common goals. That means emphasizing cooperation over competition, finding success in the success of the whole group instead of in self-achievement only. They view their leaders as coaches, mentors and colleagues rather than bosses.

Self as a Resource. Another important aspect of follower performance initiative lies in the extent to which the person treats herself or himself as a valuable but limited resource. Some followers pay little attention to their own well-being, neglecting physical, mental, and emotional health. This may yield some short-term benefits for the organization when the follower is most effective in important ways; in the long run such neglect is likely to lead to burnout or stagnation (depending on the other aspects of follower performance initiative). Followers who will be effective over the long haul recognize that they are their own most valuable resource and take care to maintain their own physical, mental, and emotional health by balancing work and other interests (e.g., family and friends, community activities and relations, physical and nutritional fitness). Leaders play a very important role in helping followers maintain this balance by modeling its importance and supporting followers' efforts to stay healthy and valuable to themselves and the organization.

Embracing Change. The other important dimension of follower initiative is the follower's orientation to change. In many cases a follower's reaction to change is to ignore it or hide from it. Change is threatening and confusing, altering the time-honored and familiar. Some followers actively take the initiative to resist change, finding ways to prevent things from being done differently. At the positive end of this dimension are the followers who look for new and better ways to do things because they are committed to continuous quality improvement and see change as the vehicle for continuous improvement. These followers see change as an opportunity for improvement for their organizations and themselves. Such followers anticipate or look for change. They can be extremely effective as agents for change, by explaining to their coworkers the advantages of doing things differently; and showing by example how different doesn't have to mean worse. Leaders who are responsible for implementing change should evaluate their followers on this dimension, looking to those who will embrace change as their vanguard.

Relationship Initiative

Relationship initiative refers to the follower's active attempts to improve his or her working relationship with the leader. People who demonstrate a high degree of relationship initiative find ways to help the leader succeed because they know that "you can't succeed if your supervisor fails."

On the relationship initiative dimension there are several questions to be explored: To what extent does the follower understand and identify with the leader's vision for the organization? Does the follower actively try to engender mutual trust with the leader? To what extent is the follower willing to communicate in a courageous fashion with the leader? How actively does the follower work to negotiate differences with the leader? At the low end of this dimension people take the relationship that they are given. At the high end they work to increase openness and understanding in order to gain a perspective that can inform their choices as a partner. The following subscales describe the relationship initiative:

Identifying with the Leader. Followers vary considerably in the extent to which they understand and empathize with the leader's perspective. Many followers simply do not. Viewing the leader as something strange and not quite human, they do not try to think about how things look from the leader's perspective or what the leader's goals or problems might be. In organizations with clear hierarchical structures and relatively strict chains of command, it is probably quite natural to see this element missing in the typical follower's approach to the leader. Followers may even be encouraged to think of their leaders as sufficiently different (i.e., superior) as to defy understanding by mere mortals. In contrast, some followers have thought more dispassionately about their leaders, understand their aspirations and styles, and have developed sufficient respect for the leader to adopt those aspirations as their own. These followers understand the leader's perspective, do what they can to help the leader succeed, and take pride and satisfaction in the leader's accomplishments. Leaders who try to make their own views, goals, aspirations and concerns understood by their followers make it much easier for their followers to adopt and identify with their perspectives.

Building Trust. Followers can also take the initiative to act in ways that will build their leader's confidence and trust in them. This means that the follower will look for and take advantage of opportunities to demonstrate to the leader that she or he is reliable, discreet, and loyal. Followers who demonstrate these qualities to their leaders will in turn be asked for their opinions and reactions to new ideas. Followers who do not seek out such opportunities for building trust, who do not understand or see as important this aspect of their relationship with their leaders, will be treated accordingly and will not be in a position to help their leaders as much as they might. Leaders can encourage followers on this by making available opportunities to demonstrate trustworthiness and by rewarding such behavior with their attention and their confidence and confidences. Mutual trust is the glue that holds the relationships between leaders and followers together.

Courageous Communication. Part of building trust includes being honest, even when that is not the easiest thing to do. This aspect of relationship initiative is important enough to consider in its own right. Some followers fear (often with good reason) being the bearer of bad news and are likely to refrain from speaking unpleasant truths. This can range from the classic notion of the yes-person to simply refraining from speaking one's mind when that might be uncomfortable for the speaker and listeners. But followers who take the initiative in their relationships with their leaders are willing to speak the truth even when others may not enjoy hearing the truth, in order to serve the goals of the organization. A follower who exhibits courageous communication takes risks in order to be honest. Followers are more likely to take risks when the leader has developed a culture where followers are not only allowed to deliver courageous communication but are expected to and are rewarded for doing so.

Negotiating Differences. Another aspect of relationship initiative concerns the follower's approach to differences that arise between leaders and followers. A follower who is oriented toward improving her or his relationship with the leader is in a position to negotiate or mediate these differences. In the case of a difference of opinion between a leader and follower, the follower may engage in open or hidden opposition to the leader's decisions, hiding his or her differences of opinion and quickly agreeing with the leader regardless of true personal opinion. Alternatively, the follower who is concerned about the leader-follower relationship will air these differences in order to have a real discussion that may persuade either party or lead to a compromise that is satisfactory to everyone. This, although desirable, can present a risk for the follower unless the leader has created an environment that encourages followers to air differences and to take a win-win negotiating approach in their interactions with their leaders. The big payoffs are outcomes that lead to creative and innovative actions that benefit leaders and followers.

DEVELOPING PARTNERS

While each of the follower styles can be effective in organizations, leaders can create the conditions that lead followers to partnership. This requires that leaders know what they are looking for in their followers. The model we have described above presents this picture. Creating the right conditions for effective followership next requires a clear understanding of practical steps that invite followers to partnership.

Sharon Moore, owner of Moore Interiors, makes a point of making room for partners in her company. When Moore Interiors reorganized and moved functions between its two buildings, the warehouse became the company's new headquarters. Sharon decided to identify the former warehouse as "Moore Interiors" in bold letters on the warehouse and gave the job of putting the name on the building to a salesman in the company. She also gave the salesman the license to figure out how to do the job, which would take a week.

As the work unfolded Sharon could see that the salesman had chosen a different approach than she originally had in mind. He was putting three-foot-tall letters six feet apart so that "Moore Interiors" would stretch across the entire face of the large building and "Beauty for Rooms" (the company's motto) would make a bold statement on the opposite side of the building. Sharon thought about redirecting the young man's efforts but then thought of the cost to personal initiative of doing so. She decided to let the salesman finish the way he had started. In the weeks after the job was done, the company received numerous compliments on the appearance of the new headquarters building. Sharon decided that the job did look better than what she had had in mind, but more important, one more salesman understood that his ideas were valued. Even more important, Sharon shared her reflections about this event with all of the employees. The wider result was that everyone understood how the owner viewed quality, initiative, and teamwork.

Those leaders who share their own thinking about why they do what they do and push their followers to think with them about why things work the way they do also push their followers to become partners. Those who encourage feedback on operations and welcome questions from their followers have a greater chance of achieving partnership. Ginnett's work shows that the difference between the best pilots in command and the others is that they directly engage each member of the crew and empower them to be active partners in the success of the mission. The best partners learn how to share what they see and think because their leaders teach them when to give their input—and when not to. Leaders who work day-to-day to create partners will find them ready when they need them, and partners who are willing to accept this role will find that they are valued by their leaders.

EPILOGUE

It is counterintuitive but true, that larger complex organizations often offer employees the greatest freedom to choose follower roles, especially if they are what Karl Weick has called "loosely coupled" organizations. In these situations, individual followers can create partnerships that significantly increase the probability of their success, even when the organization as a whole "hasn't got a clue." The best will recognize this opportunity and grab it. So think about sharing this chapter with colleagues—followers and leaders. Remember that followers who are true partners act in the best interests of the organization and their leader. You can't lose!

References

Chaleff, Ira. 2009. *The Courageous Follower: Standing Up to and for Our Leaders.* 3rd Ed. San Francisco: Berrett-Koehler Publishers, Inc.

Ginnett, R. C. 1990. "Crews as groups: Their formation and their leadership." In E. L. Wiener, B. B. Kanki, and R. L. Helmreich (Eds.), *Cockpit Resource Management.* San Diego: Academic Press.

Rosenbach, W. E., Pittman, T. S., Potter, E. H., and Baker, S. D. 1997. "The Performance and Relationship Questionnaire." Gettysburg College, Gettysburg, PA.

7

❧

Courageous Followers, Courageous Leaders

New Relationships for
Learning and Performance

Ira Chaleff

How many times have you worked in an organization in which bright, mid-level managers were frustrated by the difficulty of influencing senior executives whose leadership style was impeding organizational growth, productivity or morale?

'Young Turks,' as they are sometimes called, are often brimming with energy to innovate and test new ways of meeting organizational challenges. The senior executives, who cultural myth holds to be the change agents, are often mired in old ways of doing things with which they are comfortable. They are the roadblock, not the road, to innovation.

Alternatively, these bright, mid-level people may be dismayed to watch a new senior executive who does not fully appreciate how the company works, start reorganizing, downsizing, outsourcing or merging in ways that will not be viable. Anyone daring to question the new broom is quickly earmarked as someone who needs to go. Silence reigns. A year or two later, the board and the investors are left to clean up the mess resulting from the leader's high-handed style.

Reprinted by permission of Ira Chaleff. Copyright 2004 Ira Chaleff.

It is the quality of the relationship of leaders and followers, all the way up and down the organization chart, that makes or breaks organizations. Those lower down in the organization have more direct experience with its people, processes and customers and need to be able to influence the leaders' thinking on which way the organization should go. They cannot be intimidated by the power and trappings of office of the leaders to whom they report. Yet, as we know, they often are intimidated.

Traditional leadership theory puts the responsibility for the leader-follower relationship with the leader. In my observation, it often works the other way around. Those who work most closely with the leader, the senior 'followers' if you will, need to assume responsibility for keeping their relationship with the leader honest, authentic and courageous. 'Yes men' need not apply.

There are two distinct roles that executives and managers are called upon to play. One is the role of leader in their own right. The other is the role of courageous follower. Endless attention is paid to leadership qualities, selection, training, development and evaluation. Who ever pays attention to how well these same individuals perform their role as courageous followers? Virtually no one. Why is this?

We are a society in love with leadership and uncomfortable with follower-ship, though the subjects are inseparable. We don't honor followership. We talk pejoratively of followers being weak individuals. And we certainly don't train staff how to be strong followers who are not only capable of brilliantly supporting their leaders, but can also effectively stand up to them when their actions or policies are detrimental and need rethinking.

As a result, the orientation of those around the leader often becomes personal survival instead of group optimization. Optimum group performance requires that both leaders and followers place the organization's welfare at least on par with protecting their personal interests. As Chris Argyris of Harvard observes, in most groups the individuals are so concerned with avoiding embarrassment or personal threat, they shy away from the conversations that need to occur to fundamentally improve performance. This is the antithesis of the vaunted 'Learning Organization.' Important issues become undiscussable.

Where thinly disguised authoritarian relationships still prevail (leader dictates, follower complies or else) team members are driven down Abraham Maslow's hierarchy of motivation. Their needs for physical security and social acceptance outweigh pride in organizational achievement. Instead of risking the conversations that are needed to address leadership's own contributions to mediocre performance, they "play the game" and conform, regardless of the cost to the organization.

If leaders are exceptionally smart, they create environments in which such honest communication is the norm and rewarded. But, human nature seems to conspire against this and, most of the time, few speak truth to power. If they do so, and they get rebuffed, they don't do it again. Instead, they complain to each other and to their spouses, but no longer to the person who needs to hear the message and do something about it.

How many times have you found yourself in this position in an organization? How much do you think this type of behavior costs organizations? But if you find yourself in a follower role with a leader who is not using his or her power well, why should you risk your job by seeking to change the status quo? The simplest answer is because it is a better way to live. Win or lose, you've carried yourself with integrity and self-respect.

The more complex answer is that, if you aspire to senior leadership positions yourself, you'd better learn to take risks. Leaders who can't risk, can't lead. Here's a chance to get in practice.

How do you go about this? I believe that there is a two part answer to transforming leader-follower relations and creating the conditions in which a learning organization can emerge. The first part has to do with ourselves, the second with "the other."

At the heart of all transformation of relationships lies transformation of ourselves. This is both where we have the most power to create change and the most reluctance to confront the need for it. In this instance, the process starts with an honest examination of how we have learned to cope with authority relationships. Do we tend to be subservient? Cynical? Prickly and rebellious? Functional, but always playing it safe?

These and other patterns exert a price on the relationship. Ideally we would have mature relationships between self-confident, mutually respectful, emotionally and intellectually honest peers, each operating from a prescribed role for the common good. Often this is no more easily achieved between managers and subordinates than it is between forty year old adults and their overbearing parents. Focusing on our own end of the relationship, rather than on what is being done to us, is usually the best place to start.

Some of the key points to examine and reflect on include:

- Am I energetically pursuing the group's purpose and aligning my self-interests with it? Or, am I holding back my full contribution, including my willingness to take risks?
- Do I need to take more initiative to ensure that the group is effectively pursuing its mission? Will the way I am behaving in this relationship,

or in authority relationships generally, permit me to do that, or do I need to try new behaviors?

- What is my power based on in this situation that would enable me to take greater initiative? What combination of knowledge, skills, reputation, positional authority, networks and communication channels can I bring to bear? Who do I need to align myself with to effectively create the needed change?
- Why am I hesitant to act? Have I given up hope? Become cynical? Do I think that someone else will take the first step? Have I let myself off the hook because I raised my concern once and it wasn't acted on? Doesn't mature, responsible behavior require persistence?
- Do the perceived risks of taking the initiative require courage in order to act? If so, what are my personal sources of courage on which I can draw? If I don't know, how can I find out? Living effectively requires courage.
- Have I earned the leader's trust so that I have a platform from which to speak? If not, why not? Is my own performance not up to what it needs to be? If so, how will I remedy that?
- Do I have the skills to effectively confront the leader without making him or her defensive? Can I convey that what I am saying is in his or her interest to hear? If not, how will I develop those skills?

The clearer we become about our end of the relationship with a leader, the more effectively we can approach "the other" end. This is the second part of the answer. We can make several mistakes in this regard to which we must be alert.

One error is to rationalize away the leader's behavior. We can genuinely like the leader as an individual and admire many of his or her character traits. Because, overall, we like the leader, we tolerate the counterproductive or dysfunctional behavior. But in doing so, we let the organization go on paying a steep price for this behavior. Moreover, we are placing this leader, whom we like, at risk because sooner or later, the behavior will catch up with him and the consequences are often regrettable.

An opposite, and even greater error we can make is to lose our respect for the leader. In a leader-follower relationship that has deteriorated, much like in a deteriorated marriage, we are so painfully aware of the other's shortcomings that we lose sight of the other's strengths, struggles and value.

To be an effective change agent or partner, we need to reconnect with what is right about the leader's behavior. It is only from a platform of respect for the other that we can initiate transformation efforts without being perceived and treated as a threat. In this case, it is helpful to reflect on such questions as:

- What skills and attributes enabled the leader to attain the current leadership position? How were these adaptive in the environment in which the leader developed?
- Are there ways, with a little modification, that these skills and attributes can be better utilized to help accomplish the organization's mission? What specifically would make a difference and how can I effectively communicate that?
- What pressures and challenges is the leader under now? Are those challenges pushing the leader to rely on old 'proven' habits rather than risk new, potentially more productive behaviors?
- If the group gave the leader greater support, or a different type of support in dealing with those challenges, might there be less reliance on the dysfunctional behaviors? How can we do this?
- What in the leader's self-interest can I appeal to that would make the leader more receptive to making changes?

Answering these questions in relation to ourselves and our leaders begins a process of transformation. Barriers to organizational performance can then get discussed. Learning and growth can occur.

We can apply the same strategy towards peers whose style or performance is holding back the team. When we are receptive to both receiving and initiating honest and respectful feedback, to having difficult but necessary conversations, we can help our team break unproductive patterns and learn new, healthy ways of communicating and working together.

We spend so much of our lives with the people with whom we work. We may as well do so with elan, with a forthright style that meets the world head on. If we are willing to risk having our efforts rejected, we may be surprised at how well they work. There is great satisfaction in positively influencing a leader or an organization so that its performance and morale improves.

It is also the best training for becoming a leader who knows how to create such organizations. When will you start?

8

Follow the Leaders

Craig L. Pearce

It's a common corporate approach to a problem: Build a team of experts from different parts of the company and ask them to find a solution.

But these teams could be a lot more effective if companies took one radical step: Share leadership.

This concept, of course, flies in the face of the traditional idea of how companies should operate—one person is in charge, and the others follow. But in a team of specialists, one expert usually doesn't have the know-how to understand all the facets of the job at hand. Instead, a better approach is to share the top duties, so the person in charge at any moment is the one with the key knowledge, skills and abilities for the aspect of the job at hand. When that changes, a new expert should step to the fore.

Our research, in fact, suggests that teams that perform poorly tend to be dominated by the team leader, while high-performing teams have a shared-leadership structure. But beware: There are some risks executives run by sharing the reins. And our research suggests also that success may depend on the particular country where a business is operating.

Typically, teams are created because the company has a problem that needs to be addressed, such as devising a new product line. The company chooses one person from design, say, and others from engineering, manufacturing,

---

marketing and production. If all these people weigh in, the thinking goes, the process is more effective and the end product is better.

WHO'S THE BOSS?

But more often than not, the company makes one of those experts the sole team leader, and immediately that leader is at a knowledge disadvantage. After all, the purpose of the team is to bring together people with a diverse set of skills. So the leader often doesn't understand enough about the other team members' jobs to guide them at crucial moments. An engineer, for instance, probably isn't going to make a good leader when the team is hashing out how to market a product.

A better approach is to let the team member whose expertise is needed at the moment take the lead. The marketing expert, for instance, would be better off taking charge when the team is deciding how to sell its new idea to consumers.

Our research shows just how effective shared leadership can be. We undertook four studies of dozens of teams in a variety of industries, conducting surveys of team members and analyzing statistics about their companies. In every case, we found that shared leadership led to better results.

For example, we recently completed a study of 66 companies on the Inc. 500 list, looking at five-year growth in earnings and the number of employees, and surveying top management team members about their experiences. We found that shared leadership was a significant predictor of a company's growth rates: If a company's top management team practiced shared leadership, there was an excellent chance that the company's financials were headed up.

In some cases, companies didn't just share leadership within the top management team; they gave individual teams oversight power that was once reserved for top executives, such as whether to pursue a certain product line. Why? Senior leaders realized that they don't have enough time or relevant information to make all of the decisions in a fast-changing and complex world. Individuals down the line may be better informed and therefore more able to make the right decisions.

Take information technology, whose shelf life is measured in months. It is impossible for any single executive to be fully aware of the gamut of developments on the horizon. Software engineers know more about the ever-changing technical options than a boss would, while marketing experts have a clearer idea of what buyers are demanding from new products. So, it makes sense for companies to let teams of those workers shape new offerings, instead of relying on an executive to shoulder the burden alone.

HOW FAR CAN YOU GO?

Still, the practice of shared leadership has limits. For one, it generally requires a bit of time to develop. Shared leadership is most effective when leaders have a sense of what their teammates can do and who should be in charge at any given time. But they generally won't know that until the team has been working together for a while. So, it might be a better idea to rely on a single strong manager to run the show until the team members can suss each other out.

Personality can also cloud the issue. In some cases, team members might resist sharing the lead because of personal ambition or narcissism. Meanwhile, teams are often plagued by interdepartmental feuds among members. What if you represent the VP of marketing on the task force, and the executive has given you very specific marching orders—while someone from accounting has been given contrary instructions?

And, obviously, shared leadership can't flourish if team members don't have the necessary management skills required to lead one another effectively. A bad leader, for instance, might clumsily attempt to influence other team members and create emotional conflict—which could spiral out of control and lead to the demise of the team.

WHERE YOU LIVE MATTERS

The potential for shared leadership also varies by country, as we learned from reanalyzing data on workplace attitudes and values across 53 nations and regional groupings.

Before we go further, a caveat: What follows requires some sweeping generalizations about nations and people. Obviously, such generalizations don't apply to every person in every country. But our research suggests that the broad assertions hold a lot of truth.

We examined three categories of workplace attitudes and values. First: How much do people in a society accept unequal distribution of power in institutions and organizations?

Arab countries, Belgium, Brazil, Chile, Colombia, Costa Rica, East Africa, Ecuador, France, Greece, Guatemala, Hong Kong, Indonesia, Iran, Korea,

Malaysia, Mexico, Pakistan, the Philippines, Panama, Peru, Portugal, El Salvador, Singapore, Spain, Taiwan, Thailand, Turkey, Uruguay, West Africa, Venezuela and Yugoslavia all scored high on this measure—meaning they're characterized by centralized decision-making in organizations.

Countries with a low score are marked by egalitarianism and decentralized decision-making. In this category: Argentina, Australia, Austria, Canada, Denmark, Finland, Germany, Britain, India, Ireland, Israel, Italy, Jamaica, Japan, the Netherlands, New Zealand, Norway, South Africa, Sweden, Switzerland and the U.S.

Clearly, it's tougher to share leadership when a society is based on unequal distribution of power. Those who occupy leadership positions are less likely to share their authority, since they likely believe it is something they have earned; likewise, followers may be reluctant to share leadership because they view control as the sole prerogative of the appointed leader. Followers may also judge a leader to be weak if he or she attempts to hand over the reins.

- The Mistake: When companies put together teams of employees, they usually hamstring the group right from the start by appointing one team member to lead the crew.
- The Alternative: Leadership should be shared among team members, passing to whoever has the most expertise for the job at hand. Our research shows that when teams share leadership, their companies usually see big benefits.
- The Caveat: Shared leadership doesn't work in all situations—for instance, if the teammates haven't had time to learn each other's strengths and gauge who should be in charge at any given time. Shared leadership also faces big hurdles in some cultures, such as those that generally favor strong central authority.

Next, we examined the degree to which these countries were aggressive or nurturing. Aggressive societies have people who are assertive, materialistic and competitive. They're oriented toward the achievement of goals, at the expense of others. On the list: Arab countries, Australia, Belgium, Canada, Colombia, Ecuador, Britain, Greece, Hong Kong, India, Ireland, Jamaica, Malaysia, Mexico, New Zealand, Pakistan, the Philippines, South Africa, Switzerland, the U.S. and Venezuela.

Nurturing societies, on the other hand, are more concerned with developing the potential of all, rather than competition. Countries that scored high on this measure were Argentina, Austria, Brazil, Chile, Costa Rica, Denmark, East Africa, Finland, France, Germany, Guatemala, Indonesia, Iran, Israel, Italy, Japan, Korea, the Netherlands, Norway, Panama, Peru, Portugal, El Salvador, Singapore, Spain, Sweden, Taiwan, Thailand, Turkey, Uruguay, West Africa and Yugoslavia.

Generally, assertive societies are at a disadvantage when it comes to shared leadership. Aggressiveness may cause people to vie for control and to be unwilling to relinquish it once they have it. To get people to share leadership, the key may be to focus their natural aggression onto an external target—such as beating competitors or performance benchmarks. In other words, let them see that handing over leadership will help them beat the competition.

Finally, we looked at how much these societies were individualistic or collectivist. The former are noted for people who are self-reliant and value independence and achievement. Ranking high on this measure were Argentina, Australia, Austria, Canada, Denmark, Finland, France, Germany, Britain, India, Ireland, Israel, Italy, Jamaica, Japan, the Netherlands, New Zealand, Norway, South Africa, Sweden, Switzerland and the U.S.

People in countries with a collectivism orientation tend to gravitate toward groups—such as relatives, teams and organizations—and expect the group to take care of them in exchange for absolute loyalty. High scorers include Arab countries, Belgium, Brazil, Chile, Colombia, Costa Rica, East Africa, Ecuador, Greece, Guatemala, Hong Kong, Indonesia, Iran, Korea, Malaysia, Mexico, Pakistan, Panama, Peru, the Philippines, Portugal, El Salvador, Singapore, Spain, Taiwan, Thailand, Turkey, Uruguay, West Africa, Venezuela and Yugoslavia.

Collectivism can make it easier to introduce shared leadership, while individualism is essentially at odds with the concept. People in individualistic societies are independent and self-reliant; they enjoy personal freedom. Accordingly, they are not predisposed to work in teams, which are the building blocks of shared leadership. People in collectivistic societies, on the other hand, are oriented around groups and predisposed to help the team or organization, no matter the personal cost.

With individualistic societies, the key may be to use shared leadership only when there are clear reasons for doing so: if a particular job is complex, for instance, or especially critical to the organization. People may react badly to sharing control if the job is straightforward or routine.

Are we approaching the dusk of hierarchical leadership? Unambiguously, no. It's not a matter of choosing between hierarchical leadership and shared leadership. Instead, organizations should ask when leadership is most appropriately shared; how to develop the practice; and how to shift from a traditional management style to the new practice. By addressing these issues, we will move organizations toward the more appropriate practice of leadership in the age of knowledge work.

As all these caveats make clear, traditional leadership practices aren't going away. But the idea isn't to replace old styles with new ones overnight. Instead of seeing the matter as a black-and-white choice, companies should ask some simple—but crucial—questions. When is it a good idea to share the reins? And if we do decide to go that route, what steps can we take to make sure we're ready? Companies that apply shared leadership judiciously can see tremendous gains.

9

ço

Turbo-Charge Your
Leadership Through Mentoring

Lois J. Zachary

In today's competitive business environment, the need for continuous learning has never been greater. At the same time, the hunger for human connection and relationship has never been more palpable. It is no surprise that mentoring has become a basic leadership competency. Leaders who do not learn and do not promote learning within their organizations often end up thwarting their own efforts to lead effectively.

It is the leader's responsibility to serve as a role model, to mentor the next generation of leaders, and to make sure that continuous opportunities for learning and development are provided. When leaders strengthen themselves, they simultaneously enhance their ability to strengthen others.

GETTING IN TOUCH WITH YOURSELF AND OTHERS

In *Leadership Jazz,* Max De Pree, chairman emeritus and former CEO of Herman Miller Inc., notes that a mentoring relationship is "one of the best ways to discover one's gifts and weaknesses." Interviews I recently conducted augment De Pree's comment. One leader reported that the experience of mentoring someone outside her chain of command taught her that her division was not mentoring its people at the supervisory level effectively. As a result, she immediately addressed several key managerial inadequacies that ultimately increased the efficiency and quality of her team's efforts. Several mentors commented that mentoring relationships help them become more aware of their own communication and performance gaps. For example, one leader stated, "I learned to examine myself and the way I react to situations and became more sensitive to the needs and issues of others." Another leader, in reflecting on what he learned from his mentor, commented, "My mentoring relationship has increased my self-understanding and helped me adjust my leadership style so I can be more effective." A team leader revealed, "I am now trusting my people and other managers and sending them the message that I need their help and they can be a part of my learning."

Joe Kanfer, president and CEO of GOJO Inc., continues to have multiple mentors in his life—some from within his own business and others from the corporate and non-profit world. Kanfer considers many of his direct reports to be mentors. He hires idiosyncratic people who are "courageous enough to speak" and teach him things about himself. "A courageous person can be a great mentor to the boss, if the boss will just take time to listen," he says. "By learning from others—observing them and being open—a CEO can learn what he or she needs to do better. You learn what your direct reports are better at than you; they have a lot to teach you."

John Steinbrunner, chair of Watson Wyatt's Global Contingency Planning Task Force, mentors younger associates because it gives him an opportunity to stay in touch with their career aspirations and fears, develop the next generation of leaders, and reinforce his own learning.

Leaders like Kanfer and Steinbrunner find that through mentoring they continually gain exposure to new and diverse perspectives, improve their own coaching and listening skills, derive more meaning and satisfaction from work, and enhance—sometimes dramatically—the performance and quality of their leadership. The bottom line is that they achieve qualitatively better business results because they are more in touch with themselves and others.

GETTING STARTED ON THE RIGHT FOOT

Learning is the primary purpose, process, and product of mentoring. Relationship is the glue that binds the partnership. What distinguishes mentoring interactions from mentoring relationships is the commitment to the learning and to the relationship. Mentoring, at its fullest, is a reciprocal learning partnership in which a mentor and mentee agree to work collaboratively toward achievement of mutually defined learning goals.

Preparation is critical to building and maintaining vibrant mentoring partnerships, forging the kind of meaningful connection that sustains partnerships over time, helps the partners and the partnerships to deepen, and yields a significant return on the mentoring investment. It is tempting to skip over the preparation phase of the mentoring relationship, particularly for leaders who feel they have "been there and done that." But taking time to prepare provides a significant learning opportunity for mentors and mentees, regardless of whether their mentoring is done informally or as part of a formal program.

The lessons Steinbrunner learned from his mentoring experience at Watson Wyatt underscore the need for self-preparation. "Preparation is key," he says. "Understanding (the learning goal) helps eliminate false starts and dead-ends, and makes for more effective mentoring relationships. Preparation has forced me, as a potential mentor, to reflect on the gap of experience between what I bring to a relationship and what the mentee brings in terms of experience. You should never take your experiences for granted in mentoring another person."

When mentors and mentees prepare before they agree to a mentoring relationship, they gain clarity about what it is each is looking for in the relationship and what each is willing to contribute to it. As a result, their learning is more significant and focused, their time is better spent, and their satisfaction with the relationship is higher.

SELECTING A MENTORING PARTNER

Before deciding where to go to find a mentoring partner, some thought should be given to defining what you are looking for. Some of the more common attributes are leadership potential, expertise, accessibility, availability, professional interest, affiliation, cultural background, gender, and leadership style. Ranking the criteria helps limit the field so that you can use your current network to expand your search or more easily identify someone you want as your mentor. If someone asks you to mentor them, having criteria will help you assess whether or not this is the right mentoring relationship for you at this time.

Sometimes it takes several initial conversations with different people to find the right learning fit and a relationship that will serve to turbo-charge your leadership. Here are several factors to consider in finalizing that selection:

- *Do* ask yourself whether your potential partner will challenge your thinking and encourage you to constantly raise the bar for your own growth and development.
- *Do* base your decision on whether or not you feel there is a good *learning fit.*
- *Do* consider whether your potential mentor has the expertise, experience, time, and willingness to help you achieve your learning goals—or whether you as a mentor have the expertise, experience, time, and willingness to help another achieve his or her goals.
- *Do* consider if you would feel comfortable in a learning relationship with the potential mentor or mentee.

PREPARING THE RELATIONSHIP

There is a direct correlation between the quality of partner preparation and the development and growth of the relationship. Each partner coming to the relationship is unique. This uniqueness affects the dynamics of the relationship. It is easy for mentoring partners to make erroneous assumptions about each other unless mentor and mentee take time to prepare the relationship together.

Partner preparation is a mutual discovery process that helps prospective partners assess whether or not a learning fit exists between them. The initial conversation between the mentor and mentee merits specific attention because it sets the tone for the relationship. Preparing for a mentoring relationship need not be time-intensive but it does involve dedicating time to it.

The goal of the initial conversation is to establish a connection and determine if there is a learning fit. It is important to establish rapport, exchange information, and identify points of connection. Potential mentoring partners will want to share past mentoring experiences. It is during this conversation that the mentee, perhaps for the first time, articulates personal learning goals, expectations, and desired outcomes. It is also appropriate for mentor and mentee to share their needs, assumptions, and expectations candidly and talk about respective learning styles.

The initial conversation (which may in reality be a series of conversations) helps potential mentoring partners determine whether or not they feel comfortable working with each other and decide whether they want to move forward.

The natural tendency is to zero in on chemistry when meeting a prospective mentoring partner. If the chemistry doesn't feel right the inclination is to go

---

INITIAL CONVERSATION AGENDA
- Take time getting to know each other.
- Talk about mentoring and your mentoring experiences.
- Explore mentee's learning goals.
- Determine relationship needs, assumptions, and expectations.
- Define the deliverables.
- Discuss individual assumptions, needs, expectations, and limitations candidly.
- Consider options and opportunities for learning.

---

no further. The initial conversation should be more than a litmus test for chemistry, however. It should help mentoring partners gauge interest, understand motivation, check for understanding, and determine if there is a good learning fit.

For Marilyn Winn, senior vice president of human resources at Harrah's Entertainment, a person's desire for self-improvement and commitment to Harrah's determines her decision about mentoring. She also likes to mentor women who are assistant general managers or vice president candidates. John Steinbrunner, who also looks for commitment in those he mentors, takes the mentee's drive into account, along with his own ability to fill the mentee's knowledge gap, when deciding whether or not to get involved in a mentoring relationship.

TURBO-CHARGING YOUR PERSONAL LEADERSHIP

Leaders should periodically ask themselves two challenging questions. First, *Who is mentoring you right now?* You can find someone you can learn from at any stage of your career. No matter your position or experience, as Joe Kanfer attests, you can still find people who are better than you in some areas, people you can learn from.

Second, *Who are you mentoring?* You are missing opportunities for leadership if you are not mentoring the next generation of leaders.

For both mentors and their partners, the learning and relationship building that results from successful mentoring can turbo-charge leadership growth and development in a myriad of ways. Learning is accelerated, deepened, and broadened. Mentoring partners gain new perspectives and feedback that help clarify and challenge their thinking. Leaders feel more in touch with their people and their people feel more in touch with them.

10

c/s

When Mentoring Goes Bad

Dawn E. Chandler, Lillian Eby, and Stacy E. McManus

Most young managers view having a mentor as their ticket to the big leagues—to greater visibility, exciting assignments and big promotions. Benefits flow to mentors as well, as they enjoy broader influence when their young protégés rise to stardom.

And it's all true. Except when it isn't. Except when mentoring goes bad.

And it does go bad—in all sorts of ways and sometimes spectacularly. At one end of the spectrum are relationships that fizzle out for benign reasons, such as the pressures of daily work and personal lives, conflicting goals or a lack of shared values. But relationships also fail for not-so-benign reasons: manipulation, deceit and harassment, to name a few. Either party can be the cause—and the career trajectories of both may never be the same afterwards.

To be clear, mentoring can be invaluable, not only to protégés and mentors, but also to organizations. It is important, however, to manage the relationships appropriately and be aware of early signs of potential problems (see Exhibit 10.1).

Here is a look at some of the ways mentoring relationships go awry, followed by advice on how mentors, protégés and companies can spot warning signs sooner and create more positive experiences.

EXHIBIT 10.1—QUESTIONS TO ASK YOURSELF

1. If you are mentoring someone, are you giving them enough of your time and interesting work?
2. Are the personality and work habits of your protégé similar to yours, and if not, are you able to make sure that doesn't get in the way of working together?
3. Have you and your protégé clearly outlined his or her professional-development goals?
4. If you are being mentored, is the work interesting, and does your mentor give you credit for any projects you complete for him or her?
5. Do you feel like part of a team, and are you treated in an open, respectful manner?

If you answered no to any of these questions, your mentoring partnership may be heading for, or already in, rough waters. Discuss potential conflicts with each other, and get help from human resources to arbitrate any disagreements.

HOW MENTORING RELATIONSHIPS GO WRONG

Oil and Water. Most valuable experiences in mentoring feature trust, rapport and a general affinity between the two parties. Research has shown that the more the two have in common, especially in values and personalities, the more they will put into the relationship. Sometimes one sharp contrast can be the difference between harmony and friction. A mentor may have a habit of working long hours and weekends, for example, while the protégé prefers a 9-to-5 workday with weekends free. If neither side is willing to bend, the parties may find themselves unable to work together effectively.

Neglect of Protégés. It goes without saying (but we'll say it anyway) that for protégés to benefit, mentors must show an active interest and act in a positive way to advance their career and personal learning. Most mentors have every intention of doing that. Yet they sometimes end up neglecting their protégés.

Such mentors may be preoccupied with challenges in their own careers, excessively busy from a heavy workload or insecure about their standing in the organization. They can be evasive when called upon for advice or support, or always put their own priorities first.

It's all perfectly understandable, but that doesn't excuse the damage it does to a protégé's ego, or wasting a protégé's time. Such neglect can lead to protégés' feeling that their mentors don't value the relationship. At worst, they may withdraw from the relationship or even leave the department or organization. At the least, they will be so annoyed or disgusted or hurt that they won't be open to accepting any guidance that might occur.

Mentors Who Manipulate. Manipulation is most common when the mentor is the protégé's direct supervisor or a manager up the ladder in the same department. It's more damaging and less subtle than neglect, and it comes in three main forms: tyranny, inappropriate delegation and politicking.

Tyranny is essentially management by intimidation and has been a complaint heard repeatedly from protégés interviewed by Dr. Eby and her research colleagues over the years. It comes in many forms. A mentor, for instance, may threaten to demote a protégé unless the protégé pulls an all-nighter to fix a problem that the mentor caused. The protégé most likely will give in and work until the early morning hours, but will also so resent the mentor that the relationship will be irrevocably harmed.

Inappropriate delegation is when a mentor manipulates a protégé to do work that the mentor should be doing. But it can also involve withholding assignments. A protégé who has long awaited a particularly challenging assignment may find at the 11th hour that the mentor has decided to take the assignment. Protégés in situations like these may find their career development stymied. Too often, they end up never taking on work that will develop the skills they need to gain more responsibility and receive attention from senior management.

Politicking involves more malicious acts, like sabotage and taking undue credit. Protégés reported many instances of sabotage, including one mentor's campaigning behind the protégé's back to damage her reputation. If a mentor has a high standing and does such a thing, it can cause irreparable damage to a protégé's reputation and promotion prospects. Some said their mentors criticized them behind their backs and blamed them for mistakes that the mentors themselves made. Equally damaging: mentors who steal their protégés' ideas.

Protégés Who Manipulate. Protégés have fewer means at their disposal, but they, too, can use manipulation to benefit themselves, and sometimes to harm a mentor's reputation and career. One mentor reported a protégé who would doctor numbers, tailor justifications and say that concepts still in development had already been implemented, all to look good in front of senior managers.

The danger to the mentor here is twofold. First, any bad-mouthing could eventually tarnish a mentor's reputation, even if the source is unreliable. And second, if the protégé's exaggeration and puffery are exposed, the mentor may be held just as accountable as the protégé, if not more so. Management may decide the mentor is responsible for allowing the abuses to occur.

Sabotage Against Mentors. When protégés try to damage their mentor's career, it's typically motivated by revenge, say, for failing to win a promotion. The reason may have been subpar performance. But rather than take personal responsibility, some protégés have been known to blame the mentor for not providing adequate support.

Other times, the sabotage can be unintentional. Mentors are putting themselves on the line by saying they believe in their protégé's ability and future at the company. Such endorsements can backfire. For example, if a mentor promotes a protégé of outstanding ability who then goes on to make a major mistake—perhaps due to a personal problem that the mentor couldn't have been aware of—the mentor's judgment will be called into question as well.

Submissive Protégés. Sometimes protégés rely on their mentor too much, stifling their independent thinking and growth. It can also lead to situations in which the mentor inadvertently becomes overly controlling. In either case, the protégé's learning is hindered.

Jealous Protégés. Consider this scenario: Two employees have been with a company a long time, and at times have competed for the same assignments. Then one of them is promoted and becomes responsible for the development of his or her former peer. When that happens, it isn't hard to see why it would be difficult to create a mentoring relationship: The jealousy the rival-turned-protégé feels toward the new boss blocks any desire or ability to learn.

To make these kinds of problems much less likely, or nip them in the bud before they become serious, here are some suggestions.

Give It Structure. Whether a company has formal or informal mentoring, or both, the organization needs to provide support for mentors and protégés. Human-resources representatives should be available to provide training and help sort out any concerns that arise. HR can also help with setting goals for the relationship.

Have a Backup. It may be best for protégés to have more than one mentor at a time, and vice versa. If a mentor tries to sabotage a protégé's career, the protégé can turn to another mentor for backing. And if a protégé tries to undermine a mentor, the mentor can seek support from other protégés.

Recruit Carefully. People who volunteer are more likely to put in the time and effort necessary to fulfill their partners' expectations. Companies should also try to match mentors and protégés who have things in common, as those relationships are more likely to succeed.

Training and Orientation: Certain principles need to be communicated beforehand, whether in a formal or informal program. For example, expectations: how often to meet, what the protégé is looking for and what the mentor has to offer.

Make sure protégés understand they should be receptive to feedback, eager to learn and amiable. They also should strive to learn even outside their mentoring relationships. The more value they can bring to the relationship, the more likely the mentors will be to help them.

Both parties should be aware that their relationship will depend on trust, and that they may need to explain their actions sometimes to reduce misunderstandings. For example, if a mentor declines a requested meeting, some explanation is warranted. Otherwise, the protégé may wrongly assume the mentor is losing interest.

Both should be alerted to patterns of behavior that are likely to cause trouble. This may help them repair—or end—potentially dysfunctional relationships before they escalate into harmful ones. Both should also be taught conflict-management skills.

The Bottom Line. Before the mentoring begins, both parties need to understand what will be required to make the collaboration worthwhile. Then they should either commit wholeheartedly or opt out.

Give Feedback. Mentors can share appraisals with the protégés' supervisors, who have a vested interest in the protégés' development. If problems arise, someone from HR or another supervisor should be in the loop to give objective advice or mediate.

Prepare for the End. Everyone should be clear on the fact that mentoring eventually ends, when the protégé has learned all that he or she can, or when the mentor no longer provides guidance or satisfaction. Talking about this in advance helps to avoid misunderstandings or hurt feelings when the time comes.

— PART III —

JOURNEY

A smooth sea never made a skilled sailor.
ENGLISH PROVERB

Leadership is not an event—it is a journey. We start at different places because of our backgrounds, experiences, and interests. The destination can be a vision or a personal goal, but our inner self provides the drive to embark on the journey. Along the way, we learn from the twists and turns of the path. It can be an exciting and challenging opportunity, and it is one that we choose to engage.

Often we begin the journey quite unaware of what we are doing or where we are going. Some of us are exposed to the concept of leadership by being expected at a very early age to take charge and make decisions. Many times we are told that demonstrating good leadership is an important element of our future success. We will get more opportunities if people observe us leading, particularly in team activities. Once engaged in the competitive arena, the pressure to achieve increases, and we often find ourselves working toward the recognition and responsibility of leading.

Can leadership be taught? This is the wrong question. A more relevant question is, can leadership be learned? The answer is a resounding yes! The potential for good leadership is widely dispersed in our society, not limited to a privileged few, and learning about leadership means understanding how to recognize bad as well as good leadership. Such learning involves understanding the dynamic relationship between leader and followers, recognizing the differing contexts and situations of the leadership landscape, and realizing that the behavioral sciences, biography, the classics, economics, history, logic, and related disciplines all provide the perspective so important to comprehending and developing leadership effectiveness.

Individuals committed to improving their leadership effectiveness will take advantage of opportunities to improve their skills as speakers, debaters, negotiators, problem clarifiers, and advocates. Would-be leaders will also heed Thomas Cronin's advice to "squint with their ears." Most importantly, the developing leader learns to appreciate her or his own strengths and weaknesses. We recall Colin Powell's response to a student's question regarding how one could best prepare to be an effective leader. General Powell responded by advising students to study past and present leaders but not to get too "hung up" on role models because they need to be authentically themselves and to learn from their own mistakes. We strongly believe that leadership can be learned from multiple perspectives. We agree with John Gardner that what you learn after you know it all is what really matters.

What leaders do is important, but how they do it is of equal concern. Although much research has focused on identifying the one best leadership style, no single style or personality is best for all situations. The leader acting alone can often accomplish relatively simple tasks, but the more ambiguous and complex the situation, the greater the need for a participative style. Participatory decisions, however, are time consuming because the path to consensus is often long and tedious. When decisions must be made quickly, the leader must act alone with available information and, very often, on intuition. Intuition is not guessing; rather, it is the recollection of experiences and knowledge without conscious recognition of how the cumulative information was recalled. In the conflicts of facts versus intuition, it is seldom one or the other that is determining; instead both do.

Successful leaders with a global orientation think globally while acting locally. They must thoroughly understand not only the microcosm of their organization but also where the organization fits in the larger perspective. To create a vision of the future, the leader must understand the environment in which the organization exists today and the one in which it will exist tomorrow. Leaders serve an increasingly diverse constituency and must seek and value that diversity if they are to transform their vision into action. This vision is our destination.

Along the path of our journey, we find a myriad of leadership schools, workshops, seminars, and books presenting us with some daunting choices. Titles often reflect a current theme that attracts notice and disciples. The reality is that most are simply management tool kits attempting to suggest that everyone who adopts the message or behavior will become an effective leader. Here we often have the opportunity to make the wrong turn in our journey.

Leadership begins, first, with knowing who you are. That knowledge leads to self-confidence—understanding what you can do. Finally, with that self-confidence, you are, as noted earlier, given the opportunity to choose leadership. The important thing is that you may choose to follow or lead. The successes and failures you experience on the journey tell you what your interests are, help you to understand the process of leadership, and allow you to decide on when and where you might pursue the path of leadership.

According to Thomas Cronin, students of leadership must develop their capacities for observation, reflection, imagination, invention, and judgment. They must also learn to communicate and listen effectively and develop their abilities to gather and interpret evidence, marshal facts, and employ the most rigorous methods in the pursuit of knowledge. They need to develop an unyielding commitment to the truth balanced with a full appreciation of what remains to be learned. In a sense, these are the knowledge, skills, and abilities that they need to pick up on their journey. Students of leadership learn from mentors who lead by example and who make desirable things happen. We agree!

One observation we have made over the years is that the most effective leaders are committed to continual learning. They read, study, and constantly try to improve their capabilities as well as fulfill their personal needs. This ongoing development is what allows leaders to sharpen skills, remain sensitive to the environment, and understand the constantly changing demands of the role. We learn from our experiences on the journey.

LEADERSHIP PERSPECTIVES

"Leadership Begins with an Inner Journey" (Chapter 11), by James M. Kouzes and Barry Z. Posner, starts with the notion that we matter. We must believe in ourselves and be confident that we can lead others. The authors give us a process of internal self-discovery that leads to self-knowledge. We must know ourselves and what we value before we can lead. At the same time, Kouzes and Posner note that we must stand for something—we must have the courage of our convictions. This is a reflection of our personal values. "Who am I?" is the important question we must ask ourselves and deal with the answers because those answers will be the reason people follow (or don't follow) us. They

close by emphasizing that we must be transparent to others and recognized as
a person who is principled in words and deeds.

Richard L. Daft, in "First, Lead Yourself" (Chapter 12), suggests that we
must learn how to lead ourselves before we can lead others. Good point! He
notes that behavior starts with thought and continues with reaction. His advice
is to calm down, ask yourself questions, think before acting, review your day,
consult with others, slow your reactions, create mental pictures, talk to yourself, and develop structures; he ends with a charge to try meditation.

Barbara Kellerman and Deborah L. Rhode write in "Viable Options: Rethinking Women and Leadership" (Chapter 13) that, even after decades of
progress, women remain underrepresented in senior leadership positions. Are
they victims of discrimination, or have women chosen not to lead? This continues to be a dilemma.

In "Women and the Labyrinth of Leadership" (Chapter 14), Alice H. Eagly
and Linda L. Carli propose that the "glass ceiling" metaphor is now more
wrong than right. They suggest that women are confronted with a labyrinth
lined with historical images. They note that prejudice continues, as does a resistance to women in leadership roles. Leadership style, the demands of family
life, and the inability to build social capital continue to stifle women. They
suggest that we must continue to create awareness, change norms, reduce subjectivity in how we evaluate performance, and ensure a critical mass of women
in leadership positions.

In "Stop Holding Yourself Back" (Chapter 15), Anne Morriss, Robin J. Ely,
and Frances X. Frei identify five ways that we can unwittingly sabotage our
leadership development. They cite overemphasizing personal goals, protecting
our public image, turning competitors into enemies, going it alone, and waiting for permission as the barriers. Their purpose is to help us develop our potential as effective leaders.

11

ℭℬ

Leadership Begins with an Inner Journey

James M. Kouzes and Barry Z. Posner

Everything you will ever do as a leader is based on one audacious assumption. It's the assumption that you matter. Before you can lead others you have to lead yourself and believe that you can have a positive impact on others. You have to believe that your words can inspire and your actions can move others. You have to believe that what you do counts for something. If you don't, you won't even try. Leadership begins with you.

The quest for leadership, therefore, is first an inner quest to discover who you are and what you care about, and it's through this process of self-examination that you find the awareness needed to lead. Self-confidence is really awareness of and faith in your own powers, and these powers become clear and strong only as you work to identify and develop them. The mastery of the art of leadership comes with the mastery of the self, and so developing leadership is a process of developing the self.

Melissa Poe, a fourth grader in Nashville, Tennessee, became very concerned about the natural environment and the kind of world she and her friends might live in if people didn't start paying attention to their everyday actions. After seeing a television program about pollution that portrayed a very scary

Reprinted by permission of *Leader to Leader* (Spring 2011). Copyright 2011 Leader to Leader Institute.

future, Melissa asked the question, "Will the future be a safe place to live in when I get older?" She decided she had to do something about it. That night she wrote a letter to the president, but Melissa knew the pollution problem wouldn't wait. At home she and her family started recycling, turning lights and faucets off when they weren't in use, and planting trees. Melissa wrote more letters to newspapers, television stations, and more politicians. Melissa also started a club, called Kids F.A.C.E. (Kids For a Clean Environment) so that her friends, who'd been asking how they could help, could do projects together like writing letters, planting trees, and picking up litter. "We knew we were doing small things, but we also knew it took a bunch of small things to make a big difference," she told us.

When after several weeks she still hadn't heard back from the president, Melissa, realizing he was a busy man, felt she needed to do more to get him to see her letter. She decided to make her letter bigger so he couldn't miss it. She called up a billboard company in her home town and asked if they would put up a billboard with her letter to the president. The company donated that billboard and also connected her with other billboard companies, and in a matter of six months, over 250 billboards were put up all over the United States, at least one in each state and one just a mile from the White House.

Almost immediately, Melissa began receiving letters from other kids who were as concerned as she was about the environment. They wanted to help. Just six months after she began her journey to get people's attention about the environment, Melissa appeared on the *Today Show* to tell her story. It is here that Kids F.A.C.E. grew from a local club to a national organization. Starting with just six members at her elementary school, Kids F.A.C.E. grew to more than 2,000 club chapters in twenty-two countries and more than 350,000 members before Melissa, at age seventeen, handed over the reins to two fifteen-year-olds, saying she was too old for the job. (Today there are 500,000 members.)

Is Melissa a leader? Can someone at age nine or fifteen demonstrate the practices of exemplary leadership? Aren't those mainly abilities reserved for people in senior positions in big-time organizations?

Yes, yes, and no. Yes, Melissa is a leader. Yes, you can demonstrate leadership at any age. No, leadership is not about some position in an organization and clearly not just for those in senior positions.

A PROCESS OF INTERNAL SELF-DISCOVERY

Fast-forward to a recent leadership seminar at the Hong Kong University of Science and Technology and Olivia Lai, who told us that she was initially a little taken aback when we asked her to write about her personal best leadership experience: "Here I am, at twenty-five years of age, with four years of work experience. How could I possibly have a personal best in leadership?" After further reflection, she realized that in actuality,

> it wasn't all that hard to figure out what my personal best was and write about it. Even more surprising is that it became clear that leadership is everywhere, it takes place every day, and leadership can come from anyone. It doesn't matter that you don't have the title of "manager," "director," "CEO," to go with it. In the end, that's all they are . . . titles on business cards and company directories. Being a true leader transcends all that.
>
> Becoming a leader is a process of internal self discovery. In order for me to become a leader and become an even better leader, it's important that I first define my values and principles. If I don't know what my own values are and determine expectations for myself, how can I set expectations for others? How will I convey confidence, strong will, and empathy? Without looking within myself, it's not possible for me to look at others and recognize their potential and help others become leaders.

Through her own process of self-discovery, Olivia, like leaders everywhere, realized that becoming a leader begins when you come to understand who you are, what you care about, and why you do what you do. Developing yourself as a leader begins with knowing your own key convictions; it begins with your value system. Clarifying your own values and aspirations is a highly personal matter, and no one else can do it for you. To exhibit harmonious leadership—leadership in which your words and deeds are consonant—you must be in tune internally.

All leaders must take this inner journey. "I know who I was, who I am, and where I want to be," says Dan Kaplan, founder of Daniel Kaplan Associates and former president of Hertz Equipment Rental Corporation. "So in other words," he continues, "I know the level of commitment that I am prepared to make, and why I am personally prepared to make that level of commitment." In this vein values drive the commitment necessary to create leaders in the first place.

Dan's words reflect what leadership scholar Warren Bennis reported in his study of how successful people learned to become leaders: "To become a leader, then, you must become yourself; become the maker of your own life." Warren observes that knowing yourself is "the most difficult task any of us faces. But until you truly know yourself, strengths and weaknesses, know what you want to do and why you want to do it, you cannot succeed in any but the most su-perficial sense of the word."

Your ultimate success in business and in life depends on how well you know yourself, what you value, and why you value it. The better you know who you are and what you believe in, the better you are at making sense of the often incomprehensible and conflicting demands you receive daily. Do this, or do that. Buy this, buy that. Decide this, decide that. Support this, support that. You need internal guidance to navigate the turbulent waters in this stormy world. A clear set of personal values and beliefs is the critical controller in that guidance system.

YOU HAVE TO STAND FOR SOMETHING

People won't follow you, or even pay you much attention, if you don't have strong values. In our studies, we've asked thousands of people around the world to list the historical leaders they most admire—leaders, who if they were alive today, they could imagine themselves following willingly. Here are just a few of the names: Susan B. Anthony, Mustafa Kemal Ataturk, Jesus Christ, Mahatma Gandhi, Martin Luther King Jr., Abraham Lincoln, Nelson Mandela, Golda Meir, Mohammed, Eleanor Roosevelt, Franklin D. Roo-sevelt, Helen Suzman, Mother Teresa, and Margaret Thatcher. The entire list is populated by people with strong beliefs about matters of principle. All were passionate about what was right and just. The message is clear. People are ad-mired because of their unwavering commitment to principles. They stand for something.

People rightfully expect their leaders to have the courage of their convic-tions. They expect them to stand up for their beliefs. When leaders are clear about what they believe in, they can take strong stands and are much less likely to be swayed by every fad or opinion poll. We've all heard the expression "Leaders stand up for their beliefs." To provide a solid platform on which to stand, your beliefs must be clear to you and clearly communicated to others. When these values are matched by your deeds, then you've earned the credi-bility required for others to put their trust in you, to willingly climb up and join you on that platform, knowing they'll be supported.

When you're not clear about your personal values it's hard to imagine how you can stand up for your beliefs, isn't it? How can you speak out if you don't know what's important to you? How can you have the courage of your con-victions if you have no convictions? Leaders who aren't clear about what they believe are likely to change their position with every shift in public opinion. Without core beliefs and with only shifting positions, would-be leaders are judged as inconsistent and derided for being "political" in their behavior.

After all, who's the very first person you have to lead? Who's the first person who must be willing to follow you? You are, of course. Until you passionately believe in something it's hard to imagine that you could ever convince anyone else to believe. And if you wouldn't follow you, why should anyone else?

WHO ARE YOU?

We've asked thousands of people over the years to imagine a scenario where someone walks into the room and announces to them and their colleagues, "Hi, I'm your new leader!" At that very moment, what do you want to know from this person? What are the questions that immediately pop into your mind? While there are lots of questions someone would want to ask that individual, by far the most frequently asked is: "Who are you?"

People want to know your values and beliefs, what you really care about, and what keeps you awake at night. They want to know who most influenced you, the events that shaped your attitudes, and the experiences that prepare you for the job. They want to know what drives you, what makes you happy, and what ticks you off. They want to know what you're like as a person, and why you want to be their leader. They want to know if you play an instrument, compete in sports, go to the movies, or enjoy the theater. They want to know about your family, what you've done, and where you've traveled. They want to understand your personal story. They want to know why they ought to be following you.

So if you are the new leader who walks into that room one day, you'd better be prepared to answer the "Who are you?" question. And, to answer that question for others, you first have to answer it for yourself. In one of our leadership workshops, our colleague Spencer Clark explained himself to participants in the following way:

> I am the chief learning officer for Cadence Design Systems. I was a division president for Black and Decker, and a manager for General Electric. But these [job titles] are not who I am. If you want to know who I am, you need to understand that I grew up in Kentucky. That I was one of four sons, and we lived on a sharecropper's farm and slept in a home that had no inside plumbing. Who I am is not simply what I do. Knowing who I am has been enormously

helpful in guiding me in making decisions about what I would do and how I would do it.

As Spencer makes clear, his job resumé says very little about who he is and why he makes the decisions and takes the actions he does. He knows that there is far more to him than his work history, the titles he's had, and the positions he's held. For Spencer to become the leader that he is, he had to dig beneath the surface and find out more about the events that shaped him, the beliefs that informed him, and the values that guided him. He also knows that it's helpful for others to understand those same things before they can commit to his leadership decisions and actions.

During the last few years we've had the opportunity to co-facilitate leadership development programs with Ron Sugar, then chairman and CEO of Northrop Grumman Corporation. At the formal start of every one of these sessions, before he ever uttered a word, Ron would walk to the front of the room, sit down at a piano, and play for a few minutes.

After he'd played his last note, Ron would turn to his senior executive colleagues and ask, "Does anyone know why I began this session with playing the piano?" The point, he'd go on to explain, was that if people are going to follow you they needed to know more about you than the fact that you're their boss. They needed to know something about who you are as a person—your hopes, dreams, talents, expectations, and loves. "Leadership is personal," Ron would proclaim. "Do the people who work for and with you know if you can play the piano?" Ron would ask his colleagues. "Do they know who you are, what you care about, and why they ought to be following you?"

We were sharing this story one day with a group of people from a number of different organizations, and one participant said he could underscore just how important this point was by telling his own story about their new CEO. It seems this new chief executive was making the rounds throughout the company, talking about his vision for the firm and how people needed to execute on it:

> The CEO was there supposedly so people could get to know him. So imagine how flabbergasted everyone was when someone asked him, "What do you like to do when you are not working?" and he replied rather curtly, "That's a personal matter and not relevant; next question."
>
> But, that's the point, isn't it! Who is this guy? What does he really care about? Why should we follow—believe and trust—him if we don't know who he is? And he won't tell us!

We could all sense his exasperation. We're all just more reluctant to follow someone if they're unwilling to tell us about themselves. We start to become a little suspicious. We're less willing to trust.

WHEN TO SAY YES AND WHEN TO SAY NO

If you are ever to become a leader others will willingly follow, you must be transparent to others and known as someone who stands by your principles. And as every would-be leader has discovered, first you have to listen to your inner self in order to discover who you really are and what you are all about. There is no shortage of different interests out there competing for your time, your attention, and your approval. Before you listen to those voices, you have to listen to that voice inside that tells you what's truly important. Only then will you know when to say yes and when to say no—and mean it.

Developing leadership capacity is not about stuffing in a whole bunch of new information or trying out the latest technique. It's about leading out of what is already in your soul. It's about liberating the leader within you. It's about setting yourself free. It's about putting your ear to your heart and just listening. Clarity of values is essential in knowing which way, for each of us, is north, south, east, or west. The clearer you are, the easier it is to stay on the path you've chosen. In exploring your inner territory and finding your voice you calibrate an inner compass by which to navigate the course of your daily life and to take the first steps along the journey of making a difference,

Just as sunlight burns away the morning fog, the more light you shine on what you stand for, what you believe in, and what you care about, the more clearly you'll see those road signs pointing in the direction you want to go. Starting with the inner journey gives you the confidence to take the right turns, to make the tough decisions, to act with determination, and to take charge of your life.

12

เจ

First, Lead Yourself

Richard L. Daft

Leaders usually know the correct way to lead others, so why don't they do it? When Martha was promoted to sales manager for an advertising agency, she inherited a difficult employee who was a strong producer but whose overbearing competitiveness caused resentment among team members. Martha gathered her facts and scheduled a meeting with the prima donna. As she broached the subject of his behavior, his reaction was defensive, and she backed down. "My overwhelming sense of empathy overrode my ability to be assertive and provide strong direction." She was clearly disappointed in herself. Martha's tendency toward people pleasing overrode her ability to be assertive and do what her department—and her employee—needed. She later reflected, "It was like getting in my car to go east and the car insisted on going west, and I couldn't do anything about it."

Or consider Bob, head of a corporate manufacturing division, who promised himself and others that he would delegate more decisions. Although he was used to making all the hiring decisions himself, Bob asked the sales director to meet with candidates and make the hiring decision for a customer service position. Three weeks later, the director brought his top choice to Bob's office, along with an offer letter for Bob to sign. Dumbfounded, Bob muttered that he wanted to meet the final three candidates himself. He couldn't accept

---

Reprinted by permission of *Leader to Leader* (Spring 2011). Copyright 2011 Leader to Leader Institute.

the director's choice, someone with whom he felt little rapport, so he interviewed the other candidates and hired the person at the bottom of the director's list. "My mind has a mind of its own," he said. It was no surprise when both the sales director and new hire quit within a few months.

Leadership is often described as getting the best out of other people. But as Martha and Bob discovered, the first job of leadership is often getting the best out of yourself. For example, *Fortune* magazine reported a study of thirty-eight failed CEOs. All were good at the cognitive tasks—vision, strategy, ideas—but things broke down at execution. The CEOs' actions did not follow their stated intentions. When leaders know the smarter behavior, why do they get sidetracked into unwanted behavior? Personal mastery is a difficult thing. Most leaders today receive reasonably good feedback about how their leadership could be better. Leaders and managers typically know what they *should* be doing, *how* to do it, and *why* they should do it. Yet often their intentions and behaviors fail to align.

In my consulting and executive teaching, I have come across dozens and dozens of internal conflicts between knowing and executing. One part of a leader wants to do one thing; another part wants to do something else. The theory of constraints is very clear that the weakest link in any system will limit performance, and correcting the weak link will have a big payback in improved performance. Typical leadership weak links are reflected in the following behaviors:

- Micromanaging direct reports
- Procrastinating
- Not following through on commitments
- Making tactless remarks
- Insisting on always being right
- Overreacting and expressing inappropriate anger
- Finding fault with others and being outwardly critical
- Not celebrating and appreciating others' accomplishments
- Not listening
- Talking too much
- Not staying focused
- Showing impatience, such as interrupting others

When leaders have one of these counterproductive behaviors, they often have great difficulty achieving mastery over it. And the negative impact can be huge, because their behavior affects dozens or perhaps hundreds of other people. What is going on that leaders seem unable to alter their behavior to follow their better intentions?

THE CEO AND THE ELEPHANT

According to psychologists and neuroscientists there are two parts to the human brain, and the parts are sometimes in conflict. There is a habitual, automatic, and largely unconscious part of the brain that represents an older system. I call this "the inner elephant" because of the strength of its reactions, unconscious impulses, fears, emotional drives, and lifelong habits. The elephant is strong because its behavior is wired into your nervous system after a lifetime of conditioning. The newer system in the brain represents an intentional, reasoning, thoughtful, and largely conscious mind. This is the brain's executive function, which I am calling "the inner CEO" because it can see the objective big picture and take a balanced approach to determining the best action. The intentional CEO plays a smaller role than the unconscious habitual mind, but its higher-order choice processes can be developed to guide the inner elephant.

The older elephant part of the brain represents a marvelous internal system that has evolved to guide people safely through each day, usually without mishap. It handles memory, language, perception, communication, and other vital information processing. Probably ninety-eight percent of the time our intention and behavior are in alignment. The problem arises when this automatic system is not in alignment with our intentions or with what others want from us, as Martha and Bob discovered. The elephant's circuitry is compelling. If the elephant wants to turn left or right in search of food, it will do so, regardless of a person's conscious wish to be on a diet. Even the apostle Paul said, "I do not understand my own actions. For I do not do what I want, but I do the very thing I hate. I can will what is right, but I cannot do it" (Romans 7:15). Fortunately, even though the elephant's conditioned bad habit is wired in, potential corrective action is available from the CEO part of the brain.

RECOGNIZE YOUR TWO PARTS

Behavior starts with a thought, and there are clear differences in thoughts originating from the elephant and the CEO parts of the brain. Examples of some traits that the elephant may display compared to the inner CEO are in

TABLE 12.1—THE INNER ELEPHANT AND THE INNER CEO

Inner Elephant	Inner CEO
Monkey mind	Quiet mind
Own view	Bigger picture
Reactive	Thoughtful response
Judgmental	Cause and effect
Find fault	Open, appreciative
Feel resistance	In the flow

Table 12.1. You can learn to recognize when the elephant's dysfunctional pattern is dominant, and when your executive is in charge. Do you recognize any elements of your own behavior in Table 12.1?

The elephant part of the brain is always on. In Eastern spirituality the flow of random thoughts is called "monkey mind" because it resembles a restless monkey jumping from branch to branch. A restless or racing mind is a clear signal that your elephant is feeling fear or anxiety, and you won't be able to concentrate or think straight. The CEO mind is quiet and peaceful, able to focus on the present moment, thinking only of the task at hand. In addition, if you find yourself in a meeting fighting for your own position, with your only goal being to win the argument, these thoughts are from your elephant. Your CEO, by contrast, is interested in a bigger picture, including the opposite point of view that can be integrated into a solution.

Another quality of the elephant is instant reaction. Neuroscience tells us that the mind reacts in a small fraction of a second, especially to things it doesn't like. The instant reaction causes problems when it displays negative emotion, such as anger or impatience. Your CEO is patient and slower to respond, taking time to formulate a wise response rather than act instantly out of fear or protective self-interest. Moreover, psychologist Jonathan Haidt said that everyone has a "Like-o-meter" in their head that is constantly analyzing things for what it likes and dislikes. Right now you are likely judging what you read in this article. The elephant makes decisions based on personal like and dislike toward people or tasks. The CEO, on the other hand, detaches from personal likes and dislikes and seeks a balanced view of underlying cause-effect relationships as a basis for action.

The elephant is always scanning the environment for threats, and hence is in a mind-set of finding fault, and of resisting things it dislikes. *Negativity bias* is the term used in psychology to describe how our minds are tuned to perceive bad things more readily than good things. Evolutionary psychologists say this quality was originally a protection against predators. The inner CEO, by contrast, is able to stay open-minded, and sees people, events, and even problems through a lens of thankfulness and appreciation for whatever positive benefit they contain. Likewise, the elephant will resist, postpone, and procrastinate when facing an unwanted task, such as a needed personal confrontation, while the inner CEO feels less fear and is able to flow into and through these tasks with little hesitation.

HOW TO START LEADING YOURSELF

Recognizing the two parts is a step toward building up the CEO part of your brain. The next step is to practice using the CEO rather than the older elephant circuitry. Indeed, your elephant needs direction from your CEO to overcome its natural tendency toward overreaction, impulsiveness, procrastination, or lack of focus. The elephant thoughts stored in the brain often produce a poor leader. In other words, a residue of responses from early life conditioning may detract from an effective leadership response right now. Things go better for leaders when their inner CEO is the master and the elephant is the servant. For example, Carol Bartz, CEO of Yahoo, had a bad habit of interrupting before people could finish a sentence. She had to teach herself to take a breath, to shut up and listen. The first managerial job for Alan Mullaly, CEO of Ford, was as an engineering supervisor. His tendency to oversupervise led him to require people to show him their work, over and over again. When engineers started to quit, Mullaly changed his perspective, learned to communicate a bigger picture of mission and purpose, and encouraged those under him to be in more control of their work. Like Mullaly and Bartz, most leaders know *what* they should be doing differently. But changing yourself is not easy.

Here are some techniques to strengthen your inner CEO to have more control over your elephant's thinking and behavior. These techniques require some deliberate practice. Choose a technique that resonates for you and practice it several times to create a new groove in the CEO circuitry of your brain.

- *Calm down.* Remember, an agitated elephant is harder to control than a calm elephant. Anger, fear, frustration, and craving all give the elephant more power, so calm down before making a decision or pushing the e-mail send button. If you are procrastinating, your elephant is feeling low-level anxiety. The inner elephant is easier to manage when you are relaxed. For example, if you are procrastinating, relax rather than trying to force yourself into the task. Take three deep breaths or just sit by your task until the feeling of resistance passes. Sitting quietly by the task will calm you down, and soon you will reach out and start to work productively.

- *Ask yourself questions.* Deepak Chopra, celebrity self-help guru, teaches a leadership course at Northwestern's Kellogg Business School and recently was ordained as a Buddhist monk. The long hours of prayer, meditation, and reflection changed the way he teaches. He now counsels his clients to spend some time each day working on questions such as "What's my purpose in life?" and "What kind of contribution do I want to make to my business?" Other questions could include, "What am I feeling right now?" "What is my mood?" "What is my purpose in doing this activity?" "What outcome do I really want?" The secret to these questions is their inward focus, which is the province of the CEO part of the brain. The inner CEO can see your thoughts and what is happening within your mind and body, while the elephant brain is designed to sense the external world through the five senses. Reflecting inwardly may feel a little strange at first, but will strengthen your CEO.

- *STOP.* This acronym is a reminder to periodically stop for a moment to *Step back, Think, Organize* your thoughts, and then *Proceed.* One manager taped STOP to the crystal of her wristwatch so she would be reminded of it several times a day. STOP allows you to periodically detach from your elephant. Perhaps take a breath, clear your head, take a look around, gather yourself, and then proceed from your CEO awareness. Earlier in his career, Richard Anderson, CEO of Delta Airlines, learned to stop himself before he lost his temper when he realized he was setting the wrong tone for his organization. Breaking the anger habit was vital because everything he did as the leader was an example to those around him.

- *Review the day.* Spend ten minutes each evening reviewing the behaviors that worked and did not work during the day. To make sure you take the time to adopt this practice, schedule this activity in a quiet place and at the same time each night. At first it is hard to remember anything that happened, but with practice you will remember everything. Think about the positive CEO-type behaviors and review the negative elephant-type occurrences. As you replay incidents in your mind, you will discover more of the desired behavior repeating itself the next day while the undesired behavior will appear less often until it ultimately disappears.

- *Consult with others.* Consulting with just one person before making a decision or taking action will enlarge your elephant's thinking beyond its typical small and one-sided viewpoint. Consult with several people and your perspective will become large and balanced. Try consulting on every large or small decision for one day and witness the perspectives that emerge. Break free of the elephant's desire to believe that its own answers are always better. There is a dual benefit to consulting with others. By practicing this routine you engage others in decision making and you expand your own wisdom.

- *Slow down your reactions.* A busy manager under pressure may react too strongly to a problem. Practice a new response pattern, such as counting to ten, waiting a minute, or waiting twenty-four hours, and you will soon stop overreacting. A senior executive at an auto supply company learned to always ignore his "response one" to bad news and wait for his "response two," even if it meant responding the next day after sleeping on the topic. His response two was always wiser than his initial reaction. Jeffery Katzenberg installed a five-second delay on his reactions so others could express their views first. After deciding he didn't have to always be right, Katzenberg found that the five-second delay enabled a more robust and effective dialogue in his meetings.

- *Create a mental picture.* Visualizing a desired behavior in your mind has a powerful impact on your elephant. Spend a moment imagining how you want to give a speech, or handle a difficult conversation, and you will provide a vivid visual instruction to your elephant. Sports psychology research shows that mental rehearsal often is as effective as physical practice for improving performance. Take a few minutes to repeatedly visualize doing a dreaded task, and you will more calmly and smoothly flow through it.

- *Talk to yourself.* The practice of mentally talking to yourself in an intentional and structured way may be the hidden treasure of self-management. Offering an instruction to your elephant in the form of a well-crafted auto-suggestion tells the elephant what it needs to change. Repeating something like "I am appreciating others more," or "I am listening more carefully," or "I am delegating more responsibility," or "I am becoming more organized" twenty times morning and evening and during breaks (while driving or exercising) typically produces a noticeable change within a few days. If used extensively this type of self-talk can even reprogram a deeply held aspect of self-image or way of thinking.

- *Provide a structure.* Go to a fat camp for two weeks and you will miraculously find yourself exercising and eating a healthy diet every day until you return home. Why? The camp provides a specific structure for spending your time. Inner elephants also respond to explicit and detailed instructions from the inner executive. Therefore, get everything you are doing out of your head and written down on paper, and write down key steps and a deadline for each task. Psychologists call highly specific written steps "implementation intentions." This detailed structure makes it easier for your elephant to comply.
- *Try meditation.* Meditation quiets the active or racing mind and can awaken a deep sense of happiness. A good way to meditate is to focus your attention on an anchor object or phrase. Focus on watching your breathing or slowly repeat a word or phrase that has meaning for you. David Lynch, a director whose films include *Lost Highway* and *Mulholland Drive,* started practicing Transcendental Meditation (focus on repeating a mantra for twenty minutes twice a day). His ex-wife soon inquired, "Where did your anger go?" Lynch's anger had disappeared and was replaced with deep creativity and feelings of well-being. He still meditates twice a day thirty years later. Meditation is not for everyone. If it appeals to you, then it is important to find an approach that feels right. A good book for beginners is *The Relaxation Response* by Herbert Benson.

If you are not fulfilling your leadership potential, it may be because of a faulty habit or behavior stored in the elephant part of your brain. With practice, you can correct many shortcomings as your inner CEO becomes ascendant and takes control. You will see a change in your approach to being a leader. As you practice, you may see general signs of progress such as more self-discipline, less worry, a calm and deliberate approach, more listening and less telling, increased executive presence and focus, and concern for the long term rather than wanting everything right now.

The trick is to lead yourself first to become a first-rate leader of other people. As you find yourself more in the flow, with your rough edges softening and your faulty behaviors falling away, you are becoming the best leader that lies within you. Others will respond to the new you. Moreover, greater insight into yourself leads to greater insight into other people. You likely will begin to notice the elephant and executive within other people. With the broader perspective, patience, and grace of your inner CEO, you may find yourself passing along your wisdom to others as you coach them to lead through their inner CEO.

13

ల౩

Viable Options
Rethinking Women and Leadership

Barbara Kellerman and Deborah L. Rhode

Some forty years ago, Betty Friedan's *The Feminine Mystique* helped launch the contemporary women's movement by naming a "problem that has no name." In answer to Freud's classic question, "What do women want?" Friedan proclaimed, "We can no longer ignore that voice within women that says: 'I want something more than my husband and my children and my home.'"

Except that now, it seems, a husband and children and a home are exactly what some women want—the very women whose education and professional attainments qualify them for positions of high leadership. From *Time* to the *New York Times Magazine*, from talk shows to the water cooler, the buzz is all about women dropping out of full-time work, even at the highest professional levels, to stay home with their children. It's this "opt-out revolution," Lisa Belkin argued in the *New York Times Magazine,* and not persistent inequities and stereotypes, that account for women's underrepresentation in the leadership ranks of American business and government. As the term *opt out* implies, Belkin is at odds with Friedan. Whereas Friedan and other leaders of the women's movement stressed women's desire for something more than

Reprinted by permission of *Compass: A Journal of Leadership* (Fall 2004) published by the Kennedy School of Government at Harvard University. Copyright 2004 President and Fellows of Harvard College.

husbands, children, and well-appointed homes, Belkin and her allies claim that many women are reasonably content, for years at a stretch, with exactly that. Friedan described a society that limited women's choices; Belkin sees a society in which women are exercising choices to reject the workplace.

Jamie Gorelick, a former high-ranking official in the Clinton-era Justice Department and a member of the independent 9/11 investigative commission, might be the poster child for Belkin's revolution. In 2003, she left her position as vice chair of Fannie Mae and declined to be considered for its COO post, explaining to *Fortune* magazine that she had two children and didn't want that "pace in my life." The "dirty little secret," she added, "is that women demand a lot more satisfaction in their lives than men do."

Who is correct, Friedan or Belkin? Is the relative shortage of women leaders in government and private enterprise the result of discrimination, or have women *chosen* not to lead? The two answers, we suggest, are not mutually exclusive. Our findings do not lead us to suspend the struggle to expand women's opportunities for power, authority, and influence. Rather, we argue for reframing the problem of leadership to account for both gender *biases,* which can be addressed through greater *equity* in the workplace and in society more generally, and gender *differences,* which must be addressed through greater *diversity* in the workplace and society. To gain a sense of the interplay of the two forces, we consider where women are now, why we are where we are, and what needs to change.

PROGRESS AND FRUSTRATION

In the forty years that have passed since Friedan's manifesto, American society has experienced a transformation in gender-related attitudes, practices, and policies. About 16 percent of *Fortune* 500 corporate officers are now women; that percentage has doubled since the mid-1990s. The percentage of women holding top corporate positions—executive vice president to CEO—quadrupled during the same period, up from 2 percent to over 8 percent. Eight *Fortune* 500 companies have a female chief executive, compared with only two in 1995. Women hold fourteen Senate seats and sixty House seats in the 108th U. S. Congress. Women now constitute nearly 14 percent of members of Congress, up from 10 percent in 1992, and nearly one-quarter of the members are women of color. Twenty-one percent of college presidents are female, compared with almost none in the mid-1990s.

But progress has been partial and painfully slow. With respect to leadership, in particular, women still have a long way to go. Almost a sixth of the *Fortune* 500 companies still have no female officers. Fewer than 2 percent of corporate offices are held by African-American, Asian-American, or Hispanic women. The vast majority of women in top jobs in corporate America hold staff jobs rather than the line positions that typically produce CEOs. Women account for just 6 percent of the top corporate earners. In academia, women faculty members earn 14 percent less than men. Despite four decades of equal opportunity legislation, the workforce remains segregated and stratified by gender. Women are overrepresented at the bottom and underrepresented at the top, even controlling for educational qualifications. The best-trained women are still concentrated in different kinds of jobs from men—jobs with less pay, status, and power. As for politics and government, the United States ranks fifty-ninth in the world in electing women leaders. Congress gained three fewer women since the mid-1990s than it did in the single 1992 election, the fabled "year of the woman." Fewer women ran for state legislative offices in 2000 than did in 1992, and the number of women in state politics has been stagnant at about 20 percent since the mid-1990s. What accounts for such persistent and pervasive disparities? Why, forty years after Friedan wrote of the problem that has no name, have we done so well at labeling the problem but are still so far from solving it?

For one thing, gender bias has not been—and cannot be—legislated away. Women remain underrepresented in positions of leadership in part because of the mismatch between the characteristics traditionally associated with women and the characteristics traditionally associated with leadership. As Rakesh Khurana has observed, the Great Man model of leadership—the heroic savior—is still with us. And the term *man* is not used generically. Although recent theories of leadership stress interpersonal qualities commonly associated with women, such as cooperation and collaboration, most qualities associated with leaders are still masculine: dominance, authority, driving ambition, unflinching decisiveness, fierce determination, and so on.

Such expectations of leaders confront women with a double standard and a double bind. They may appear too soft, unable, or unwilling to make the tough calls required in the positions of greatest influence. Or if they mimic the male model, they are often viewed as strident and overly aggressive. An overview of more than a hundred studies confirms that women are rated lower when they adopt stereotypically masculine authoritative styles, particularly when the evaluators are men or when the woman's role is one typically occupied by men. Since other research suggests that individuals with masculine styles are more likely to emerge as leaders than those with feminine styles, women face trade-offs that men do not. Even in experimental situations where male and female performances are objectively equal, women are held to higher standards, and their competence is rated lower.

Many women internalize these stereotypes, which create a self-fulfilling prophecy. Researchers consistently find that most women see themselves as less deserving of rewards than men are for the same performance. On average, female workers are also less willing to take the risks, or to seek the challenges, that would equip them for leadership roles.

Commentators who focus on women's choice to leave the workplace typically fail to acknowledge the social forces that constrain it. Women are, and are expected to be, the primary caregivers, especially of the very young and very old. Many men are committed to equality more in principle than in practice; they are unwilling or (in their own view) unable to structure their lives to promote it. If, as Belkin and others insist, women are choosing not to run the world, it is partly because, to paraphrase Gloria Steinem, men are choosing not to run the washer-dryer.

Double standards in domestic roles are deeply rooted in cultural attitudes, managerial policies, and social priorities. Fewer than 15 percent of *Fortune* 100 companies offer the same paid parental leave to fathers as to mothers, and an even smaller percentage of men take any extended period of time away from their jobs for family reasons. As one director of professional development noted, the traditional expectation was that fathers with newborn infants would "just go to the hospital, take a look, and come right back to work." This pattern no longer holds, but workplaces that only grudgingly accommodate mothers can be even more resistant to fathers. Daddy tracks are noticeable for their absence. As one man put it, it is now "okay [for fathers] to say that they would like to spend more time with the kids, but it is not okay to do it, except once in a while."

As long as work-family issues are seen as problems primarily for women, potential solutions are likely to receive inadequate attention in decision making structures still dominated by men. Within those structures, caretaking is considered primarily an individual rather than a social responsibility, adding to women's work in the home and limiting their opportunities in the world outside it. America is almost alone among industrialized nations in failing to guarantee paid parental leaves. And high-quality, affordable child care is unavailable for many women attempting to work their way up the leadership ladder.

Since the mid-1960s we have made more progress in getting women access to roles traditionally occupied by men than in getting men to assume domestic roles traditionally occupied by women. And we have made even less progress in altering social policy to accommodate the needs of both sexes on family-related issues. The resilience of traditional gender patterns is reflected in two especially telling sets of statistics. Three-quarters of women have a spouse or a partner with a full-time job; three-quarters of men have a spouse or a partner who spends at least part time at home. Almost a fifth of women with graduate or professional degrees are not in the paid labor force; only 5 percent of similarly credentialed men have opted out.

WHAT PRICE POWER?

Various researchers have attempted to find a biological basis for this achievement gap. But for every piece of data that supports the hypothesis that gender roles are biologically determined, there are at least as many data to challenge it. More compelling is a growing body of research that challenges conventional views that women want just what men want. Put another way, if women are underrepresented in leadership positions, the reason is not simply that men stand in their way. Recent surveys indicate that many women, especially women with young children, are not sufficiently determined to get to the top. For a variety of reasons, women are often ambivalent about seeking power and making the sacrifices necessary to obtain it.

There is countervailing evidence for this hypothesis as well. A recent survey by Catalyst, a New York research group that studies gender and workplace issues, reports that a majority of senior executives want to become their employer's chief executive. The numbers remain roughly the same whether the respondents are male or female, childless or not. Those findings, says Catalyst, seem to challenge "the assertion that there aren't more women at the top because they don't want to be there." But it is important to note that the survey sample consisted of those who already had made the choices necessary to become senior executives.

Belkin's small sample was skewed in the other direction. It consisted of an Atlanta book group of full-time homemakers with Princeton degrees, a group of San Francisco mothers with MBAs, and "countless" readers with whom the author had corresponded. All were well educated and economically privileged women who could afford to choose to leave the paid workforce because their high-earning partners chose differently. Such selective samples preclude definitive conclusions.

Countering both the Catalyst and the Belkin arguments are studies that suggest that at least some differences in women's and men's positions in the workplace reflect different choices, many of which involve small children. A recent *Fortune* magazine article described a number of such studies and then raised the heretical question: "Do women lack power in business because they just don't want it enough?"

As the article acknowledged, the very question comes treacherously close to blaming the victim. But the signs that women have mixed feelings about conventional measures of workplace achievement are too striking to ignore. For example, Catalyst recently reported that about a quarter of women not yet in senior posts say they don't want those jobs. About a fifth of the hundred-odd women who have appeared on the *Fortune* 500 over the past five years have left their prestigious positions, generally of their own volition. And a recent survey by *Fast Company* identifies a significant minority of high-ranking women who have not opted out entirely but have chosen a life less consumed by work—which means, among other things, a life less consumed by leadership.

Such studies reinforce a conclusion unnerving to many feminists: When women aren't in positions that carry the greatest power, authority, and influence, it is not always because women can't get them; it is sometimes because they don't want them. The question is why. At least some of the reasons take us back to the gender roles and stereotypes with which we began.

First and foremost, forever foremost, there are the children. Women both bear the children and remain their primary caretakers. Most women want to have at least one child, and they are increasingly aware that involved parenting is difficult for anyone at the top.

The difficulties of reconciling family and leadership responsibilities are starkly demonstrated by the demographics. Fully 42 percent of high-achieving women in corporate America are childless at the age of forty. Moreover, among those who do have children, 40 percent feel that their husbands create more work around the house than they contribute. Men, in contrast, do not experience the same conflict between success and parenting or, to put it more pointedly, between leadership and parenting. In one representative survey, 79 percent of high-achieving men reported wanting children—and 75 percent had them.

Motherhood, it is apparent, entails more significant personal and professional implications than does fatherhood, which in turn affects access to leadership. More women than men drop out of the paid workforce, typically for periods ranging from several months to several years. More women than men work part time. And more women than men leave large organizations to strike out on their own for jobs with fewer and more flexible hours.

Yet family considerations are not the only reason that women appear less committed than men to climbing the leadership ladder. The gender biases noted earlier take a toll as well. Women who do seek leadership are slammed for seeming overly ambitious or aggressive. Others decline to risk the negative evaluations that such "unfeminine" styles evoke.

That's not the whole story, though. Many women are less professionally ambitious than men because they are more personally ambitious than men. They dream of making a difference in ways that are personally more meaningful than achievement in conventional corporate and professional settings. Many women also have personal commitments and interests that seem impossible to reconcile with the all-consuming demands of leadership roles.

THE PATH TO LEADERSHIP

Of course, only economically privileged women confront such questions as whether to work, how much to work, and whether to pursue leadership roles in the paid labor force or in the community. Yet the women who have those options also tend to be the ones with the greatest education and the best chance of achieving leadership positions. They were expected to be the role models, and if they did hold positions of power they could, in theory at least, create change for the benefit of others. Ruth Mandel, a pioneer in the field of women's studies, has well captured the current dilemma, an impasse partly created by women who could aim higher, but opt not to:

Nothing will change the picture of leadership and perhaps the practice of leadership unless women themselves choose to pursue leadership. In the United States, far and away, this matter of women's choice stands as the single greatest remaining challenge to achieve parity for women in leadership. . . . I am not saying that women at one time were choosing to lead and now are not. I am saying that today women can enter a path to leadership that has been cleared of many of the old impediments. They confront more opportunities and options than ever before. Nonetheless, women must choose to walk the path.

We have argued that the reasons for women's still-limited access to power, authority, and influence reflects both gender *biases* and gender *differences*. For women to gain ground at the leadership level, they must pursue two related but distinct strategies. Women must fight against gender biases by demanding equity; and they must fight for recognition of gender differences by demanding accommodation of diversity. These battles should be intertwined, fought simultaneously, and planned strategically, with tactics that are both political and legal.

The goals that women should be fighting for are substantially the same as those that inspired the contemporary women's movement. They include:

- Changes in public policy concerning equal opportunity enforcement, affirmative action, quality child and elder care, paid family leave, and meaningful part-time work
- Changes in organizational policies that increase those organizations' commitment to equity and diversity and that place a priority on accommodating workers with significant family, community, or other socially valued commitments
- Changes in the academy to support research on gender-related issues, particularly the socialization patterns, workplace practices, and public policies that could promote gender equality and a better quality of life for both sexes
- Changes in individual and group behaviors that will revitalize the women's movement and enable it to work more effectively toward shared goals

To promote those goals, the law can be an important tool, but its effectiveness should not be overstated and the need for its reform should not be underestimated. Legal prohibitions on sex-based discrimination and harassment, and legal entitlements concerning family leave and affirmative action, remain crucial forces in the struggle for equal employment opportunity. Multimillion-dollar victories in class action lawsuits like those against Merrill Lynch, Salomon Smith Barney, and Morgan Stanley, as well as the pending litigation against Wal-Mart, send a powerful message about the price of gender inequities. Women must continue to pursue such remedies while also pressing for changes that would make the law more effective in enhancing employment opportunities. As experts have frequently noted, our current legal framework is a highly inadequate response to "second-generation" sex discrimination, which is based less on demonstrable prejudice than on unconscious stereotypes and workplace structures that are gender neutral in form but not in fact. For the vast majority of victims, the difficulties of proof are insurmountable, or the financial and psychological costs of litigation are prohibitive. Women who pursue more informal internal remedies often experience an arbitration or mediation system stacked against them; employers control the system and are generally adept at minimizing the risk of adverse decisions, substantial financial liability, and unfavorable publicity. For victims who lack the resources to pursue litigation, federal and state enforcement agencies are a poor backup; their resources are insufficient to pursue more than a small fraction of complaints. And even the rare women who win in court often end up losing in life, given the informal blacklisting and unflattering personal disclosures that may result from litigation.

Many hard-won legal guarantees remain limited in scope. The federal Family and Medical Leave Act still leaves more than half the labor force unprotected. It provides job security only to those who can afford to take unpaid leave and excludes individuals who work for small employers or in part-time positions. And temporary-leave provisions do little to solve the long-term needs of those with substantial child-rearing or elder-care responsibilities.

There are no simple solutions. Gender-related laws remain too limited in scope and too expensive in application to reach most of the causes of women's underrepresentation in leadership positions. But we can certainly work to make those laws more effective and accessible. We can insist on greater resources for governmental enforcement agencies. We can provide financial contributions to women's rights organizations that litigate important cases and lobby for essential reforms. We can press for legislative mandates and workplace policies that will ensure more equitable informal dispute resolution systems. And we can support candidates for political and judicial positions who are committed to gender equality and the legal strategies that might help achieve it. Expanding parental leave entitlements and child-care programs, creating tax incentives for family-friendly workplace policies, and mandating more affirmative action in fields where women are underrepresented are obvious priorities for a society that is committed to equal opportunity in practice as well as principle.

Legal reforms cannot be obtained without political strategies. Our agenda, although ambitious, should be viewed in context. We do not see most American women as downtrodden. We realize that more than a few American women control large sums of money and that many (ourselves included) have very good jobs. And we are certainly aware that, by global standards, the overwhelming majority of American women are extremely well off. But in terms of basic gender equity, American women still have a long way to go. And neither governmental policy nor business practices ensure that women (or men for that matter) can care adequately for their families and participate actively in their communities while exercising leadership roles.

Women are not well positioned to address that problem. Despite their numerical majority, women still lack the positions of influence, in both the public and the private sectors, necessary to achieve the agenda set forth above. That, in turn, means that women need to employ the strategies most readily available to those without conventional sources of leverage. We refer to three in particular:

First, women must envision themselves as agents of change. Instead of reconciling ourselves to unequal burdens in the home and to unequal pay, status, and power in the world outside, we need to demand gender equity and the strategies necessary to achieve it.

Second, women must be ready, willing, and able to take a stand. The first step is a revival of old-fashioned consciousness-raising. We need to increase awareness of gender inequities and inspire a passion for challenging them. This will, in turn, require some willingness to assume short-term risks in the interest of long-term gains. As political theorists and activists across the globe remind us, there are no substitutes for speaking truth to power. Of course, that strategy must be selective. In order to reach positions of influence, women need to target their efforts and pick battles that they have some prospect of winning. But the challenge is to succeed within organizations without losing the capacity or commitment to change them. Silence in the face of inequality can only perpetuate it.

Third, women must take collective action. Fundamental change begins with individual commitment, but it requires group efforts. Women need to be more strategic in forging alliances and enlisting the collaboration of other individuals, small groups, and large organizations in the interest of common causes. Since the 1960s, both national and grassroots women's groups, all with their own particular missions and constituencies, have dramatically increased in size and number. But there has been insufficient unity even around key issues, as well as equally insufficient attempts to involve women from different points along the socioeconomic and demographic spectrum.

We need also to include men in our struggle. Women must insist, endlessly it seems, that the most crucial women's issues are issues not only for women. They are concerns in which both sexes have a stake. Increasing numbers of men want more balance in their lives. And their families, communities, and workplaces would benefit greatly if they achieved it. As a growing body of research makes clear, balanced lives serve bottom lines; they reduce employers' training and recruitment expenses and improve workers' health and productivity. A diverse workforce serves equally important objectives. In today's increasingly competitive global economy, no organization can secure long-term success with policies that penalize half the talent pool for leadership.

We cannot know with any certainty what, in an ideal world, women would truly want. But in this far from perfect world, we know well enough what women do not want—enough to forge a constructive agenda for reform. Forcing professionals of either sex to opt on or off leadership tracks as they are currently structured is not the answer. Choice on these terms is not a solution. It is part of the problem.

14

e⁄ɔ

Women and the Labyrinth
of Leadership

Alice H. Eagly and Linda L. Carli

If one has misdiagnosed a problem, then one is unlikely to prescribe an effective cure. This is the situation regarding the scarcity of women in top leadership. Because people with the best of intentions have misread the symptoms, the solutions that managers are investing in are not making enough of a difference.

That there is a problem is not in doubt. Despite years of progress by women in the workforce (they now occupy more than 40 percent of all managerial positions in the United States), within the C-suite they remain as rare as hens' teeth. Consider the most highly paid executives of *Fortune* 500 companies—those with titles such as chairman, president, chief executive officer, and chief operating officer. Of this group, only 6 percent are women. Most notably, only 2 percent of the CEOs are women, and only 15 percent of the seats on the boards of directors are held by women. The situation is not much different in other industrialized countries. In the 50 largest publicly traded corporations in each nation of the European Union, women make up, on average, 11 percent of the top executives and 4 percent of the CEOs and heads of boards.

Just seven companies, or 1 percent, of *Fortune* magazine's Global 500 have female CEOs. What is to blame for the pronounced lack of women in positions of power and authority?

In 1986 the *Wall Street Journal*'s Carol Hymowitz and Timothy Schellhardt gave the world an answer: "Even those few women who rose steadily through the ranks eventually crashed into an invisible barrier. The executive suite seemed within their grasp, but they just couldn't break through the glass ceiling." The metaphor, driven home by the article's accompanying illustration, resonated; it captured the frustration of a goal within sight but somehow unattainable. To be sure, there was a time when the barriers were absolute. Even within the career spans of 1980s-era executives, access to top posts had been explicitly denied. Consider comments made by President Richard Nixon, recorded on White House audiotapes and made public through the Freedom of Information Act. When explaining why he would not appoint a woman to the U.S. Supreme Court, Nixon said, "I don't think a woman should be in any government job whatsoever . . . mainly because they are erratic. And emotional. Men are erratic and emotional, too, but the point is a woman is more likely to be." In a culture where such opinions were widely held, women had virtually no chance of attaining influential leadership roles.

Times have changed, however, and the glass ceiling metaphor is now more wrong than right. For one thing, it describes an absolute barrier at a specific high level in organizations. The fact that there have been female chief executives, university presidents, state governors, and presidents of nations gives the lie to that charge. At the same time, the metaphor implies that women and men have equal access to entry- and midlevel positions. They do not. The image of a transparent obstruction also suggests that women are being misled about their opportunities, because the impediment is not easy for them to see from a distance. But some impediments are not subtle. Worst of all, by depicting a single, unvarying obstacle, the glass ceiling fails to incorporate the complexity and variety of challenges that women can face in their leadership journeys. In truth, women are not turned away only as they reach the penultimate stage of a distinguished career. They disappear in various numbers at many points leading up to that stage.

Metaphors matter because they are part of the storytelling that can compel change. Believing in the existence of a glass ceiling, people emphasize certain kinds of interventions: top-to-top networking, mentoring to increase board memberships, requirements for diverse candidates in high-profile succession horse races, litigation aimed at punishing discrimination in the C-suite. None of these is counterproductive; all have a role to play. The danger arises when they draw attention and resources away from other kinds of interventions that might attack the problem more potently. If we want to make better progress, it's time to rename the challenge.

WALLS ALL AROUND

A better metaphor for what confronts women in their professional endeavors is the labyrinth. It's an image with a long and varied history in ancient Greece, India, Nepal, native North and South America, medieval Europe, and elsewhere. As a contemporary symbol, it conveys the idea of a complex journey toward a goal worth striving for. Passage through a labyrinth is not simple or direct, but requires persistence, awareness of one's progress, and a careful analysis of the puzzles that lie ahead. It is this meaning that we intend to convey. For women who aspire to top leadership, routes exist but are full of twists and turns, both unexpected and expected. Because all labyrinths have a viable route to the center, it is understood that goals are attainable. The metaphor acknowledges obstacles but is not ultimately discouraging.

If we can understand the various barriers that make up this labyrinth, and how some women find their way around them, we can work more effectively to improve the situation. What are the obstructions that women run up against? Let's explore them in turn.

Vestiges of Prejudice

It is a well-established fact that men as a group still have the benefit of higher wages and faster promotions. In the United States in 2005, for example, women employed full-time earned 81 cents for every dollar that men earned. Is this true because of discrimination or simply because, with fewer family demands placed on them and longer careers on average, men are able to gain superior qualifications? Literally hundreds of correlational studies by economists and sociologists have attempted to find the answer.

One of the most comprehensive of these studies was conducted by the U.S. Government Accountability Office. The study was based on survey data from 1983 through 2000 from a representative sample of Americans. Because the same people responded to the survey repeatedly over the years, the study provided accurate estimates of past work experience, which is important for explaining later wages.

The GAO researchers tested whether individuals' total wages could be predicted by sex and other characteristics. They included part-time and full-time employees in the surveys and took into account all the factors that they could estimate and that might affect earnings, such as education and work experience. Without controls for these variables, the data showed that women earned about 44 percent less than men, averaged over the entire period from 1983 to 2000. With these controls in place, the gap was only about half as large, but still substantial. The control factors that reduced the wage gap most were the different employment patterns of men and women: Men undertook more hours of paid labor per year than women and had more years of job experience.

Although most variables affected the wages of men and women similarly, there were exceptions. Marriage and parenthood, for instance, were associated with higher wages for men but not for women. In contrast, other characteristics, especially years of education, had a more positive effect on women's wages than on men's. Even after adjusting wages for all of the ways men and women differ, the GAO study, like similar studies, showed that women's wages remained lower than men's. The unexplained gender gap is consistent with the presence of wage discrimination.

Similar methods have been applied to the question of whether discrimination affects promotions. Evidently it does. Promotions come more slowly for women than for men with equivalent qualifications. One illustrative national study followed workers from 1980 to 1992 and found that white men were more likely to attain managerial positions than white women, black men, and black women. Controlling for other characteristics, such as education and hours worked per year, the study showed that white men were ahead of the other groups when entering the labor market and that their advantage in attaining managerial positions grew throughout their careers. Other research has underscored these findings. Even in culturally feminine settings such as nursing, librarianship, elementary education, and social work (all specifically studied by sociologist Christine Williams), men ascend to supervisory and administrative positions more quickly than women.

The findings of correlational studies are supported by experimental research, in which subjects are asked to evaluate hypothetical individuals as managers or job candidates, and all characteristics of these individuals are held constant except for their sex. Such efforts continue the tradition of the Goldberg paradigm, named for a 1968 experiment by Philip Goldberg. His simple, elegant study had student participants evaluate written essays that were identical except for the attached male or female name. The students were unaware that other students had received identical material ascribed to a writer of the other sex. This initial experiment demonstrated an overall gen-

der bias: Women received lower evaluations unless the essay was on a feminine topic. Some forty years later, unfortunately, experiments continue to reveal the same kind of bias in work settings. Men are advantaged over
equivalent women as candidates for jobs traditionally held by men as well as
for more gender-integrated jobs. Similarly, male leaders receive somewhat
more favorable evaluations than equivalent female leaders, especially in roles
usually occupied by men.

Interestingly, however, there is little evidence from either the correlational
or the experimental studies that the odds are stacked higher against women
with each step up the ladder—that is, that women's promotions become pro-
gressively less likely than men's at higher levels within organizations. Instead,
a general bias against women appears to operate with approximately equal
strength at all levels. The scarcity of female corporate officers is the sum of
discrimination that has operated at all ranks, not evidence of a particular obstacle to advancement as women approach the top. The problem, in other
words, is not a glass ceiling.

Resistance to Women's Leadership

What's behind the discrimination we've been describing? Essentially, a set of
widely shared conscious and unconscious mental associations about women,
men, and leaders. Study after study has affirmed that people associate women
and men with different traits and link men with more of the traits that connote
leadership. Kim Campbell, who briefly served as the prime minister of Canada
in 1993, described the tension that results: "I don't have a traditionally female
way of speaking. . . .I'm quite assertive. If I didn't speak the way I do, I
wouldn't have been seen as a leader. But my way of speaking may have grated
on people who were not used to hearing it from a woman. It was the right
way for a leader to speak, but it wasn't the right way for a woman to speak. It
goes against type."

In the language of psychologists, the clash is between two sets of associations: communal and agentic. Women are associated with communal qualities,
which convey a concern for the compassionate treatment of others. They include being especially affectionate, helpful, friendly, kind, and sympathetic,
as well as interpersonally sensitive, gentle, and soft-spoken. In contrast, men
are associated with agentic qualities, which convey assertion and control. They
include being especially aggressive, ambitious, dominant, self-confident, and
forceful, as well as self-reliant and individualistic. The agentic traits are also
associated in most people's minds with effective leadership—perhaps because

a long history of male domination of leadership roles has made it difficult to separate the leader associations from the male associations.

As a result, women leaders find themselves in a double bind. If they are highly communal, they may be criticized for not being agentic enough. But if they are highly agentic, they may be criticized for lacking communion. Either way, they may leave the impression that they don't have "the right stuff" for powerful jobs.

Given this double bind, it is hardly surprising that people are more resistant to women's influence than to men's. For example, in meetings at a global retail company, people responded more favorably to men's overt attempts at influence than to women's. In the words of one of this company's female executives, "People often had to speak up to defend their turf, but when women did so, they were vilified. They were labeled 'control freaks'; men acting the same way were called 'passionate.'"

Studies have gauged reactions to men and women engaging in various types of dominant behavior. The findings are quite consistent. Nonverbal dominance, such as staring at others while speaking to them or pointing at people, is a more damaging behavior for women than for men. Verbally intimidating others can undermine a woman's influence, and assertive behavior can reduce her chances of getting a job or advancing in her career. Simply disagreeing can sometimes get women into trouble. Men who disagree or otherwise act dominant get away with it more often than women do.

Self-promotion is similarly risky for women. Although it can convey status and competence, it is not at all communal. So while men can use bluster to get themselves noticed, modesty is expected even of highly accomplished women. Linguistics professor Deborah Tannen tells a story from her experience: "This [need for modesty] was evident, for example, at a faculty meeting devoted to promotions, at which a woman professor's success was described: She was extremely well published and well known in the field. A man commented with approval, 'She wears it well.' In other words, she was praised for not acting as successful as she was."

Another way the double bind penalizes women is by denying them the full benefits of being warm and considerate. Because people expect it of women, nice behavior that seems noteworthy in men seems unimpressive in women. For example, in one study, helpful men reaped a lot of approval, but helpful women did not. Likewise, men got away with being unhelpful, but women did not. A different study found that male employees received more promotions when they reported higher levels of helpfulness to coworkers. But female employees' promotions were not related to such altruism.

While one might suppose that men would have a double bind of their own, they in fact have more freedom. Several experiments and organizational studies have assessed reactions to behavior that is warm and friendly versus dominant and assertive. The findings show that men can communicate in a warm or a dominant manner, with no penalty either way. People like men equally well and are equally influenced by them regardless of their warmth.

It all amounts to a clash of assumptions when the average person confronts a woman in management. Perhaps this is why respondents in one study characterized the group of "successful female managers" as more deceitful, pushy, selfish, and abrasive than "successful male managers." In the absence of any evidence to the contrary, people suspect that such highly effective women must not be very likable or nice.

Issues of Leadership Style

In response to the challenges presented by the double bind, female leaders often struggle to cultivate an appropriate and effective leadership style—one that reconciles the communal qualities people prefer in women with the agentic qualities people think leaders need to succeed. Here, for instance, is how Marietta Nien-hwa Cheng described her transition to the role of symphony conductor: "I used to speak more softly, with a higher pitch. Sometimes my vocal cadences went up instead of down. I realized that these mannerisms lack the sense of authority. I strengthened my voice. The pitch has dropped. . . . I have stopped trying to be everyone's friend. Leadership is not synonymous with socializing."

It's difficult to pull off such a transformation while maintaining a sense of authenticity as a leader. Sometimes the whole effort can backfire. In the words of another female leader, "I think that there is a real penalty for a woman who behaves like a man. The men don't like her and the women don't either." Women leaders worry a lot about these things, complicating the labyrinth that they negotiate. For example, Catalyst's study of *Fortune* 1000 female executives found that 96 percent of them rated as critical or fairly important that they develop "a style with which male managers are comfortable."

Does a distinct "female" leadership style exist? There seems to be a popular consensus that it does. Consider, for example, journalist Michael Sokolove's profile of Mike Krzyzewski, head coach of the highly successful Duke University men's basketball team. As Sokolove put it, "So what is the secret to Krzyzewski's success? For starters, he coaches the way a woman would. Really." Sokolove proceeded to describe Krzyzewski's mentoring, interpersonally sensitive, and highly effective coaching style.

More scientifically, a recent meta-analysis integrated the results of 45 studies addressing the question. To compare leadership skills, the researchers adopted a framework introduced by leadership scholar James MacGregor Burns that distinguishes between transformational leadership and transactional leadership. Transformational leaders establish themselves as role models by gaining followers' trust and confidence. They state future goals, develop plans to achieve those goals, and innovate, even when their organizations are generally successful. Such leaders mentor and empower followers, encouraging them to develop their full potential and thus to contribute more effectively to their organizations. By contrast, transactional leaders establish give-and-take relationships that appeal to subordinates' self-interest. Such leaders manage in the conventional manner of clarifying subordinates' responsibilities, rewarding them for meeting objectives, and correcting them for failing to meet objectives. Although transformational and transactional leadership styles are different, most leaders adopt at least some behaviors of both types. The researchers also allowed for a third category, called the laissez-faire style—a sort of nonleadership that concerns itself with none of the above, despite rank authority.

The meta-analysis found that, in general, female leaders were somewhat more transformational than male leaders, especially when it came to giving support and encouragement to subordinates. They also engaged in more of the rewarding behaviors that are one aspect of transactional leadership. Meanwhile, men exceeded women on the aspects of transactional leadership involving corrective and disciplinary actions that are either active (timely) or passive (belated). Men were also more likely than women to be laissez-faire leaders, who take little responsibility for managing. These findings add up to a startling conclusion, given that most leadership research has found the transformational style (along with the rewards and positive incentives associated with the transactional style) to be more suited to leading the modern organization. The research tells us not only that men and women do have somewhat different leadership styles, but also that women's approaches are the more generally effective—while men's often are only somewhat effective or actually hinder effectiveness.

Another part of this picture, based on a separate meta-analysis, is that women adopt a more participative and collaborative style than men typically favor. The reason for this difference is unlikely to be genetic. Rather, it may be that collaboration can get results without seeming particularly masculine. As women navigate their way through the double bind, they seek ways to project authority without relying on the autocratic behaviors that people find so jarring in women. A viable path is to bring others into decision making and to lead as an encouraging teacher and positive role model. (However, if there is not a critical mass of other women to affirm the legitimacy of a participative style, female leaders usually conform to whatever style is typical of the men—and that is sometimes autocratic.)

Demands of Family Life

For many women, the most fateful turns in the labyrinth are the ones taken under pressure of family responsibilities. Women continue to be the ones who interrupt their careers, take more days off, and work part-time. As a result, they have fewer years of job experience and fewer hours of employment per year, which slows their career progress and reduces their earnings.

In one study of Chicago lawyers, researchers sought to understand why women were much less likely than men to hold the leadership positions in large law firms—the positions that are most highly paid and that confer (arguably) the highest prestige. They found that women were no less likely than men to begin their careers at such firms but were more likely to leave them for positions in the public sector or corporate positions. The reasons for their departures were concentrated in work/family trade-offs. Among the relatively few women who did become partner in a firm, 60 percent had no children, and the minority who had children generally had delayed childbearing until attaining partner status.

There is no question that, while men increasingly share housework and child rearing, the bulk of domestic work still falls on women's shoulders. We know this from time-diary studies, in which people record what they are doing during each hour of a 24-hour day. So, for example, in the United States married women devoted 19 hours per week on average to housework in 2005, while married men contributed 11 hours. That's a huge improvement over 1965 numbers, when women spent a whopping 34 hours per week to men's five, but it is still a major inequity. And the situation looks worse when child care hours are added.

Although it is common knowledge that mothers provide more child care than fathers, few people realize that mothers provide more than they did in earlier generations—despite the fact that fathers are putting in a lot more time than in the past. National studies have compared mothers and fathers on the amount of their primary child care, which consists of close interaction not combined with housekeeping or other activities. Married mothers increased their hours per week from 10.6 in 1965 to 12.9 in 2000, and married fathers increased theirs from 2.6 to 6.5. Thus, though husbands have taken on more domestic work, the work/family conflict has not eased for women; the gain has been offset by escalating pressures for intensive parenting and the increasing time demands of most high-level careers.

Even women who have found a way to relieve pressures from the home front by sharing child care with husbands, other family members, or paid workers may not enjoy the full workplace benefit of having done so. Decision makers often assume that mothers have domestic responsibilities that make it inappropriate to promote them to demanding positions. As one participant in a study of the federal workforce explained, "I mean, there were two or three names [of women] in the hat, and they said, 'I don't want to talk about her because she has children who are still home in these [evening] hours.' Now they don't pose that thing about men on the list, many of whom also have children in that age group."

Underinvestment in Social Capital

Perhaps the most destructive result of the work/family balancing act so many women must perform is that it leaves very little time for socializing with colleagues and building professional networks. The social capital that accrues from such "nonessential" parts of work turns out to be quite essential indeed. One study yielded the following description of managers who advanced rapidly in hierarchies: Fast-track managers "spent relatively more time and effort socializing, politicking, and interacting with outsiders than did their less successful counterparts . . . [and] did not give much time or attention to the traditional management activities of planning, decision making, and controlling or to the human resource management activities of motivating/reinforcing, staffing, training/developing, and managing conflict." This suggests that social capital is even more necessary to managers' advancement than skillful performance of traditional managerial tasks.

Even given sufficient time, women can find it difficult to engage in and benefit from informal networking if they are a small minority. In such settings, the influential networks are composed entirely or almost entirely of men. Breaking into those male networks can be hard, especially when men center their networks on masculine activities. The recent gender discrimination lawsuit against Wal-Mart provides examples of this. For instance, an executive retreat took the form of a quail-hunting expedition at Sam Walton's ranch in Texas. Middle managers' meetings included visits to strip clubs and Hooters restaurants, and a sales conference attended by thousands of store managers featured a football theme. One executive received feedback that she probably would not advance in the company because she didn't hunt or fish.

MANAGEMENT INTERVENTIONS THAT WORK

Taking the measure of the labyrinth that confronts women leaders, we see that it begins with prejudices that benefit men and penalize women, continues with particular resistance to women's leadership, includes questions of leadership style and authenticity, and—most dramatically for many women—features the challenge of balancing work and family responsibilities. It becomes clear that a woman's situation as she reaches her peak career years is the result of many turns at many challenging junctures. Only a few individual women have made the right combination of moves to land at the center of power—but as for the rest, there is usually no single turning point where their progress was diverted and the prize was lost.

What's to be done in the face of such a multifaceted problem? A solution that is often proposed is for governments to implement and enforce antidiscrimination legislation and thereby require organizations to eliminate inequitable practices. However, analysis of discrimination cases that have gone to court has shown that legal remedies can be elusive when gender inequality results from norms embedded in organizational structure and culture. The more effective approach is for organizations to appreciate the subtlety and complexity of the problem and to attack its many roots simultaneously. More specifically, if a company wants to see more women arrive in its executive suite, it should do the following:

Increase people's awareness of the psychological drivers of prejudice toward female leaders, and work to dispel those perceptions. Raising awareness of ingrained bias has been the aim of many diversity-training initiatives, and no doubt they have been more helpful than harmful. There is the danger they will be undermined, however, if their lessons are not underscored by what managers say and do in the course of day-to-day work.

Change the long-hours norm. Especially in the context of knowledge work, it can be hard to assess individuals' relative contributions, and managers may resort to "hours spent at work" as the prime indicator of someone's worth to the organization. To the extent an organization can shift the focus to objective measures of productivity, women with family demands on their time but highly productive work habits will receive the rewards and encouragement they deserve.

Reduce the subjectivity of performance evaluation. Greater objectivity in evaluations also combats the effects of lingering prejudice in both hiring and promotion. To ensure fairness, criteria should be explicit and evaluation processes designed to limit the influence of decision makers' conscious and unconscious biases.

Use open-recruitment tools, such as advertising and employment agencies, rather than relying on informal social networks and referrals to fill positions. Recruitment from within organizations also should be transparent, with postings of open positions in appropriate venues. Research has shown that such personnel practices increase the numbers of women in managerial roles.

Ensure a critical mass of women in executive positions—not just one or two women—to head off the problems that come with tokenism. Token women tend to be pegged into narrow stereotypical roles such as "seductress," "mother," "pet," or "iron maiden." (Or more colorfully, as one woman banker put it, "When you start out in banking, you are a slut or a geisha.") Pigeonholing like this limits women's options and makes it difficult for them to rise to positions of responsibility. When women are not a small minority, their identities as women become less salient, and colleagues are more likely to react to them in terms of their individual competencies.

Avoid having a sole female member of any team. Top management tends to divide its small population of women managers among many projects in the interests of introducing diversity to them all. But several studies have found that, so outnumbered, the women tend to be ignored by the men. A female vice president of a manufacturing company described how, when she or another woman ventures an idea in a meeting, it tends to be overlooked: "It immediately gets lost in the conversation. Then two minutes later, a man makes the same suggestion, and it's 'Wow! What a great idea!' And you sit there and think, 'What just happened?'" As women reach positions of higher power and authority, they increasingly find themselves in gender-imbalanced groups—and some find themselves, for the first time, seriously marginalized. This is part of the reason that the glass ceiling metaphor resonates with so many. But in fact, the problem can be present at any level.

Help shore up social capital. As we've discussed, the call of family responsibilities is mainly to blame for women's underinvestment in networking. When time is scarce, this social activity is the first thing to go by the wayside. Organizations can help women appreciate why it deserves more attention. In particular, women gain from strong and supportive mentoring relationships and connections with powerful networks. When a well-placed individual who possesses greater legitimacy (often a man) takes an interest in a woman's career, her efforts to build social capital can proceed far more efficiently.

Prepare women for line management with appropriately demanding assignments. Women, like men, must have the benefit of developmental job experiences if they are to qualify for promotions. But, as one woman executive wrote, "Women have been shunted off into support areas for the last thirty years, rather than being in the business of doing business, so the pool of women trained to assume leadership positions in any large company is very small." Her point was that women should be taught in business school to insist on line jobs when they enter the workforce. One company that has taken up the challenge has been Procter & Gamble. According to a report by Claudia Deutsch in the *New York Times,* the company was experiencing an executive attrition rate that was twice as high for women as for men. Some of the women reported having to change companies to land jobs that provided challenging work. P&G's subsequent efforts to bring more women into line management both improved its overall retention of women and increased the number of women in senior management.

Establish family-friendly human resources practices. These may include flextime, job sharing, telecommuting, elder care provisions, adoption benefits, dependent child care options, and employee-sponsored on-site child care. Such support can allow women to stay in their jobs during the most demanding years of child rearing, build social capital, keep up to date in their fields, and eventually compete for higher positions. A study of 72 large U.S. firms showed (controlling for other variables) that family-friendly HR practices in place in 1994 increased the proportion of women in senior management over the subsequent five years.

Allow employees who have significant parental responsibility more time to prove themselves worthy of promotion. This recommendation is particularly directed to organizations, many of them professional services firms, that have established "up or out" career progressions. People not ready for promotion at the same time as the top performers in their cohort aren't simply left in place—they're asked to leave. But many parents (most often mothers), while fully capable of reaching that level of achievement, need extra time—perhaps a year or two—to get there. Forcing them off the promotion path not only reduces the number of women reaching top management positions, but also constitutes a failure by the firm to capitalize on its early investment in them.

Welcome women back. It makes sense to give high-performing women who step away from the workforce an opportunity to return to responsible positions when their circumstances change. Some companies have established "alumni" programs, often because they see former employees as potential sources of new business. A few companies have gone further to activate these networks for other purposes, as well. (Procter & Gamble taps alumni for innovation purposes; Booz Allen sees its alumni ranks as a source of subcontractors.) Keeping lines of communication open can convey the message that a return may be possible.

Encourage male participation in family-friendly benefits. Dangers lurk in family-friendly benefits that are used only by women. Exercising options such as generous parental leave and part-time work slows down women's careers. More profoundly, having many more women than men take such benefits can harm the careers of women in general because of the expectation that they may well exercise those options. Any effort toward greater family friendliness should actively recruit male participation to avoid inadvertently making it harder for women to gain access to essential managerial roles.

Managers can be forgiven if they find the foregoing list a tall order. It's a wide-ranging set of interventions and still far from exhaustive. The point, however, is just that: Organizations will succeed in filling half their top management slots with women—and women who are the true performance equals of their male counterparts—only by attacking all the reasons they are absent today. Glass ceiling–inspired programs and projects can do just so much if the leakage of talented women is happening on every lower floor of the building. Individually, each of these interventions has been shown to make a difference. Collectively, we believe, they can make all the difference.

THE VIEW FROM ABOVE

Imagine visiting a formal garden and finding within it a high hedgerow. At a point along its vertical face, you spot a rectangle—a neatly pruned and inviting doorway. Are you aware as you step through that you are entering a labyrinth? And, three doorways later, as the reality of the puzzle settles in, do you have any idea how to proceed? This is the situation in which many women find themselves in their career endeavors. Ground-level perplexity and frustration make every move uncertain.

Labyrinths become infinitely more tractable when seen from above. When the eye can take in the whole of the puzzle—the starting position, the goal, and the maze of walls—solutions begin to suggest themselves. This has been the goal of our research. Our hope is that women, equipped with a map of the barriers they will confront on their path to professional achievement, will make more informed choices. We hope that managers, too, will understand where their efforts can facilitate the progress of women. If women are to achieve equality, women and men will have to share leadership equally. With a greater understanding of what stands in the way of gender-balanced leadership, we draw nearer to attaining it in our time.

IS IT ONLY A QUESTION OF TIME?

It is a common perception that women will steadily gain greater access to leadership roles, including elite positions. For example, university students who are queried about the future power of men and women say that women's power will increase. Polls have shown that most Americans expect a woman to be elected president or vice president within their lifetimes. Both groups are extrapolating women's recent gains into the future, as if our society were on a continuous march toward gender equality.

But social change does not proceed without struggle and conflict. As women gain greater equality, a portion of people react against it. They long for traditional roles. In fact, signs of a pause in progress toward gender equality have appeared on many fronts. A review of longitudinal studies reveals several areas in which a sharp upward trend in the 1970s and 1980s has been followed by a slowing and flattening in recent years (for instance, in the percentage of managers who are women). The pause is also evident in some attitudinal data—like the percentage of people who approve of female bosses and who believe that women are at least as well suited as men for politics.

Social scientists have proposed various theories to explain this pause. Some, such as social psychologist Cecilia Ridgeway, believe that social change is activating "people's deep seated interests in maintaining clear cultural understandings of gender difference." Others believe progress has reached its limit given the continuing organization of family life by gender, coupled with employer policies that favor those who are not hampered by primary responsibility for child rearing.

It may simply be that women are collectively catching their breath before pressing for more change. In the past century, feminist activism arose when women came to view themselves as collectively subjected to illegitimate and unfair treatment. But recent polls show less conviction about the presence of discrimination, and feminism does not have the cultural relevance it once had. The lessening of activism on behalf of all women puts pressure on each woman to find her own way.

15

⁊ↄ

Stop Holding Yourself Back

Anne Morriss, Robin J. Ely, and Frances X. Frei

From the world's poorest communities to the corner offices of its largest corporations, ambitious employees struggle with the same basic challenge: how to gain the strength and insights not just to manage but to lead. For more than a decade, from three different perspectives, we have been investigating what gets in the way. Robin conducts research on race, gender, and leadership; Frances focuses on coaching senior executives; and Anne works on unleashing social entrepreneurs around the world.

We've worked with hundreds of leaders in the public, private, and nonprofit sectors, in industries spanning more than 30 fields, and in more than 50 countries at various stages of development. Amid all the diversity, one very clear pattern has emerged: Organization builders, fire starters, and movement makers are unintentionally stopping themselves from becoming exceptional leaders. As a result, companies aren't getting the best from their people, and employees are limiting their opportunities.

Why does this happen? We've identified five major barriers.

BARRIER I: OVEREMPHASIZING PERSONAL GOALS

True leadership is about making *other* people better as a result of your presence—and making sure your impact endures in your absence. That doesn't

Reprinted by permission of *Harvard Business Review* (January-February 2011). Copyright 2011 Harvard Business School Publishing Corporation. All rights reserved.

mean leaders are selfless. They have personal goals—to build status, a professional identity, and a retirement plan, among other things.

But the narrow pursuit of those goals can lead to self-protection and self-promotion, neither of which fosters other people's success.

One leader we studied fell into this destructive behavior after a long, successful run at a number of software companies. Troy's bosses had always valued his drive and accountability. But when customer complaints began pouring into the service division he was managing, he pinned the blame on the "mediocrity" of the product development division, claiming that his team had to support an inferior product.

Troy's COO disagreed and began to hint that Troy's job was on the line: After all, the complaints had started accumulating on his watch. To shore up his position, Troy started working to win over senior colleagues one by one—"picking them off," as he put it—by asking for feedback on his performance. His strategy worked to some extent. Senior management recognized that he was committed to improving his leadership skills. But the customer service problems just got worse. People began trashing the company on influential blogs, and demands for refunds kept rising. The more Troy worked to save his job, the harder his job became.

Troy had a leadership breakthrough when one of his service representatives asked for help resolving the growing conflict with the product development team. The rep's despair triggered a shift in Troy's thinking—away from worrying about his own position and toward healing the split between the two divisions. Troy hosted a series of cross-team meetings and made sure that both groups felt heard. By the third meeting, the teams were brainstorming about ways to solve the service problem together, by improving the software and helping customers learn how to better use it.

Like other effective leaders, Troy changed his focus from protecting himself to supporting the members of his team and making sure that customers were happy. Within a few weeks, demands for refunds began to decrease, even though the company hadn't yet made any upgrades to the product.

The decision to focus on others can feel dangerous. It forces you to take your eyes off your own welfare and to stop scanning the horizon for predators. Risk aversion is a protective mechanism wired into our DNA; that's why security concerns generally trump impact. But all breakthrough leaders find ways to tame their security impulses. Most are amazed by the energy and meaning they discover when they no longer define themselves by their personal needs and fears.

Making other people a priority is perhaps most challenging for emerging leaders—especially women and minorities, who may feel heightened pressure to protect their interests in a world that seems (and often is) rigged against them. When societal attitudes contain built-in questions about your competence, it takes a lot of energy to keep trying to prove those attitudes wrong.

We don't underestimate this challenge. But if your goal is to lead, our advice is the same no matter who you are: First, *get over yourself.* Start with a commitment to make another person, or an entire team, better—and then go back for the skills and resources to pull it off.

BARRIER 2: PROTECTING YOUR PUBLIC IMAGE

Another common impediment to leadership is being overly distracted by your image—that ideal self you've created in your mind. Sticking to the script that goes along with that image takes a lot of energy, leaving little left over for the real work of leadership.

There are more-nuanced costs as well. Once you've crafted your persona and determined not to veer from it, your effectiveness often suffers. The need to be seen as intelligent can inhibit learning and risk taking, for instance. The need to be seen as likable can keep you from asking tough questions or challenging existing norms. The need to be seen as decisive can cause you to shut down critical feedback loops.

One woman we interviewed, Anita, was an executive vice president in charge of the regional performance of a large retail company. The public image she'd created—tough, decisive, analytical—had been a powerful instrument in advancing her career. But it left little room for her humanity—an essential part of the leadership equation.

Anita thought that using intuition was intellectually lazy; she was known for the phrase "Show me the data." When in-store analytics suggested that the company gained little advantage from long-term employees, Anita ordered some store managers to replace experienced salespeople with lower-paid part-timers. The experiment reduced payroll costs, but it wreaked havoc on the culture and service experience in those stores—an outcome the data didn't immediately reveal.

Store managers tried to communicate their frustration to Anita, but the interactions invariably went badly. She pushed back on any concerns that weren't supported by numbers and recklessly concluded that her managers simply feared change. Their resignations started to roll in. Like many leaders, Anita

EXHIBIT 15.1—LEADERSHIP DIAGNOSTIC: ARE YOU HAVING MAXIMUM
IMPACT?

For most of us, the high-impact leader lurking inside comes out only on our best
days. If you find yourself in this category—if you're not getting the leadership trac-
tion you want—ask yourself these questions. If most of your answers are "no," you
may be getting in your own way.

Overemphasizing Personal Goals

- Do I spend most of my time as a
  manager thinking about what
  other people in the organization
  need to succeed?
- Does the "best version" of my
  employees show up in my presence?
- Does their best version endure in
  my absence?

Protecting Your Public Image

- Do I ever stop monitoring myself
  and simply do my job?
- Have I been willing to "look
  bad" in the service of my team or
  organization?
- Do I explicitly model the attitudes and behaviors I want others in my organization to adopt?

had decided she could be tough or empathetic—but not both. She was unable
to hear feedback, particularly from people below her, or to risk looking bad
by making a high-profile course correction. And so she lost some of the company's best managers.

Once the turnover on her team reached 50%, however, Anita decided she
had to take action. Inspired by an exercise in an executive education program
she'd attended, she thought about teams she'd been part of that had worked
together well. She then spoke with some of the people involved in an attempt
to figure out why. Her conversation with her high school volleyball coach rat-
tled her. He gave this advice: "If you want your people to care what you think,
first make it clear that you care what *they* think." Within a few days, Anita
reached out to one of the managers who had just resigned, a woman with a
decade of experience making retail spaces work. She invited the manager to
come back and help her repair the damage. Their collaboration was a professional turning point for Anita.

This type of journey is not uncommon. At some point in their leadership
trajectory, ambitious people must choose between image and impact, between
looking powerful and empowering others. They must choose, in effect, between impersonating a leader and being one (see Exhibit 15.1).

BARRIER 3: TURNING COMPETITORS INTO ENEMIES

One particularly toxic behavior is the act of turning those you don't get along with into two-dimensional enemies. Distorting other people is a common response to conflict, but it carries significant leadership costs. It severs your links to reality, making you reliably incapable of exerting influence. As you turn others into caricatures, you risk becoming a caricature yourself.

Consider Sarah, the COO of a global medical devices company. She specialized in integrating acquired business, and she was unambiguously great at her job. But she became easily frustrated by the "incompetence" of coworkers, including Max, the CFO. Sarah was quick to dismiss his abilities, having decided that he was out of his league and held his position only because he fawned over other senior leaders, particularly the CEO. She began to dislike everything about him—his voice, his ridiculous cufflink collection, his goatee.

Sarah started to rethink her judgment only when she was seated next to Max on a flight from London to the U.S. Forced to engage, she learned the reason for his apparent sycophancy—he was concerned about the CEO's credibility with investors and senior managers. By the time the plane landed, Sarah and Max were not only mapping out a plan to present the CEO more effectively but also talking about working together on business opportunities in Asia. Just as important, the conversation made Sarah realize that her hastily formed aversion had caused her to miss out on valuable chances to collaborate with a worthy colleague.

Circumstances forced Sarah to humanize Max, but we recommend a more pro-active approach. Take a hard look at how you interact with colleagues whose agendas seem opposed to your own. Recognize that these colleagues are real people who may even become your allies.

BARRIER 4: GOING IT ALONE

Most people opt out of leadership for perfectly good reasons. The road, by definition, is unsafe. It leads to change, not comfort. Troy, the software service division manager, found it deeply unsettling to try working in a brand-new way. Eventually, though, he learned how to cope with his fears: by relying on the advice and support of select friends and family members. We call these people "the team."

Troy's team played a key role in his shift from focusing on his own career to helping his colleagues succeed. After more than a few sleepless nights, Troy decided to host a casual dinner for the people whose opinions he valued most: a sister, two friends from college, and a software entrepreneur he'd met at a recent Ironman competition. Halfway into the appetizer course, he put aside his pride, described his problem, and asked for advice.

His new triathlete friend, Raj, pushed Troy to stop worrying so much about his own job and instead try to break down the organizational silos that were making his life difficult and threatening the company as well. Troy initially resisted the idea, but the next day he decided to change his behavior according to what he called "Raj's intervention." The collaborative culture he created in his division and with the product development division became a model for other groups in the company. To this day Troy continues the monthly dinner ritual so that he and his "team" of family and friends can keep sharing problems and ideas.

We heard similar stories from other effective leaders. Almost all of them have a strong team that helps provide perspective, grounding, and faith. Your team members can be family, colleagues, friends, mentors, spouses, partners. The litmus test: Does the leader in you regularly show up in their presence? Find the people who believe in your desire and ability to lead. Fall in love with them. Or at least meet them for drinks on a regular basis (see Exhibit 15.2).

BARRIER 5: WAITING FOR PERMISSION

Like risk aversion, patience can be a valuable evolutionary gift. It's a main ingredient in discipline and hope. It helps us uncover the root cause of problems. It keeps us from hurting someone at the DMV.

But patience can be a curse for emerging leaders. It can undermine our potential by persuading us to keep our heads down and soldier on, waiting for someone to recognize our efforts and give us the proverbial tap on the shoulder—a better title and formal authority.

The problem with this approach is that healthy organizations reward people who decide on their own to lead. Power and influence are intimate companions, but their relationship isn't the one we tend to imagine. More often than not, influence leads to power, not the other way around.

Most of the exceptional leaders we've studied didn't wait for formal authority to begin making changes. They may have ended up in a corner office, but their leadership started elsewhere. In one way or another, they all simply began to use whatever informal power they had.

EXHIBIT 15.2—BARRIERS TO EXCEPTIONAL LEADERSHIP

Turning Competitors Into Enemies	Going It Alone	Waiting for Permission
• Is it rare for me to feel defensive, insecure, or judgmental?	• Do I have a core group of people who help me make important decisions?	• Is it possible to make a difference from my current position?
• Is it rare for people to feel defensive, insecure, or judgmental around me?	• Do I have people around me who can handle both my audacity and my insecurities?	• Do I have control over when I'll be able to have a meaningful impact?
• Is my environment generally free of people I can't stand to be around?	• Do the most important people in my life participate in my leadership dreams?	• Could I become a leader before other people see me as one?

A personal trainer named Jon was in the middle of a workout session when he made the decision to lead. One morning, while he was trying to help a client lose her post-pregnancy weight, his mind kept wandering to a teenager he knew, and especially to worries that he might have joined a gang. In the middle of counting crunches, Jon realized he wanted to do something different with his life.

He sketched out his vision that night. He knew that weightlifting could appeal to young people at risk for gang involvement, so he decided to start a program that would offer them physical empowerment, independence, and community, and help them build self-esteem. Two years later Inner City Weightlifting was serving more than a hundred kids in East Boston. Its gyms are among the few places in the city where rival gang members come together peacefully. Jon is now poised to expand the concept to other cities.

Jon's career change was not a logical pivot, at least not from an outside perspective. He was young, he was inexperienced with youth development programs, and he'd grown up with limited exposure to urban life. His friends and family thought he was crazy to give up his lucrative personal-training practice for what seemed to them a pipe dream. But Jon was impatient, unwilling to wait until he'd gained experience and legitimacy. He went for it anyway, and the program's early results gave him enough influence to recruit students, schools, parents, and funders.

Jon's story holds a lesson for every aspiring leader: You must simply begin.

OUR CLOSING PLEA

We're sharing this research because we're quite selfishly invested in having you get out of your own way. We want to live in a world—we want our children to grow up in a world—in which your talents are fully unleashed on the issues that matter most. You should learn to recognize and overcome the self-imposed obstacles to your impact. The rest of us need you on the front lines, building better organizations.

PART IV

HAZARDS

Leadership development can be viewed as a long journey through challenging terrain.

BILL GEORGE AND ANDREW MCLEAN

Yes, the leadership journey travels through challenging terrain with many potential obstacles, detours, potholes, and hazards presented along the way. Successfully navigating these potential pitfalls takes skill, persistence, and, yes, even a bit of luck. And as we've discussed previously, there is no ultimate, final pinnacle to the journey, as even the most seasoned and successful leaders continue to face hazards that need to be navigated. In fact, at times success can dull our senses, lead to complacency, and create self-delusion and hubris and therefore be the greatest hazard of all. How ironic that our fundamental goal as a leader can be a curse rather than a blessing. Fortunately, having a better appreciation for the potential hazards in the leadership journey allows us to better overcome them.

So, what are the primary hazards along the way? Interestingly, they're mostly inside us. True, there are real, objective hazards on the path, but it's how we react to these obstacles and situations that ultimately determines our success as leaders. And it's not about being perfect during the developmental journey, as mistakes along the way can be some of the best learning tools and preventive medicine for avoiding major pitfalls later in our leadership careers.

In essence, it might be fair to say that paradox is the biggest hazard leaders deal with along the journey. Mistakes can be good and bad, depending on when they occur and how leaders deal with them. Success is the ultimate goal, but it can lead to demise. Acquiring power is essential, but wielding it appropriately creates many challenges. And as leaders rise up the ladder, they tend to become much more isolated and solitary, yet this is when they need the most critical, candid feedback from their followers.

Thus, to be successful, leaders must develop both the internal capacity and the external systems and relationships to effectively deal with these hazards. Leaders must always remain good listeners and open to criticism to keep from becoming isolated and unapproachable; they must always remember that success is a team effort and not fall prey to self-centered, ego-driven delusions of individual greatness. Leaders must continue to learn and develop, as the world within which they lead is constantly changing and they must never forget their inner moral compass to make sure their actions always align with doing the right thing.

Externally, leaders need to create a culture of integrity and candor, as we'll discuss more in Part V. Such a culture helps followers internalize the ultimate purpose and ideals of the organization, and it creates an atmosphere in which followers are expected to give and are rewarded for candid and even very critical feedback. In fact, this may be the most important aspect differentiating "good" and "bad" leaders, as the latter rarely, if ever, encourage and reward contrarian views, whereas the former constantly seek it out both formally and informally. Such an environment is characterized by mutual trust between leaders and followers. So, as we've seen before, successful leadership requires successful followership.

In sum, there are many potential hazards we face on the leadership journey, but they are also part of our education as a leader. The key is to recognize that these hazards exist and constantly be aware of the warning signs. For some, having a person close to them who will be candid and direct will help when they begin to ignore the signs and stray from the path. Study leaders of any ilk so that you learn how to keep alert for the hazards and temptations that lie just outside the path to effective leadership.

LEADERSHIP PERSPECTIVES

Bill George and Andrew McLean outline many hazards to which potential leaders may fall prey in "Why Leaders Lose Their Way" (Chapter 16). Fortunately, the path is somewhat forgiving, and, in fact, a potential leader's mistakes ultimately may make him or her a better leader. The key, according to George and McLean, is for potential leaders to engage in honest self-introspection, be open to blunt feedback, and have a robust sense of purpose.

In Chapter 17, "'Success': A Leadership Trap," Pierre Casse and Eoin Banahan argue that many times success can be a curse rather than a blessing. They suggest that it's almost inevitable, at least to some degree, that the "sweet taste of success" dulls the senses and leads to some level of complacency. Furthermore, success provides confirmation to leaders about their wisdom and abilities, which often leads to self-delusion and an ego trip. But success is not bad per se; how it's perceived and acted upon can be.

In "The Disabling Shadow of Leadership" (Chapter 18), Bill McCabe suggests that leaders cast a shadow visible to all but themselves. Thus, if leaders want to transform their own performance and their followers' effectiveness, they must try to understand how their shadow might be getting in the way. In fact, many leaders are unconscious of the unintended but large—and potentially negative—impact their leadership style has on their peers, followers, and stakeholders. And it's not just the autocratic leader who casts a large shadow; it's the soft and gentle leader, too.

In Chapter 19, Michael Maccoby explores "Narcissistic Leaders: The Incredible Pros, the Inevitable Cons." He describes the paradox that narcissists are good for organizations where people with vision and courage are needed but bad for organizations when these same visionary leaders refuse to listen to the advice of those around them when faced with challenges. Effective leaders all have some degree of ego, but the narcissistic leader must be cautious. To overcome the potential hazards associated with being a narcissist, such leaders, Maccoby suggests, would be wise to find a trusted sidekick to bring balance and rationality. No doubt we need narcissistic leaders to create vision for today's organizations, but they need to understand and accept their own limits.

Part IV closes with Robert J. Allio's "Bad Leaders: How They Get That Way and What to Do About Them." In this piece Allio ties together many of the usual suspects hindering leadership: narcissism, weakness of will, self-interest, misguided values. However, he extends these into a model examining leaders' trajectories as they move from idealism to realism during their leadership journey. Some keep their integrity and become pragmatic leaders, whereas others take a more venal path and end up fallen stars. And, like many of the other pieces suggest, followers need to share some of the blame for bad leaders, as they are complicit if they don't provide critical feedback.

16

ॐ

Why Leaders Lose Their Way

Bill George and Andrew McLean

One of the most perplexing management mysteries of our times is, "Why do so many developing leaders either fail to reach their full potential or cross the line into destructive or even unethical actions?" Another way of asking this question is, "How do successful leaders learn to recognize and avoid destructive behavior?" To find out, we interviewed successful leaders and studied the case histories of failed leaders. Our study of unsuccessful leaders revealed a pattern: the failed leaders couldn't lead themselves. On their leadership journey these high potential managers adopted a set of personal behaviors that worked temporarily but were unsustainable in the long run.

In contrast, our interviews of 125 successful, authentic leaders revealed that all of them faced significant personal development hazards on their journey. Being human, they faced a number of leadership temptations: to blame others for failure, to win excessive monetary rewards or enhanced titles, to gain affirmation of their unique abilities, and to achieve success quickly.

Through these interviews with successful leaders and our study of failed leaders, we identified a number of distinctive destructive behaviors that result from these temptations. Leadership development, therefore, can be viewed as a long journey though challenging terrain. Authentic leaders either learn to

Reprinted by permission of *Strategy and Leadership* (Vol. 35, No. 3, 2007). Copyright 2007 Emerald Group Publishing Limited.

avoid the temptations or to overcome the personality flaws that lead to these destructive behaviors; leaders who lose their way do not.

The good news is that developing leaders can make mistakes and fall prey to these hazards, yet regain their footing and continue on their developmental journey. In fact, their mistakes, especially those that come early in their careers, are highly beneficial in their developmental process and reduce the likelihood of making major mistakes when reaching the pinnacle of power. If emerging leaders are aware of these hazards and willing to devote sufficient time to their personal development, they will be less likely to become enmeshed in destructive patterns and more likely to persevere and emerge as authentic leaders.

MOVING THROUGH THE HERO
STAGE OF LEADERSHIP DEVELOPMENT

As we examined the way successful leaders told their life histories, we realized that the early chapters of their stories fit the pattern of what mythologist Joseph Campbell has called, "the Hero's Journey."[1] Many leaders we interviewed described their early life as if it were the quest of an all-conquering hero. Leaders told us they began their careers with a primary focus on themselves—their skills, performance, achievements and rewards.

Surprisingly, we found in our interviews with these successful leaders that the hero role was representative of only their early leadership development. The hero's job—doing impressive deeds, facing challenges alone, and gaining notice—initially seemed their best route to success. But acting as a hero was just a stage that the successful managers moved through on their journey to authentic leadership. The heroic model of leadership turns out to be merely an early stage—one with risks, temptations, misbehaviors—and one that needs to be outgrown.

As our interviews revealed, leaders who move beyond the hero stage learn to focus on others, gain a sense of a larger purpose, foster multiple support networks, and develop mechanisms to keep perspective and stay grounded. For example, Xerox CEO Anne Mulcahy, in spite of her success in turning the company around, routinely deflects most media attention. To explain why, she told about receiving a telephone call from her mentor, former CEO David Kearns, when she was in the darkest hours of trying to keep the company out of bankruptcy and fending off an SEC investigation. "Mulcahy, do you believe all that bull they are writing about you in the newspapers?" Kearns asked her.

"No, David," Mulcahy replied calmly. "Good," responded Kearns. "Then don't believe it when they start writing about you as the savior of Xerox."

Many of the perils of the hero stage are well described by Novartis CEO Daniel Vasella in a *Fortune* magazine interview:

> Once you get under the domination of making the quarter—even unwittingly . . . you'll begin to sacrifice things that are important and may be vital for your company over the long term. The culprit that drives this cycle isn't the fear of failure so much as it is the craving for success. . . . For many of us the idea of being a successful manager is an intoxicating one. It is a pattern of celebration leading to belief, leading to distortion. When you achieve good results, you are typically celebrated, and you begin to believe that the figure at the center of all that champagne toasting is yourself. You are idealized by the outside world, and there is a natural tendency to believe that what is written is true.[2]

THE FIVE PERILS

From our interviews we found five perils of the leadership journey, distinctive destructive behaviors that tend to occur in the hero stage of managers' early careers. The five are: being an imposter; rationalizing; glory seeking; playing the loner; and being a shooting star. In the following examples, the disguised cases are of real failed leaders at major firms.

Being an Imposter

Imposters frequently lack self-awareness and self-esteem. They may have little appetite for self-reflection and consequently defer personal development. They rise through organizational ranks with a combination of cunning and aggression. Imposters use these strategies to achieve positions of power, but then have little sense of how to use that power for the good of the organization. In effect, they have been too busy besting their competitors to learn how to lead. Leaders who succumb to this hazard embrace the politics of getting ahead and letting no one stand in their way. They are the ultimate political animals, adept at figuring out who their competitors are and then eliminating them one by one (see Exhibit 16.1).

Having acquired power, imposters may not be confident of how to use it. They are beset with doubts about handling the responsibilities of leadership.

EXHIBIT 16.1—THE CASE OF THE IMPOSTER CEO

Rising through the ranks of "Automation Inc.," Harry always seemed on top of his game, very cool and rarely worried. He developed superb relationships with his bosses—often golfing, hunting and fishing with company board members. The dinner parties at his home were glamorous affairs, featuring rare French wines and gourmet foods. On the job he rarely became involved in the details of his business, delegating all issues to his subordinates while he built relationships with his peers and bosses. He set extremely conservative goals to ensure that he never missed a financial plan, but was able to convince his bosses that his goals were challenging. Although his track record never produced growth in either revenues or profits, he persuaded Automation's board to promote him to CEO of this $10 billion company.

Once Harry was in the CEO's chair, some severe operational problems arose, causing the company to fall short of expectations. This situation caused him to feel like an imposter who did not belong in his job. He was racked with self-doubts and paralyzed from taking action to correct the obvious problems. Rather than face the criticism of the company's shareholders and launch a major cost-cutting effort, Harry instead initiated negotiations to sell the company. As the situation worsened and external calls for action intensified, he announced its sale for a very modest premium, including a $100 million severance package for himself. He was unable to protect his former employees, however, as 10,000 of them in the company's hometown, including his entire corporate staff, lost their jobs.

Because their greatest strength is besting internal opponents, they are often paranoid that underlings are out to get them.

Some imposters may be unable to act decisively because they are paralyzed by doubt. Their inaction leads to poor results and external challenges, so they will likely attack their critics and cut themselves off from internal feedback. Their most competent subordinates move on to greener pastures when it becomes obvious that they have failed to have influence on their leader. Meanwhile, people remaining in the organization tend to keep their heads down and wait for their leaders to make decisions.

Rationalizing

These leaders are unable to admit their mistakes for fear of being considered a failure or of losing their jobs. As a result of their inability to take responsibility for setbacks and failures, they rationalize their problems away. To outsiders, rationalizers always appear on top of the issues. When things don't go their way, they tend to blame external forces or subordinates or offer facile answers to their problems. Worse yet, they may attempt to cover them up or deny them. They rarely step up and take responsibility (see Exhibit 16.2).

As rationalizers find themselves facing greater challenges, they transmit pressure to their subordinates instead of modulating it. When pressuring subordinates fails to produce the desired results, they resort to short-term strategies

EXHIBIT 16.2—THE CASE OF THE RATIONALIZER CEO

The CEO of "Retail, Inc.," Charlie always had a confident answer for everything. No matter how bad things were at his company, he was on the move, acquiring new businesses, negotiating deals, and courting customers. Asked about his mediocre results, he tended to blame them on the economy or unfair competitive actions, but his answers never squared with reality. Under increasing external pressure to produce results, he steadily cut back on the company's customer service, the very thing that had given it competitive advantage. As competitors took advantage of his moves to gain share at Retail's expense, he pointed to increasing earnings while criticizing the stock market's focus on his company's tepid revenues. To offset the sagging revenues, he reduced maintenance of his stores, leading to a shabby appearance. As results worsened, he de-emphasized the company's core retail business and attempted to shift to the wholesale business. It didn't work. Under increasing pressure from shareholders, his board forced him to resign. Even after his termination, he was unwilling to acknowledge the problems he created, attempting to take credit for the successful turnaround launched by his successor.

such as cutting funding for research, growth initiatives, and organization building in order to hit immediate goals. Eventually, these short-term actions begin to catch up with them. They are then likely to borrow from the future to make today's numbers look good, or to stretch accounting rules, rationalizing that they can make it up in the future.

Ultimately, they become the victims of their own rationalizations, as do their depleted organizations. The misdeeds of rationalizers have become all too apparent in recent years. The high stock prices of the 1990s, based on ever higher expectations of revenue growth, led many executives to play the game of meeting stock market expectations while sacrificing the long-term value of their companies and their own reputations.

Glory Seeking

Leaders who seek glory are motivated by a need for acclaim. The hazard of being derailed by glory-seeking stems from the need for external reinforcement of their self-worth. Money, fame, glory, and power are their goals, as they pursue visible signs of success. Often it seems more important to them to be known as powerful business leaders than to build organizations of lasting value (see Exhibit 16.3).

For a leader stuck in the trap of glory-seeking, however, the thirst for fame is unquenchable. Leaders who are perpetually dissatisfied cannot be effective, and they are prone to try to divert more and more resources—money, fame, glory and power—from their organization to their own use.

EXHIBIT 16.3—THE CASE OF THE GLORY-SEEKING CEO

Michael arrived at "Innovation, Inc." to the acclaim of the media and analysts. He repeatedly captured headlines as one of the most successful new CEOs of his generation. Although Innovation was a modest company that prided itself on egalitarianism and no frills, he built a fancy new office suite for himself, complete with a gym and an executive dining room, and convinced his board to purchase a large private jet exclusively for his use. A master at public speaking, each year he gave more than one hundred speeches outside the company. Yet he never had time to talk to the innovators who had made the company so successful.

Insiders commented that they could go for months without seeing him in the company headquarters or wandering through its laboratories. He loved high level customer contacts, but rarely took time to talk to sales people to find out why the company's products weren't selling. Quarter after quarter, the company missed its financial expectations, yet he never took responsibility, preferring to blame his subordinates and even firing them on the spot. Eventually, the results were so bad that the board was forced to ask for his resignation.

Playing the Loner

In the heroic stage of the leadership journey, it is perilous to think that leadership is a solitary pursuit. When leaders adopt the loner role they avoid forming close relationships, fail to seek out mentors, and don't create support networks. As a result they are cut off from appropriate feedback (see Exhibit 16.4).

In a competitive world where leaders are evaluated on their individual merits, it stands to reason that aspiring leaders would take care to develop their own resources, husband their own ideas, and trust only their own judgment. Yet without wise counsel, loners are prone to making major mistakes. This, too, is a self-reinforcing trap. When results elude them and criticism of their leadership grows, they retreat to the bunker. They have few personal support structures to draw upon to get through challenging times. They become rigid in pursuing their objectives, not recognizing it is their behavior that makes it impossible to reach their goals. Meanwhile, their organizations unravel or their personal lives crumble.

Being a Shooting Star

Leaders who fall into the shooting star trap lack the grounding of an integrated life. The lives of shooting star leaders center entirely on their careers. To observers, they are always on the go, traveling incessantly to get ahead. They rarely make time for family, friendships, their communities, or even themselves. Much-needed sleep and exercise are continually deferred. As they run ever faster, their stress mounts (see Exhibit 16.5).

The increasing pace of organizational life, fueled by information technology, globalization and hyper-competition, creates a growing demand for tal-

EXHIBIT 16.4—THE CASE OF THE SOLITARY LEADER

Simon never seemed comfortable in the CEO's chair. He joined "Financial Services, Inc." after consulting for the company for many years and devising its strategy. He maneuvered a clever merger with a larger company and negotiated his way into the top job. Once there, he surrounded himself with loyal subordinates, moving away from the larger company's well-honed meritocracy. He refused to hear bad news, blaming subordinates for problems and often firing bearers of bad tidings. Under pressure, he would retire to his office, close the door and ruminate by himself for many hours. He seemed genuinely uncomfortable when interacting with the company's customers or revenue producers. Over time, many key executives departed from the company. In their place he promoted inexperienced subordinates whose knowledge and capability were questionable. Eventually, employees revolted and went to the board, explaining why the company was declining and threatening to resign en masse. Faced with a palace revolution, Financial's board decided it had to make a change in leadership. As compensation, the board voted him an additional $50 million cash bonus.

---

ented people interested in moving onto the fast track. High achievement and top leadership come to those who start early and run fast.

Yet shooting stars move up so rapidly in their careers that they never have time to learn from their mistakes. A year or two into any job, they are ready to move on, before they have had to confront the results of their decisions. When they see problems of their making coming back to haunt them, their anxiety rises and so does the urgency to move to a new position. If their employer doesn't promote them, they are off to another organization. One day they find themselves at the top, overwhelmed by an intractable set of problems. At this point, they are prone to impulsive or even irrational decisions, and have no grounding in their lives that enables them to cope in a rational manner. Eventually, shooting stars flame out.

THE NEED FOR SELF-DEVELOPMENT

These five hazards of the hero stage of leadership development arise from ill-conceived attempts by leaders to disguise or ignore their humanity. No one is immune to the seductions or pressures of leadership that create these five types of destructive behaviors. By undertaking a dedicated process of self-development, authentic leaders, such as the 125 leaders interviewed for our research, are able to navigate these hazards as they progress in their careers and stay grounded in the process.

To do this they viewed the leadership journey as a human journey. To initiate this learning process, they should first ask themselves five fundamental questions:

EXHIBIT 16.5—THE CASE OF THE SHOOTING STAR CONSULTANT

Sarah was the rising superstar at "Consulting, Inc." She was entirely dedicated to her clients, spending months at a time on their premises, as she received top marks for client satisfaction and for garnering follow-on contracts. She was so busy flying around the country that she had little time for her personal life, her husband, or her two young children. The latter were cared for by her nanny, as her husband also traveled frequently. To progress in her career, she often entertained clients at glamorous resorts around the country on weekends, further separating herself from her family. Physically exhausted, emotionally drained, and distraught over the hollowness of her existence, she decided she had no choice but to resign from her job and focus on her family.

---

1. Who am I, and what are my strengths and developmental needs?
2. What motivates me to lead?
3. What is the purpose of my leadership?
4. Who can I rely upon for real feedback and support?
5. How can I sustain myself in this leadership role?

Honest answers to these questions enable the individual to avoid or overcome the five hazards of leadership. There is nothing wrong with desiring the rewards of leadership as long as they are combined with a deeper desire to serve something greater than oneself.

As we discovered when our interviewees told their early stories, they initially framed their lives in the model of an all-conquering hero. But many of our participants went on to identify the true beginning of their leadership as the point in time when they realized they needed to empower others in order to achieve their leadership goals. This moment of personal discovery made them see that authentic leadership entails empowering leaders throughout their organizations, enabling their development, taking responsibility for mistakes but offering others the credit for success, and engaging in work with a larger purpose.

EMBRACE THE LESSONS OF FAILURE

While many leaders have a deep-seated fear of failure, the irony is that they learn the most from their failures. David Pottruck, former CEO of Charles Schwab, relishes the opportunity to learn from every experience. "You don't have to be perfect," he said. "You can start off on a bad path and recover. You can turn most failures into successes if you ask yourself, what can I learn from this so that I can do better the next time?" Pottruck believes that the key to learning from failure is to avoid denial and be honest with yourself. "If you're open, you can learn a lot more from failure than success," he says: "When you're successful, you take it for granted and move on to the next thing. Failure forces you to reflect. What went wrong? How could I have done this better? It's an opportunity for you to take responsibility. The path of least resistance is to blame it on someone else. I failed many times but learned from each experience and usually managed to come back stronger. I kept plugging away and eventually was successful."

AT ALL COSTS, KEEP PERSPECTIVE

While self-knowledge arises most dramatically from life experiences—notably the experience of failure—it is also continually available in a leader's surroundings, provided the leader is able to take advantage of it.

So, how do leaders keep perspective and stay grounded? Here are some suggestions for personal development gleaned from our interviews:

- Be honest with yourself and listen to honest critics.
- Take responsibility for failures, but share successes with others.
- Have several blunt, honest people you trust close to you to tell the truth.
- Maintain strong personal relationships with people who care about you.
- Foster a strong inner world, including a robust sense of purpose.

KEVIN SHARER: A LEADER GETS BACK ON TRACK

Can leaders recover after losing their way? Let's look at the story of a talented leader who hit some hazards and rebounded. In 1989, Kevin Sharer, now Amgen's chairman and CEO, faced failure for the first time after he jumped ship from GE to join the telecommunications company MCI where he thought he had a shot at the top job within two years.

At age forty, Sharer was running a major GE business when the headhunters came looking for a new head of sales and marketing for MCI. "The CEO race is wide open," MCI's vice chairman assured Sharer, who seized the opportunity. Upon joining the company, however, Sharer learned that the chief operating officer was in line for the top slot and didn't welcome competition from an ambitious young hotshot. With just six weeks on the job, Sharer said, "I marched into the chairman's office and proposed a restructuring of MCI's sales organization." His proposal alienated senior executives who had spent their careers building MCI and its sales team, and because he lacked telecommunications experience Sharer had little credibility.

Desperate to escape, Sharer telephoned Jack Welch about returning to GE. Welch wasn't happy with the sudden way Sharer had bailed out of GE. "Hey, Kevin, forget you ever worked here," Welch replied. "At that moment," Sharer recalled, "I knew I had been cast adrift. It was a gut-wrenching two years for me, the most challenging and unhappy time of my professional life. I'm not a good knife fighter, and I was getting outmaneuvered. At first I went into denial. Then I became defeatist and cynical." Sharer later observed, "I learned that whether you are right or not, there is a price to be paid for arrogance."

Sharer recognized changes he needed to make. "In retrospect, the MCI experience wasn't all bad," he said. "I learned what a truly competitive company can do, and I learned about entrepreneurship and innovation. A tough experience like that gives you genuine empathy for other people." Two years after joining MCI, a letter came across Sharer's desk asking if he knew anyone who could be president of Amgen. After expressing interest, he landed the number two position at Amgen. Sharer then focused on learning the business before taking charge and listened to the wisdom and experience of his colleagues: "By being patient, I became an insider before I started making changes. I learned the business from the ground up, made calls with sales representatives, and showed my desire to learn."

Sharer spent seven years patiently understudying CEO Gordon Binder before becoming CEO. So far his efforts to become an authentic leader have paid off handsomely for Sharer and for Amgen. In his first six years as CEO, Amgen's revenues grew at a 25 percent clip, with earnings and its market capitalization increasing rapidly. "It is vitally important that you love what you do because if you don't, you won't do your best," Sharer told us. "When I was at MCI, I never had an emotional connection with low-priced long distance. [At Amgen] . . . if somebody walks up to you and says, 'Your product saved my life,' the power of that connection is enormous."

MANAGING THE LEADERSHIP JOURNEY

Ultimately, responsibility for leadership development lies with the individual leader. Even as distinguished a leader as Jeff Immelt, chairman and CEO of General Electric, noted when he faced the greatest crisis of his career in GE's plastics business, "Leadership is a long journey into your soul. It's not like anyone can tell you how to do it."

Organizations can take steps to foster the individual development of leaders. Many leading organizations are shifting their leadership development programs away from the historic focus on the development of competencies, characteristics, skills and styles to emphasize the process of self-development. They do so with long-term programs for leaders to develop themselves as authentic leaders and to acknowledge the importance of their life histories in determining their leadership. Organizations are fostering necessary support systems for their leaders, using mentoring, one-to-one coaching, 360-degree feedback, participation in leadership discussion groups, and support for a healthy work/life balance.

Corporate managers who have successfully traveled the leadership journey can be an organization's most adaptive and flexible resource. Avoiding the five hazards of the early leadership period is the first part of the journey's challenge. The equally crucial second part is encouraging the development of leaders with a diverse set of perspectives, capacities and capabilities.

Notes

1. Campbell, Joseph, *The Hero's Journey*, Phill Cousineau (Ed.), Harper & Row, San Francisco, CA, 1990.

2. Vasella, Daniel, and Clifton Leaf, "Temptation is all around us," *Fortune*, Vol. 146, No. 10, pp. 109–16, 2002, full text accessed via Academic Search Premier (accessed November 18, 2002).

Bill George would like to acknowledge the work of two of his colleagues, Diana Mayer and Peter Sims, who did a majority of the interviews that this article is based on.

17

✌

"Success"

A Leadership Trap

Pierre Casse and Eoin Banahan

A careful examination of successful leaders reveals that they are able to adjust their behavior to the requirements of the time.

If success is to be sustainable, the leader must be able to adjust his behavior according to the demands of each situation to which he is exposed. It is critical to be able to anticipate when a situation calls for new attitudes, new assumptions and related behaviors and to have the courage to change despite the fact that such risks will inevitably require swimming against the tide.

There are some highly visible examples. Look at Michael Dell, who had the courage to recognize that success in today's personal computer market is not about mass production but mass customization. He recognizes the importance of adjusting behavior to focus on building a relationship with the individual customer.

Similarly, Richard Branson, at the Virgin Group, recognizes that power has shifted from the producer to the consumer and leadership behavior must reflect that.

Leaders like Dell, Branson and Steve Jobs at Apple are successful now because they are responding to the requirements of the time. So long as they continue to do so, they increase their chances of success.

Reprinted by permission of *Training Journal* (May 2010).

Indeed many leaders are able to do so at least once in their career. They catch the wave and revel in the glory that success brings. But then, almost inevitably, they fall into the trap: the sweet taste of success dulls their senses and they begin to believe they are somehow invincible. They remain in a leadership mode that proves inappropriate, unsuccessful and ultimately destructive, leading eventually to their own demise.

Let's consider the typical process through which many leaders progress. Although simple, it's extremely subtle and destructive. It involves these three critical steps:

1. The leader faces a challenging situation and recognizes the need for different attitudes and behaviors that will effectively address the requirements in order to turn the situation around.
2. As a result of the leader's actions, the challenge is successfully addressed and the situation is transformed. Crisis is averted and the leader is praised for his acumen and initiative.
3. Many leaders forget that the situation has now been transformed by their actions and, as a result, new attitudes and behaviors are now necessary if they are to build on their success for the longer term. Instead, they persist with outdated behaviors, erroneously believing that what has proved successful in the past will continue to be so. They are struck down by the curse of leadership success.

Let's consider three all-too-common illustrations of the curse of leadership success in action.

THE COACHING THAT WENT TOO WELL

A leader has invested time and energy in coaching a team member. The leader recognized the team member's potential, had faith in his abilities but identified deficiencies in his level of competency.

The support and help provided proved such a success that the team member has grown; he is now ready to stand on his own two feet and move forward alone.

However, the leader can't let go and persists in playing the coaching role. It has proved so successful thus far; why change now? He is overdoing it and, as a result, the team member is upset because he feels he doesn't trust him enough to let him fly solo.

In such a case, the team member has two choices: either he confronts the leader and highlights the fact that now his behavior is inappropriate given the new situation or, for the sake of peace and tranquility, he accepts his persistent behavior and resigns himself to being over-coached.

THE LEADER WHO HAS LOST IT

A leader has proved very effective in managing his business unit and team. He took over a few months earlier and everybody at the top of the company has been impressed by how quickly he has settled in and come to terms with the demands of his new position. Senior management is impressed with his success and is considering him as a potential high flyer.

However, lately it seems that something has gone wrong. Suddenly he seems unstable. The confidence with which he has made decisions seems to have evaporated. His management reports are late and his team members are complaining that he is not giving enough time and attention to their issues and concerns.

Everyone is puzzled and wonders how such a good leader can lose it so quickly and so completely.

THE SUCCESSFUL TURNAROUND

The situation is bad and requires some tough decisions and drastic actions. A leader has been appointed by top management to deal with the crisis. He is a turnaround leader: someone who is used to dealing with highly ambiguous situations requiring quick thinking and a commitment to action. He can act swiftly and has the courage to act brutally, if the situation requires it.

After a few months, it becomes clear that the situation is better. The crisis has been addressed and the actions of the leader have proved a huge success. Top management has acknowledged his outstanding performance and asked him to ease up and adjust his approach to the requirements of the new stable situation.

But it seems that he cannot do it. He is a turnaround leader and will remain so since this is what has brought him success thus far. He cannot see why he should change what has been a winning approach.

What these three scenarios illustrate is that at the heart of the curse of leadership success lies the following three critical maladies:

- Self-delusion
- Complacency
- Ego trip

SELF-DELUSION

Leaders perceive success as a confirmation of their wisdom and know-how. It is proof positive that they have what it takes. They float high on a cloud of hype and hyperbole. They revel in the glory of their own making. They have made it and there is no question that they deserve the recognition that success brings them.

The problem is that, although it may be true that their behavior has brought them success this time, they invariably fail to realize that success today is no guarantee of success tomorrow. Despite what they may think, they have not found the secret of alchemy. Moreover, what worked well in one situation can prove a severe handicap in a different one.

This self-delusion can be detrimental. For instance, the leader may begin to believe in his invincibility and, as a result, reject those who disagree or dissent. He surrounds himself with a "clique" of people who agree with everything he says and does, thus fuelling the self-delusion ever further. He becomes insulated from reality and ever more convinced that reality is the way it is because that is the way he wants it to be.

If such attitudes and behavior persist, the endgame is unavoidable as the leader hurtles headlong towards his inevitable doom.

COMPLACENCY

The successful leader does not think it necessary to challenge his basic assumptions. He feeds on his success and feels comfortable with the *status quo*. Everything is as it should be and will remain so, or so he thinks.

Such complacency can lead to some major disasters, particularly if the successful leader has been rewarded with more power. To challenge him is difficult, risky and, in many cases, useless. He is the only one who really knows and it's his way, or the highway.

EGO TRIP

It is often the case that deep down inside, and sometimes it is not so deep inside, the leader knows he should change. He is clever enough to be aware of the new balance in the situation and the need to reinvent himself but that requires actions that can be very difficult for the leader who has been the origin of a big success.

He will have to admit that:

- What worked in the past is no longer valid.
- He is lost and does not have the new answers.
- He needs help.

To admit such truths is an assault on the leader's ego, made all the more severe if he has decided to progress up the ladder on the basis of his past success.

THE CURSE OF LEADERSHIP SUCCESS AND YOU

Are you suffering from the curse of leadership success? Here is a simple self-assessment exercise that can give you an idea of your tolerance to success. It's purely subjective so, whatever the outcome, you will have to decide if, and how, it may apply to you. The purpose of the exercise is to give you food for thought.

Please answer each question in Exhibit 17.1 with a "yes" or "no." Be honest with yourself.

Debriefing

Profile one (15 yes or more): This is a really good position to be in. In fact, it may be too good. There is a chance that you are overdoing it and challenging yourself, and others, in such a systematic and constant way that it has become counter-productive. The environment that you create is highly ambiguous and unstable. A minimum of stability is always required in any leadership situation—the art of leadership is to decide what to change and what *not* to change.

Profile two (eight to 14 yes): This could imply that you are able to question your own behavior and change it even when the situation looks good. The risk of such an attitude could be that you are perceived by those around you as hesitant and undecided. It is critical, then, that you ensure your partners and associates understand why you are doing what you are doing, including "fixing it when it is not broken."

Profile three (one to seven yes): Either you have never been successful (and therefore have never experienced the success trap) or you have a natural aversion to

EXHIBIT 17.1—SELF-ASSESSMENT OF TOLERANCE TO SUCCESS

In general . . .	Yes	No
1. Am humble when winning a contest	___	___
2. Challenge myself regularly and systematically	___	___
3. Do not overwhelm people with my success stories	___	___
4. Play it down when achieving my objectives	___	___
5. Am ready to share the recognition that goes with a successful project	___	___
6. Am open to ideas that are different to mine	___	___
7. Like to learn from a good action	___	___
8. Enjoy reinventing myself	___	___
9. Am not afraid of facing the unknown	___	___
10. Keep inviting people to disagree with me	___	___
11. Know that a good accomplishment today is not a guarantee of success for tomorrow	___	___
12. Realize that success can be a source of complacency	___	___
13. Do not believe that winning once is good enough	___	___
14. Have no major problem with bad news	___	___
15. Realize that success does not last (forever)	___	___
16. Feel uncomfortable when things go too smoothly	___	___
17. Can face my mistakes openly and candidly	___	___
18. Am not afraid of losing face	___	___
19. Like to celebrate a success and move on very quickly afterwards	___	___
20. Think that success is a very relative thing anyway	___	___
TOTAL	___	___

adjusting your behavior to new requirements. You believe that what's good today will always be good. Be careful—a reluctance to question your assumptions could cost you dearly.

MANAGING SUCCESS

Success is not bad in itself. It's the way it is perceived and built upon by the leader that counts. Leaders who have been successful over time develop a set of practical ways to cope with success:

- They recognize that it is not an end in itself but a by-product of something much more important, namely the contribution they, and others, make to creating a better world.

- They understand that it is a collaborative achievement. Although the right ideas may have originated from them, others were involved in their development and execution, and deserve credit too.
- They take the praise and adulation with a grain of salt and recognize their good fortune and privilege for what it is.
- They are flexible and open to question and suggestion. They are the leaders of a fast-changing world. Their motto is "success is just another challenge."

In conclusion, although experience shows that there is an inherent danger in success of which leaders should be aware, they should welcome it as an opportunity to reassess their attitudes and behaviors, and use it as a springboard for new ways of thinking and behaving.

18

ℰↃ

The Disabling Shadow
of Leadership

Bill McCabe

There was an advertisement run not so long ago for Tabasco sauce. You may
have seen it. In the advertisement God was shown sitting in the heavens on a
cloud shaking the sauce onto a sandwich and clearly relishing the prospect of
his fiery snack. However, as he was shaking the bottle he was also quite unaware that drops of the sauce were falling onto the earth below, causing havoc
and destruction.

So it is with leaders everywhere. Leaders focus on what they see as important and are typically quite unconscious of the unintended but massive impact
they are having on their colleagues, teams, and clients. We call this outcome
of their actions the unconscious impact of their shadow(s). But why is this
impact of their shadow important?

The answer is that an autocratic command-and-control approach in business is no longer appropriate. To be successful, leaders today have to find ways
to engage people's ideas, energy, and inspiration, and this means they will also
have to build much stronger relationships—and what will prevent such relationships from occurring is their shadow.

Let me give you a real-life example of a leader I have worked with who became very aware of the impact his shadow was having on his effectiveness.

Reprinted from *Manager: British Journal of Administrative Management* (April-May
2005). Copyright 2005 The Institute of Administrative Management.

EXHIBIT 18.1—CASE STUDY ONE

Graham Cooke is factory general manager with Unilever Ice Cream and Frozen Food in Lowestoft, England. In his early career he achieved results by being a capable, forceful, and task-oriented manager. There was nothing unusual about this, but he had developed something of a reputation in the business, and when he took up a new role to drive through a large IT change project, he discovered that his new team were extremely concerned about how he might manage them. Graham Cooke recognized that he needed to change, and my work with him started by focusing on his shadow. I helped him to become more aware of the impact he was having on others and helped him to see that he had different choices based on the future that he wanted to create for himself. This understanding—that a greater awareness of the impact we make leads to a clearer choice around what future we want to create—is a critical one for leaders to grasp.

We may think that we have choice all the time, but I would suggest that most of us are, in fact, governed by judgment. We are always assessing what is right or wrong, good or bad. We base decisions not on what we want to create in the future but on what we have learned through experience in the past. But if we want to change, there has to be a radical interruption in this normal way of looking and responding. This interruption starts with a deep self-inquiry into how we impact on others at the moment and whether our intended impact is the same as that experienced by our colleagues (see Exhibit 18.1).

SOFT AND GENTLE

To give you another example of how this principle plays out in real life, let me highlight the case of the leader who is perceived by his or her team as being too soft. The leader may believe that his or her style is one that helps to empower staff, but the shadow of such a leadership style may impact the team profoundly.

In such cases people in the team will often start to go "off message"—doing their own things in their own way. There may also be a continual sense of crisis in the team caused by a leadership that isn't clear enough or engaging enough.

The point here is that it isn't only strong leaders who cast a shadow. All leaders do. We may have a particular leadership style, but our shadow will affect others, and when we are unaware, it can seriously compromise people's engagement in work and their business effectiveness (see Exhibit 18.2).

TACKLING YOUR SHADOW

So, if you are a leader, how do you start to tackle your shadow? Your lever is this: to build fierce self-awareness of the way you behave around people. This requires

EXHIBIT 18.2—CASE STUDY TWO

This example of the shadow in action underlines the problems that can be caused. Take the case of the managing director (MD) whose team reported regularly that sales and results were in line with projections. Then, just two months before the end of the year, the sales team reported that they were in fact running more than £500,000 behind target. The MD exploded. How could this happen? Why hadn't he been told earlier? What were all the meetings about? The answer he got was that people were afraid to tell him about the real state of affairs because of his temper. In this real-life example the MD saw in that moment that his shadow had led his people to present him with key information in such a way that he wouldn't have reason to blow up. Unfortunately, their approach had exacerbated the situation. He would have needed the information much earlier in the year in order to do something about it—but the weakness of his relationships with his key people had let him down, and these relationships were his responsibility all along.

---

you to get information about your impact on others, and you can use coaching, 360-degree questionnaires, or structures like action-learning groups to begin to get such feedback. However, you can make this even more real, right now, by looking at people with whom you do not have a strong relationship.

Take a moment to think of your manager or your manager's boss when you are about to present important information about your team, department, or performance. What spin do you put on that information? How does your attitude and behavior differ in a meeting where your boss is present and in a meeting where she or he isn't present? Do you feel you need to look after that relationship?

And now recognize that you have that same impact on the people who report directly to you. Some of your colleagues—those with whom you have strong relationships—may feel energized and inspired by your leadership. But don't kid yourself. There will be others who feel drained, demotivated, or even intimidated by you. Where this is the case you have an extraordinary opportunity for growth.

CONCLUSION

So how aware are you of your shadow? It is absolutely up to you to decide whether you want to look at it or not. But if you are prepared to continue leading, unaware of its impact, then don't be surprised when you achieve results you don't intend.

Alternatively, take your courage in your hands, adopt ways that help you to see the shadow that you cast, and start to make different choices about the impact you want to have in the world.

19

ℰↄ

Narcissistic Leaders
The Incredible Pros, the Inevitable Cons

Michael Maccoby

Many leaders dominating business today have what psychoanalysts call a narcissistic personality. That's good news for companies that need passion and daring to break new ground. But even productive narcissists can be dangerous for organizations. Here is some advice on avoiding the dangers.

There's something new and daring about the CEOs who are transforming today's industries. Just compare them with the executives who ran large companies in the 1950s through the 1980s. Those executives shunned the press and had their comments carefully crafted by corporate PR departments. But today's CEOs—superstars such as Bill Gates, Andy Grove, Steve Jobs, Jeff Bezos, and Jack Welch—hire their own publicists, write books, grant spontaneous interviews, and actively promote their personal philosophies. Their faces adorn the covers of magazines like *Business Week, Time,* and *The Economist.* What's more, the world's business personalities are increasingly seen as the makers and shapers of our public and personal agendas. They advise schools on what kids should learn and lawmakers on how to invest the public's money. We look to them for thoughts on everything from the future of e-commerce to hot places to vacation.

There are many reasons today's business leaders have higher profiles than ever before. One is that business plays a much bigger role in our lives than it used to, and its leaders are more often in the limelight. Another is that the business world is experiencing enormous changes that call for visionary and charismatic leadership. But my twenty-five years of consulting both as a psychoanalyst in private practice and as an adviser to top managers suggest a third reason, namely, a pronounced change in the personality of the strategic leaders at the top. As an anthropologist, I try to understand people in the context in which they operate, and as a psychoanalyst, I tend to see them through a distinctly Freudian lens. Given what I know, I believe that the larger-than-life leaders we are seeing today closely resemble the personality type that Sigmund Freud dubbed narcissistic. "People of this type impress others as being 'personalities,'" he wrote, describing one of the psychological types that clearly fall within the range of normality. "They are especially suited to act as a support for others, to take on the role of leaders, and to give a fresh stimulus to cultural development or damage the established state of affairs."

Throughout history, narcissists have always emerged to inspire people and to shape the future. When military, religious, and political arenas dominated society, it was figures such as Napoleon Bonaparte, Mahatma Gandhi, and Franklin Delano Roosevelt who determined the social agenda. But from time to time, when business became the engine of social change, it, too, generated its share of narcissistic leaders. That was true at the beginning of this century, when men like Andrew Carnegie, John D. Rockefeller, Thomas Edison, and Henry Ford exploited new technologies and restructured American industry. And I think it is true again today.

But Freud recognized that there is a dark side to narcissism. Narcissists, he pointed out, are emotionally isolated and highly distrustful. Perceived threats can trigger rage. Achievements can feed feelings of grandiosity. That's why Freud thought narcissists were the hardest personality types to analyze. Consider how an executive at Oracle described his narcissistic CEO Larry Ellison: "The difference between God and Larry is that God does not believe he is Larry." That observation is amusing, but it is also troubling. Not surprisingly, most people think of narcissists in a primarily negative way. After all, Freud named the type after the mythical figure Narcissus, who died because of his pathological preoccupation with himself.

Yet narcissism can be extraordinarily useful—even necessary. Freud shifted his views about narcissism over time and recognized that we are all somewhat narcissistic. More recently, psychoanalyst Heinz Kohut built on Freud's theories and developed methods of treating narcissists. Of course, only professional clinicians are trained to tell whether narcissism is normal or pathological. In this article, I discuss the differences between productive and unproductive narcissism but do not explore the extreme pathology of borderline conditions and psychosis.

Leaders such as Jack Welch and George Soros are examples of productive narcissists. They are gifted and creative strategists who see the big picture and find meaning in the risky challenge of changing the world and leaving behind a legacy. Indeed, one reason we look to productive narcissists in times of great transition is that they have the audacity to push through the massive transformations that society periodically undertakes. Productive narcissists are not only risk takers willing to get the job done but also charmers who can convert the masses with their rhetoric. The danger is that narcissism can turn unproductive when, lacking self-knowledge and restraining anchors, narcissists become unrealistic dreamers. They nurture grand schemes and harbor the illusion that only circumstances or enemies block their success. This tendency toward grandiosity and distrust is the Achilles' heel of narcissists. Because of it, even brilliant narcissists can come under suspicion for self-involvement, unpredictability, and—in extreme cases—paranoia.

It's easy to see why narcissistic leadership doesn't always mean successful leadership. Consider the case of Volvo's Pehr Gyllenhammar. He had a dream that appealed to a broad international audience—a plan to revolutionize the industrial workplace by replacing the dehumanizing assembly line caricatured in Charlie Chaplin's *Modern Times*. His wildly popular vision called for team-based craftsmanship. Model factories were built and publicized to international acclaim. But his success in pushing through these dramatic changes also sowed the seeds of his downfall. Gyllenhammar started to feel that he could ignore the concerns of his operational managers. He pursued chancy and expensive business deals, which he publicized on television and in the press. On one level, you can ascribe Gyllenhammar's falling out of touch with his workforce simply to faulty strategy. But it is also possible to attribute it to his narcissistic personality. His overestimation of himself led him to believe that others would want him to be the czar of a multinational enterprise. In turn, these fantasies led him to pursue a merger with Renault, which was tremendously unpopular with Swedish employees. Because Gyllenhammar was deaf to complaints about Renault, Swedish managers were forced to take their case public. In the end, shareholders aggressively rejected Gyllenhammar's plan, leaving him with no option but to resign.

Given the large number of narcissists at the helm of corporations today, the challenge facing organizations is to ensure that such leaders do not self-destruct or lead the company to disaster. That can take some doing because it is very hard for narcissists to work through their issues—and virtually impossible for them to do it alone. Narcissists need colleagues and even therapists if they hope to break free from their limitations. But because of their extreme independence and self-protectiveness, it is very difficult to get near them. Kohut maintained that a therapist would have to demonstrate an extraordinarily profound empathic understanding and sympathy for the narcissist's feelings in order to gain his trust. On top of that, narcissists must recognize that they can benefit from such help. For their part, employees must learn how to recognize—and work around—narcissistic bosses. To help them in this endeavor, let's first take a closer look at Freud's theory of personality types.

THREE MAIN PERSONALITY TYPES

Although Freud recognized that there are an almost infinite variety of personalities, he identified three main types: erotic, obsessive, and narcissistic. Most of us have elements of all three. We are all, for example, somewhat narcissistic. If that were not so, we would not be able to survive or assert our needs. The point is, one of the dynamic tendencies usually dominates the others, making each of us react differently to success and failure.

Freud's definitions of personality types differed over time. When talking about the erotic personality type, however, Freud generally did not mean a sexual personality but rather one for whom loving and above all being loved is most important. These types of individual are dependent on those people they fear will stop loving them. Many erotics are teachers, nurses, and social workers. At their most productive, they are developers of the young as well as enablers and helpers at work. As managers, they are caring and supportive, but they avoid conflict and make people dependent on them. They are, according to Freud, outer-directed people.

Obsessives, in contrast, are inner-directed. They are self-reliant and conscientious. They create and maintain order and make the most effective operational managers. They look constantly for ways to help people listen better, resolve conflict, and find win-win opportunities. They buy self-improvement books such as Stephen Covey's *The Seven Habits of Highly Effective People*. Obsessives are also ruled by a strict conscience: They like to focus on continuous improvement at work because it fits in with their sense of moral improvement.

EXHIBIT 19.1—FROMM'S FOURTH PERSONALITY TYPE

Not long after Freud described his three personality types in 1931, psychoanalyst Erich Fromm proposed a fourth personality type, which has become particularly prevalent in today's service economy. Fromm called this type the "marketing personality," and it is exemplified by the lead character in Woody Allen's movie *Zelig*, a man so governed by his need to be valued that he becomes exactly like the people he happens to be around.

Marketing personalities are more detached than erotics and so are less likely to cement close ties. They are also less driven by conscience than obsessives. Instead, they are motivated by a radar-like anxiety that permeates everything they do. Because they are so eager to please and to alleviate this anxiety, marketing personalities excel at selling themselves to others.

Unproductive marketing types lack direction and the ability to commit themselves to people or projects. But when productive, marketing types are good at facilitating teams and keeping the focus on adding value as defined by customers and colleagues. Like obsessives, marketing personalities are avid consumers of self-help books. Like narcissists, they are not wedded to the past. But marketing types generally make poor leaders in times of crisis. They lack the daring needed to innovate and are too responsive to current, rather than future, customer demands.

As entrepreneurs, obsessives start businesses that express their values, but they lack the vision, daring, and charisma it takes to turn a good idea into a great one. The best obsessives set high standards and communicate very effectively. They make sure that instructions are followed and costs are kept within budget. The most productive are great mentors and team players. The unproductive and the uncooperative become narrow experts and rule-bound bureaucrats.

Narcissists, the third type, are independent and not easily impressed. They are innovators, driven in business to gain power and glory. Productive narcissists are experts in their industries, but they go beyond this expertise. They also pose the critical questions. They want to learn everything about everything that affects the company and its products. Unlike erotics, they want to be admired, not loved. And unlike obsessives, they are not troubled by a punishing superego, so they are able to aggressively pursue their goals. Of all the personality types, narcissists run the greatest risk of isolating themselves at the moment of success. And because of their independence and aggressiveness, they are constantly looking out for enemies, sometimes degenerating into paranoia when they are under extreme stress. (For more on personality types, see Exhibit 19.1.)

STRENGTHS OF THE NARCISSISTIC LEADER

When it comes to leadership, personality type can be instructive. Erotic personalities generally make poor managers: They need too much approval. Obsessives make better leaders: They are your operational managers, critical and cautious. But it is narcissists who come closest to our collective image of great leaders. There are two reasons: They have compelling, even gripping, visions for companies, and they have an ability to attract followers.

Great Vision

I once asked a group of managers to define a leader. "A person with vision" was a typical response. Productive narcissists understand the vision thing particularly well, because they are by nature people who see the big picture. They are not analyzers who can break up big questions into manageable problems; they aren't number crunchers either (these are usually the obsessives). Nor do they try to extrapolate to understand the future: They attempt to create it. To paraphrase George Bernard Shaw, some people see things as they are and ask why; narcissists see things that never were and ask why not.

Consider the difference between Bob Allen, a productive obsessive, and Mike Armstrong, a productive narcissist. In 1997, Allen tried to expand AT&T to reestablish the end-to-end service of the Bell System by reselling local service from the regional Bell operating companies (RBOCs). Although this was a worthwhile endeavor for shareholders and customers, it was hardly earth shattering. By contrast, through a strategy of combining voice, telecommunications, and Internet access by high-speed broadband telecommunication over cable, Mike Armstrong has "created a new space with his name on it," as one of his colleagues puts it. Armstrong is betting that his costly strategy will beat out the RBOCs' less expensive solution of digital subscriber lines over copper wire. This example illustrates the different approaches of obsessives and narcissists. The risk Armstrong took is one that few obsessives would feel comfortable taking. His vision is galvanizing AT&T. Who but a narcissistic leader could achieve such a thing? As Napoleon—a classic narcissist—once remarked, "Revolutions are ideal times for soldiers with a lot of wit—and the courage to act."

As in the days of the French Revolution, the world is now changing in astounding ways; narcissists have opportunities they would never have in ordinary times. In short, today's narcissistic leaders have the chance to change the very rules of the game. Consider Robert B. Shapiro, CEO of Monsanto. Shapiro described his vision of genetically modifying crops as "the single most successful introduction of technology in the history of agriculture, including the plow" (*New York Times*, August 5, 1999). This is certainly a huge claim—there are still many questions about the safety and public acceptance of genetically engineered fruits and vegetables. But industries like agriculture are desperate for radical change. If Shapiro's gamble is successful, the industry will be transformed in the image of Monsanto. That's why he can get away with painting a picture of Monsanto as a highly profitable "life sciences" company—even though Monsanto's stock fell 12 percent from 1998 to the end of the third quarter of 1999. (During the same period, the S&P was up 41 percent.) Unlike Armstrong and Shapiro, it was enough for Bob Allen to win against his competitors in a game measured primarily by the stock market. But narcissistic leaders are after something more. They want—and need—to leave behind a legacy.

Scores of Followers

Narcissists have vision—but that's not enough. People in mental hospitals also have visions. The simplest definition of a leader is someone whom other people follow. Indeed, narcissists are especially gifted in attracting followers, and more often than not, they do so through language. Narcissists believe that words can move mountains and that inspiring speeches can change people. Narcissistic leaders are often skillful orators, and this is one of the talents that makes them so charismatic. Indeed, anyone who has seen narcissists perform can attest to their personal magnetism and their ability to stir enthusiasm among audiences.

Yet this charismatic gift is more of a two-way affair than most people think. Although it is not always obvious, narcissistic leaders are quite dependent on their followers: They need affirmation, and preferably adulation. Think of Winston Churchill's wartime broadcasts or JFK's "Ask not what your country can do for you" inaugural address. The adulation that follows from such speeches bolsters the self-confidence and conviction of the speakers. But if no one responds, the narcissist usually becomes insecure, overly shrill, and insistent—just as Ross Perot did.

Even when people respond positively to a narcissist, there are dangers. That's because charisma is a double-edged sword: It fosters both closeness and isolation. As he becomes increasingly self-assured, the narcissist becomes more spontaneous. He feels free of constraints. Ideas flow. He thinks he's invincible. This energy and confidence further inspire his followers. But the very adulation that the narcissist demands can have a corrosive effect. As he expands, he listens even less to words of caution and advice. After all, he has been right before, when others had their doubts. Rather than try to persuade those who disagree with him, he feels justified in ignoring them—creating further isolation. The result is sometimes flagrant risk taking that can lead to catastrophe. In the political realm, there is no clearer example of this than Bill Clinton.

Despite the warm feelings their charisma can evoke, narcissists are typically not comfortable with their own emotions. They listen only for the kind of information they seek. They don't learn easily from others. They don't like to teach but prefer to indoctrinate and make speeches. They dominate meetings with subordinates. The result for the organization is greater internal competitiveness at a time when everyone is already under as much pressure as they can possibly stand. Perhaps the main problem is that the narcissist's faults tend to become even more pronounced as he becomes more successful (see Exhibit 19.2).

Sensitive to Criticism

Because they are extraordinarily sensitive, narcissistic leaders shun emotions as a whole. Indeed, perhaps one of the greatest paradoxes in this age of teamwork and partnering is that the best corporate leader in the contemporary world is the type of person who is emotionally isolated. Narcissistic leaders typically keep others at arm's length. They can put up a wall of defense as thick as those in the Pentagon. And given their difficulty with knowing or acknowledging their own feelings, they are uncomfortable with other people expressing theirs—especially their negative feelings.

Indeed, even productive narcissists are extremely sensitive to criticism or slights, which feel to them like knives threatening their self-image and their confidence in their visions. Narcissists are almost unimaginably thin-skinned. Like the fairy-tale princess who slept on many mattresses and yet knew she was sleeping on a pea, narcissists—even powerful CEOs—bruise easily. This is one reason that narcissistic leaders do not want to know what people think of them unless this opinion is causing them a real problem. They cannot tolerate dissent. In fact, they can be extremely abrasive with employees who doubt them or with subordinates who are tough enough to fight back. Steve Jobs, for example, publicly humiliates subordinates. Thus, although narcissistic leaders often say that they want teamwork, what that means in practice is that they want a group of yes-men. As the more independent-minded players leave or are pushed out, succession becomes a particular problem.

Poor Listeners

One serious consequence of this oversensitivity to criticism is that narcissistic leaders often do not listen when they feel threatened or attacked. Consider the response of one narcissistic CEO I had worked with for three years who

EXHIBIT 19.2—THE RISE AND FALL OF A NARCISSIST

The story of Jan Carlson, the former CEO of the Scandinavian airline SAS, is an almost textbook example of how a narcissist's weaknesses can cut short a brilliant career. In the 1980s, Carlson's vision of SAS as the businessperson's airline was widely acclaimed in the business press; management guru Tom Peters described him as a model leader. In 1989, when I first met Carlson and his management team, he compared the ideal organization to the Brazilian soccer team—in principle, there would be no fixed roles, only innovative plays. I asked the members of the management team if they agreed with this vision of an empowered front line. One vice president, a former pilot, answered no. "I still believe that the best organization is the military," he said. I then asked Carlson for his reaction to that remark. "Well," he replied, "that may be true, if your goal is to shoot your customers."

That rejoinder was both witty and dismissive; clearly, Carlson was not engaging in a serious dialogue with his subordinates. Nor was he listening to other advisers. Carlson ignored the issue of high costs, even when many observers pointed out that SAS could not compete without improving productivity. He threw money at expensive acquisitions of hotels and made an unnecessary investment in Continental Airlines just months before it declared bankruptcy.

Carlson's story perfectly corroborates the often-recorded tendency of narcissists to become overly expansive and hence isolated at the very pinnacle of their success. Seduced by the flattery he received in the international press, Carlson's self-image became so enormously inflated that his feet left the ground. And given his vulnerability to grandiosity, he was propelled by a need to expand his organization rather than develop it. In due course, as Carlson led the company deeper and deeper into losses, he was fired. Now he is a venture capitalist helping budding companies. And SAS has lost its glitter.

---

asked me to interview his immediate team and report back to him on what they were thinking. He invited me to his summer home to discuss what I had found. "So what do they think of me?" he asked with seeming nonchalance. "They think you are very creative and courageous," I told him, "but they also feel that you don't listen." "Excuse me, what did you say?" he shot back at once, pretending not to hear. His response was humorous, but it was also tragic. In a very real way, this CEO could not hear my criticism because it was too painful to tolerate. Some narcissists are so defensive that they go so far as to make a virtue of the fact that they don't listen. As another CEO bluntly put it, "I didn't get here by listening to people!" Indeed, on one occasion when this CEO proposed a daring strategy, none of his subordinates believed it would work. His subsequent success strengthened his conviction that he had nothing to learn about strategy from his lieutenants. But success is no excuse for narcissistic leaders not to listen.

Lack of Empathy

Best-selling business writers today have taken up the slogan of "emotional competencies"—the belief that successful leadership requires a strongly developed sense of empathy. But although they crave empathy from others, productive narcissists are not noted for being particularly empathetic themselves. Indeed, lack of empathy is a characteristic shortcoming of some of the most charismatic and successful narcissists, including Bill Gates and Andy Grove. Of course, leaders do need to communicate persuasively. But a lack of empathy did not prevent some of history's greatest narcissistic leaders from knowing how to communicate—and inspire. Neither Churchill, de Gaulle, Stalin, nor Mao Tse-tung was empathetic. And yet they inspired people because of their passion and their conviction at a time when people longed for certainty. In fact, in times of radical change, lack of empathy can actually be a strength. A narcissist finds it easier than other personality types to buy and sell companies, to close and move facilities, and to lay off employees—decisions that inevitably make many people angry and sad. But narcissistic leaders typically have few regrets. As one CEO says, "If I listened to my employees' needs and demands, they would eat me alive."

Given this lack of empathy, it's hardly surprising that narcissistic leaders don't score particularly well on evaluations of their interpersonal style. What's more, neither 360-degree evaluations of their management style nor work-shops in listening will make them more empathic. Narcissists don't want to change—and as long as they are successful, they don't think they have to. They may see the need for operational managers to get touchy-feely training, but that's not for them.

There is a kind of emotional intelligence associated with narcissists, but it's more street smarts than empathy. Narcissistic leaders are acutely aware of whether or not people are with them wholeheartedly. They know whom they can use. They can be brutally exploitive. That's why, even though narcissists undoubtedly have "star quality," they are often unlikable. They easily stir up people against them, and it is only in tumultuous times, when their gifts are desperately needed, that people are willing to tolerate narcissists as leaders.

Distaste for Mentoring

Lack of empathy and extreme independence make it difficult for narcissists to mentor and be mentored. Generally speaking, narcissistic leaders set very little store by mentoring. They seldom mentor others, and when they do they typically want their protégés to be pale reflections of themselves. Even those narcissists like Jack Welch who are held up as strong mentors are usually more interested in instructing than in coaching.

Narcissists certainly don't credit mentoring or educational programs for their own development as leaders. A few narcissistic leaders such as Bill Gates may find a friend or consultant—for instance, Warren Buffet, a super-productive obsessive—whom they can trust to be their guide and confidant. But most narcissists prefer "mentors" they can control. A thirty-two-year-old marketing vice president, a narcissist with CEO potential, told me that she had rejected her boss as a mentor. As she put it, "First of all, I want to keep the relationship at a distance. I don't want to be influenced by emotions. Second, there are things I don't want him to know. I'd rather hire an outside consultant to be my coach." Although narcissistic leaders appear to be at ease with others, they find intimacy—which is a prerequisite for mentoring—to be difficult. Younger narcissists will establish peer relations with authority rather than seek a parent-like mentoring relationship. They want results and are willing to take chances arguing with authority.

An Intense Desire to Compete

Narcissistic leaders are relentless and ruthless in their pursuit of victory. Games are not games but tests of their survival skills. Of course, all successful managers want to win, but narcissists are not restrained by conscience. Organizations led by narcissists are generally characterized by intense internal competition. Their passion to win is marked by both the promise of glory and the primitive danger of extinction. It is a potent brew that energizes companies, creating a sense of urgency, but it can also be dangerous. These leaders see everything as a threat. As Andy Grove puts it, brilliantly articulating the narcissist's fear, distrust, and aggression, "Only the paranoid survive." The concern, of course, is that the narcissist finds enemies that aren't there—even among his colleagues.

AVOIDING THE TRAPS

There is very little business literature that tells narcissistic leaders how to avoid the pitfalls. There are two reasons. First, relatively few narcissistic leaders are interested in looking inward. And second, psychoanalysts don't usually get close enough to them, especially in the workplace, to write about them. (The noted psychoanalyst Harry Levinson is an exception.) As a result, advice on leadership focuses on obsessives; this is the reason that so much of it is about creating teamwork and being more receptive to subordinates. But as we've already seen, this literature is of little interest to narcissists, nor is it likely to help subordinates understand their narcissistic leaders. The absence of managerial literature on narcissistic leaders doesn't mean that it is impossible to devise strategies for dealing with narcissism. In the course of a long career counseling CEOs, I have identified three basic ways in which productive narcissists can avoid the traps of their own personality.

Find a Trusted Sidekick

Many narcissists can develop a close relationship with one person, a sidekick who acts as an anchor, keeping the narcissistic partner grounded. However, given that narcissistic leaders trust only their own insights and view of reality, the sidekick has to understand the narcissistic leader and what he is trying to achieve. The narcissist must feel that this person, or in some cases persons, is practically an extension of himself. The sidekick must also be sensitive enough to manage the relationship. Don Quixote is a classic example of a narcissist who was out of touch with reality but who was constantly saved from disaster by his "squire," Sancho Panza. Not surprisingly, many narcissistic leaders rely heavily on their spouses, the people they are closest to. But dependence on spouses can be risky, because they may further isolate the narcissistic leader from his company by supporting his grandiosity and feeding his paranoia. I once knew a CEO in this kind of relationship with his spouse. He took to ac-

---

EXHIBIT 19.3—WORKING FOR A NARCISSIST

Dealing with a narcissistic boss isn't easy. You have to be prepared to look for another job if your boss becomes too narcissistic to let you disagree with him. But remember that the company is typically betting on his vision of the future—not yours. Here are a few tips on how to survive in the short term:

- Always empathize with your boss's feelings, but don't expect any empathy back. Look elsewhere for your own self-esteem. Understand that behind his display of infallibility, there hides a deep vulnerability. Praise his achievements and reinforce his best impulses, but don't be shamelessly sycophantic. An intelligent narcissist can see through flatterers and prefers independent people who truly appreciate him. Show that you will protect his image, inside and outside the company. But be careful if he asks for an honest evaluation. What he wants is information that will help him solve a problem about his image. He will resent any honesty that threatens his inflated self-image and is likely to retaliate.
- Give your boss ideas, but always let him take the credit for them. Find out what he thinks before presenting your views. If you believe he is wrong, show how a different approach would be in his best interest. Take his paranoid views seriously; don't brush them aside— they often reveal sharp intuitions. Disagree only when you can demonstrate how he will benefit from a different point of view.
- Hone your time-management skills. Narcissistic leaders often give subordinates many more orders than they can possibly execute. Ignore the requests he makes that don't make sense. Forget about them. He will. But be careful: Carve out free time for yourself only when you know there's a lull in the boss's schedule. Narcissistic leaders feel free to call you at any hour of the day or night. Make yourself available, or be prepared to get out.

---

cusing loyal subordinates of plotting against him just because they ventured a few criticisms of his ideas.

It is much better for a narcissistic leader to choose a colleague as his sidekick. Good sidekicks are able to point out the operational requirements of the narcissistic leader's vision and keep him rooted in reality. The best sidekicks are usually productive obsessives. Gyllenhammar, for instance, was most effective at Volvo when he had an obsessive COO, Hakan Frisinger, to focus on improving quality and cost, as well as an obsessive HR director, Berth Jonsson, to implement his vision. Similarly, Bill Gates can think about the future from the stratosphere because Steve Ballmer, a tough obsessive president, keeps the show on the road. At Oracle, CEO Larry Ellison can afford to miss key meetings and spend time on his boat contemplating a future without PCs because he has a productive obsessive COO in Ray Lane to run the company for him. But the job of sidekick entails more than just executing the leader's ideas. The sidekick also has to get his leader to accept new ideas. To do this, he must be able to show the leader how the new ideas fit with his views and serve his interests. (For more on dealing with narcissistic bosses, see Exhibit 19.3.)

Indoctrinate the Organization

The narcissistic CEO wants all his subordinates to think the way he does about the business. Productive narcissists—people who often have a dash of the obsessive personality—are good at converting people to their point of view. One of the most successful at this is GE's Jack Welch. Welch uses toughness to build a corporate culture and to implement a daring business strategy, including the buying and selling of scores of companies. Unlike other narcissistic leaders such as Gates, Grove, and Ellison, who have transformed industries with new products, Welch was able to transform his industry by focusing on execution and pushing companies to the limits of quality and efficiency, bumping up revenues and wringing out costs. In order to do so, Welch hammers out a huge corporate culture in his own image—a culture that provides impressive rewards for senior managers and shareholders.

Welch's approach to culture building is widely misunderstood. Many observers, notably Noel Tichy in *The Leadership Engine,* argue that Welch forms his company's leadership culture through teaching. But Welch's "teaching" involves a personal ideology that he indoctrinates into GE managers through speeches, memos, and confrontations. Rather than create a dialogue, Welch makes pronouncements (either be the number one or two company in your market or get out), and he institutes programs (such as Six Sigma quality) that become the GE party line. Welch's strategy has been extremely effective. GE managers must either internalize his vision, or they must leave. Clearly, this is incentive learning with a vengeance. I would even go so far as to call Welch's teaching brainwashing. But Welch does have the rare insight and know-how to achieve what all narcissistic business leaders are trying to do, namely, get the organization to identify with them, to think the way they do, and to become the living embodiment of their companies.

Get into Analysis

Narcissists are often more interested in controlling others than in knowing and disciplining themselves. That's why, with very few exceptions, even productive narcissists do not want to explore their personalities with the help of insight therapies such as psychoanalysis. Yet since Heinz Kohut, there has been a radical shift in psychoanalytic thinking about what can be done to help narcissists work through their rage, alienation, and grandiosity. Indeed, if they can be persuaded to undergo therapy, narcissistic leaders can use tools such as psychoanalysis to overcome vital character flaws.

Consider the case of one exceptional narcissistic CEO who asked me to help him understand why he so often lost his temper with subordinates. He lived far from my home city, and so the therapy was sporadic and very unorthodox. Yet he kept a journal of his dreams, which we interpreted together either by phone or when we met. Our analysis uncovered painful feelings of being unappreciated that went back to his inability to impress a cold father. He came to realize that he demanded an unreasonable amount of praise and that when he felt unappreciated by his subordinates, he became furious. Once he understood that, he was able to recognize his narcissism and even laugh about it. In the middle of our work, he even announced to his top team that I was psychoanalyzing him and asked them what they thought of that. After a pregnant pause, one executive vice president piped up, "Whatever you're doing, you should keep doing it, because you don't get so angry anymore." Instead of being trapped by narcissistic rage, this CEO was learning how to express his concerns constructively.

Leaders who can work on themselves in that way tend to be the most productive narcissists. In addition to being self-reflective, they are also likely to be open, likable, and good-humored. Productive narcissists have perspective; they are able to detach themselves and laugh at their irrational needs. Although serious about achieving their goals, they are also playful. As leaders, they are aware of being performers. A sense of humor helps them maintain enough perspective and humility to keep on learning.

THE BEST AND WORST OF TIMES

As I have pointed out, narcissists thrive in chaotic times. In more tranquil times and places, however, even the most brilliant narcissist will seem out of place. In his short story *The Curfew Tolls,* Stephen Vincent Benet speculates on what would have happened to Napoleon if he had been born some thirty years earlier. Retired in prerevolutionary France, Napoleon is depicted as a lonely artillery major boasting to a vacationing British general about how he could have beaten the English in India. The point, of course, is that a visionary born in the wrong time can seem like a pompous buffoon.

Historically, narcissists in large corporations have been confined to sales positions, where they use their persuasiveness and imagination to best effect. In settled times, the problematic side of the narcissistic personality usually conspires to keep narcissists in their place, and they can typically rise to top management positions only by starting their own companies or by leaving to lead startups. Consider Joe Nacchio, formerly in charge of both the business and consumer divisions of AT&T. Nacchio was a super-salesman and a popular leader in the mid-1990s. But his desire to create a new network for business customers was thwarted by colleagues who found him abrasive, self-promoting, and ruthlessly ambitious.

In 1998, Nacchio left AT&T to become CEO of Qwest, a company that is creating a long-distance fiber-optic cable network. Nacchio had the credibility—and charisma—to sell Qwest's initial public offering to financial markets and gain a high valuation. Within a short space of time, he turned Qwest into an attractive target for the RBOCs, which were looking to move into long-distance telephony and Internet services. Such a sale would have given Qwest's owners a handsome profit on their investment. But Nacchio wanted more. He wanted to expand—to compete with AT&T—and for that he needed local service. Rather than sell Qwest, he chose to make a bid himself for local telephone operator U.S. West, using Qwest's highly valued stock to finance the deal. The market voted on this display of expansiveness with its feet: Qwest's stock price fell 40 percent between June 1999, when he made the deal, and the end of the third quarter of 1999. (The S&P index dropped 5.7 percent during the same period.)

Like other narcissists, Nacchio likes risk—and sometimes ignores the costs. But with the dramatic discontinuities going on in the world today, more and more large corporations are getting into bed with narcissists. They are finding that there is no substitute for narcissistic leaders in an age of innovation. Companies need leaders who do not try to anticipate the future so much as create it. But narcissistic leaders—even the most productive of them—can self-destruct and lead their organizations terribly astray. For companies whose narcissistic leaders recognize their limitations, these will be the best of times. For other companies, these could turn out to be the worst.

20

ల౨

Bad Leaders
How They Get That Way and
What to Do About Them

Robert J. Allio

Over the past few years, the media has chronicled the misadventures of a mug
book full of corporate scoundrels. Some of the notables making lurid headlines
were Kenneth Lay and Jeffrey Skilling, former Enron executives, Dennis Kozlowski, former CEO of Tyco, and convicted WorldCom chief executive
Bernard J. Ebbers. But should these scandals make us reflect on the wider
problems of corporate leadership? True, such convicted malefactors total just
a small percentage of the Fortune 500. But there are also many CEOs who
have been forced to resign in recent years because they failed leadership 101,
and a scandal involving the backdating of options has raised questions about
the judgment of even remarkable leaders like Steve Jobs of Apple. As one in-
dication of the widespread climate of disenchantment with leadership, *Business
Week* now publishes a feature on the year's "worst leaders."[1]

So it's not clear whether we're witnessing an epidemic of misbehavior, or
merely watching corporate leadership under more intensive scrutiny in the post
Sarbanes-Oxley environment. But in either case, several fundamental questions
need to be answered. They include: Why aren't bad leaders recognized long

Reprinted by permission of *Strategy and Leadership* (Vol. 35, No. 3, 2007). Copyright
2007 Emerald Group Publishing Limited.

FIGURE 20.1—THE TRAJECTORY OF THE LEADER OVER TIME

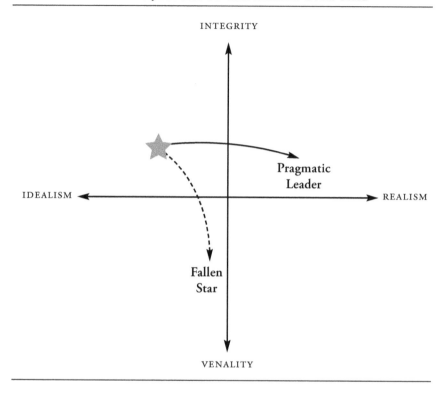

before they bring woe to shareholders? Why isn't the process of anticipating who will be a good leader failsafe? And how can organizations deal with a brilliant candidate who obviously lacks important leadership skills but seems to be capable of delivering impressive results?

Over time it is easy to distinguish bad leaders from good ones. Good leaders find strategies that do right by all the stakeholders. They manage by influence rather than coercion, and they encourage change rather than resisting it. Effective leaders exhibit both proficiency and integrity.

In contrast, leaders who are toxic, corrupt, or simply misguided damage the interests and welfare of the stakeholders. They inflict pain and suffering on their organizations, and on the individuals who follow them, including employees and shareholders.

The challenge is to determine in advance which potential leader will work for the stakeholders and which one will damage their interests. It's a difficult judgment because many corporate and government leaders begin as idealistic visionaries, imbued with a strong view of how to lead their organization into the future. They also initially demonstrate a strong sense of integrity. But their career trajectory often follows one of two scenarios (see Figure 20.1).[2]

In the best of cases, idealistic leaders retain their aspirations, but adversity or resource limitations temper their idealism; they become tough pragmatists, yet may still give their direct reports a chance to express alternative views.

All too often, however, they act out an alternative scenario. The would-be visionary, seduced by power and a growing sense of certitude, first becomes isolated and then gets lost. When plans fail to deliver wins, the leader grows tyrannical, wields power wrongly, and devolves into a fallen star and self-serving "decider," often surrounded by fawning acolytes.

WHERE DO BAD LEADERS COME FROM?

How do we explain the deviation of leaders from the path of righteousness? And why do they so often disappoint us? Consider five possibilities:

Personality Disorder

One need not be a trained psychiatrist to recognize the manifestation of personality disorder in many leaders. Narcissism seems to be a common syndrome among failed leaders; individuals exhibit a pattern of grandiosity, a need for admiration, and a lack of empathy.[3] Other symptoms include an overdeveloped expectation of entitlement, as exemplified by Jack Welch of GE and Dennis Kozlowski of Tyco. GE's board forced Welch to relinquish a variety of extravagant personal perks after he retired, while the Justice Department sent Kozlowski to prison for grand larceny, conspiracy, and falsifying corporate records.

Recent executive salary trends reveal how pervasive the entitlement neurosis is across corporate America.[4] The compensation of the average CEO has escalated to 411 times the compensation of the average worker, a dramatic increase from 1980, when CEOs commanded compensation only 42 times that of the average worker. What's worse, compensation no longer appears to correlate with performance. Forbes now compiles an annual list of the most overpaid CEOs in the S&P 500—those whose rewards were most negatively correlated with change in shareholder value.[5] Making the top ten last year were the CEOs of Interpublic, OfficeMax, Biogen Idec, Gateway, Marsh &

McLennan, Comcast, Schering-Plough, Sanmina-SCI, LSI Logic, and East-
man Kodak.

Narcissistic leaders often take advantage of others to achieve their own ends.
They believe that their uniqueness excuses them from the ethical codes that
bind others. They relish the pleasure of power, and are overtaken with a lust
for more. They crave glory: success plus recognition. Power corrupts them,
and absolute power corrupts them absolutely.

Not all narcissists are bad leaders, to be sure. Some, like Andrew Carnegie,
Henry Ford, and John D. Rockefeller were exceptionally productive. In modern times, some narcissistic CEOs have bold visions, attract devoted followers,
and inspire their organizations to accomplish great things.[6]

In his exhaustive review of the field, Clive Roland Boddy reports that the
key defining characteristics of organization psychopaths include a lack of conscience and an inability to experience the feelings of others.[7] These psychopaths constitute approximately one percent of the population. But because
of their charm and networking skills, they have a "knack of getting employed
and climbing the organizational hierarchy."

Akrasia

Socrates proposed centuries ago the concept of akrasia, or weakness of will. If
one judges an action to be the best course of action, why would a person
choose anything else? Socrates concluded that "no one goes willingly towards
the bad." But our intuition and personal experience suggest otherwise. Sometimes our appetites appear to overwhelm us (why not take one more bite of
the apple?). Or in other cases we find it easy to place just one more bet on the
game or postpone an important task one more day. And cognitive dissonance
may delude us into embracing less attractive alternatives.

Moral philosopher Harry Frankfurt offers a simple explanation for why a
person who knows the right course of action nonetheless appears to freely
choose the wrong path: he cites the influence of "first-order desires" that interfere with the fulfillment of "higher-order desires." These higher-order desires reflect our true needs; those who fail to honor these desires run the risk
of behaving recklessly.

An equally plausible rationale for akrasia or incontinent behavior is that
we fall prey to a lapse in judgment. In doing so we temporarily believe that
the worse course of action is better because we have not evaluated fully all
the implications and consequences of our actions, but have inadvertently
sub-optimized.[8]

Misguided Values

Some leaders simply choose their own interests above all else; they consciously act in ways that serve their own purposes. Machiavelli is their mentor. In *The Prince*, based on observations of his patron, Cesare Borgia, he advocates the use of power as a tool and deems cultivation of fear to be more important than love. Conquer by force, he tells us. Commit all your crimes against the people at the start of the regime. Be a lion (strong and ruthless) and a fox (sly and duplicitous).[9]

Economist Adam Smith concluded that individuals who attend to only their own gain would in fact promote the public interest.[10] They would be led, as if by an invisible hand, to achieve the best good for all. Were Smith a witness to recent history, he might well revise his opinion, for it seems clear that individuals who make decisions based only on self-interest may unwittingly damage the welfare of the system.

Perhaps former UnitedHealth Group chief executive William McGuire fell into this trap when he greedily backdated millions of dollars of incentive stock options. McGuire was a free rider—a man who takes a little more (a free ride on the bus) on the assumption that it won't matter and no one will notice. After the UnitedHealth board forced McGuire to resign in October 2006, the firm began the painful process of restating its financial statements, and its market value plummeted.

Avoidance of Reality

Some leaders resist facing the facts. Among the many historical examples are Procter & Gamble's denial of toxicity in its Rely Tampons, Perrier's rejection of evidence that its bottled water contained benzene, and Coca Cola's refusal to accept responsibility for illness caused by contaminated Cokes drunk by schoolchildren in Belgium.

Executives in the Big Three of the US automobile industry have blundered before, but even today, as Toyota and other foreign manufacturers seize market share, the leaders of Ford, GM, and Chrysler grumble about an undervalued yen, high costs of materials, and excessive health care costs. They appear unable to conceive of any scenario that would allow them to surmount these burdens. (How about a better car?)

Deficiencies of perspective are a common corollary. Leaders who emphasize short-term performance (earnings per share this year) may well compromise long-term performance and survival. They often exhibit "risk myopia"; they place greater focus on imminent crises while ignoring longer-term potential cataclysm until it's too late. And often leaders are reluctant to accept change— the possibility that new technologies or shifts in consumer needs dictate a change in corporate policy and strategy.

The Complicity of Followers

In any organization, followers can have as much influence on a leader as does a leader on the followers. Followers often abdicate responsibility and become sycophants or toadies. Leaders and followers often share a folie à deux, a collective madness that allows each side to accept uncritically common goals and behavior.

When leaders are charged with misfeasance or malfeasance, the role of followers often doesn't get the attention it deserves. But followers always share culpability for their leader's misdeeds, often as a result of their crimes of obedience. As Barbara Kellerman notes, followers seek safety, certainty, and self-reservation.[11]

HOW TO CURB THE EMERGENCE OF BAD LEADERSHIP

How, asks historian James MacGregor Burns, "can we subdue the voracious, crafty, and inescapable beast of power?"[12] The starting point is the leader selection process. Corporations usually select their leaders from a pool of candidates who have been tested in managerial jobs for decades. So why do the vainglorious ones get recruited? Aren't there signs of egotistic or self-serving behavior in evidence before they are chosen? Are their direct reports and front-line workers being interviewed?

Boards of directors have a particular responsibility to make informed decisions, rather than simply looking for imperial rulers who may be narcissistic but are expected to turn around the organization by imposing their will on rebellious organizations.

Boards also need to review their other practices. For example, two-thirds of the CEOs in US corporations also hold the title of chairman. By separating the roles of the CEO and the chairman, they will reduce the risk of bad decisions. Boards can also help by establishing term limits for directors, and assuring that a leadership-succession plan is in place. They must install appropriate performance metrics and monitor progress at regular intervals.

Once a candidate is in place, further measures can be taken to lessen the risk of bad leadership. Here are recommendations for both leaders and followers:

Advice for Leaders

- *Determine what stakeholders value:* Leaders need to confirm the legitimacy of their path by formulating and publishing a complete description of their proposed strategy and long-range vision. The response from stakeholders will help confirm or refute the plan, and good leaders adapt to new information.
- *Listen to other views:* The tendency of leaders to make bad judgments can be tempered if they establish a network of peers and others who can give them guidance and feedback. Leaders must encourage alternative perspectives and tolerate dissent, even from the rebels in the ranks.
- *Rely on the team:* Team support is essential if the leader's vision is to be implemented. And evidence supports conclusively the superiority of group decisions over individual decisions (although "group think" is always a peril). Teams also can help leaders build scenarios that consider alternative futures and clarify the implications of taking different paths.
- *Foster a culture of integrity:* High-performing organizations like Johnson & Johnson, Southwest Airlines, and Starbucks have developed an explicit set of values and code of behavior. Actions that reinforce the code are rewarded; transgressions are punished. Ultimately the ethic of the enterprise becomes internalized, and its members intuitively do the right thing.
- *Cultivate personal awareness:* This is the greatest challenge, for leaders, often isolated from stakeholders, can be seduced by power; they find it easy to lie to themselves to accommodate their appetites or world views. Leaders must learn to balance intuition with data, confidence with context, personal needs with the greater good.

Advice for Followers

- *Give feedback:* The feedback must be strong and fearless, although giving feedback can be risky, for bad leaders rarely encourage contrarian views. If the leader does not want to listen, the ultimate strategy for a follower may be to find another job.

    Nevertheless, followers cannot simply watch the ship go down. Shareholders of Home Depot were infuriated by CEO Bob Nardelli's arrogance at the firm's 2006 annual meeting (he refused to answer questions about the company's performance). Nardelli later apologized, promised to be more forthcoming, and promised to alter his approach to shareholder meetings. But the board had seen enough and in January 2007 sent him packing.

- *Develop coalitions:* There is strength in numbers. By identifying allies and taking collective action, followers speak with [a] louder voice and can accelerate the pace of change. A balance of power will provide protection against the perils of bureaucracy and over-centralization.
- *Regulate the organization:* When self-regulation fails, governing bodies must step in to protect the rights of the stakeholders. A recent example of this intervention was the Sarbanes-Oxley Act of 2002, passed to address the spate of accounting scandals at Enron, Tyco, WorldCom, Computer Associates, and elsewhere. The legislation requires independent auditing, certification of reports by CEOs and CFOs, and protection for whistleblowers.

CONCLUSIONS

We appear to be suffering today from a plague of bad leadership in both the private and public sector. Whom can we blame for this epidemic? The primary culprits are those who appoint leaders that exhibit personality disorders, akrasia, flawed values, and detachment from reality—and then tolerate bad leadership when it manifests. But followers cannot evade some level of responsibility.

Leaders and followers enjoy a symbiotic relationship. The interaction between them can either produce great success or exacerbate failure. By more conscientious adherence to an explicit moral code, more consistent communication and transparency, and greater attention to the needs of all the stakeholders, we can close the gap and help leaders do the right thing.

Notes

1. *Business Week,* December 18, 2006.

2. Adapted from Daniel Chirot's superlative study of tyranny: *Modern Tyrants,* The Free Press, 1994.

3. American Psychiatric Association, *Diagnostic and Statistical Manual of Mental Disorders,* 1994.

4. The Corporate Library's 2006 Pay Survey, The Corporate Library, September 29, 2006.

5. Elizabeth MacDonald, "Executive Sweets," Forbes.com, November 7, 2006.

6. Michael Maccoby, "Narcissistic leaders: The incredible pros, the inevitable cons," *Harvard Business Review,* Vol. 78, January 2000.

7. Clive Roland Boddy, "The dark side of management decisions: Organizational psychopaths," *Management Decision,* Vol. 44, No. 10, 2006.

8. Neuroscience research supports this hypothesis. Brain scans show that the limbic system is more active when immediate gratification is possible. Evaluation of longer-range options stimulates activity in another part of the brain, and these two modules may actually compete with each other.

9. Niccolò Machiavelli, *The Prince,* 1513.

10. Adam Smith, *The Wealth of Nations,* 1776.

11. Barbara Kellerman, *Bad Leadership,* Harvard Business School Press, 2004.

12. James MacGregor Burns, *Leadership,* Harper & Row, 1978.

PART V

SOUL

Leadership is a long journey into your soul.

JEFF IMMELT

Leadership is a potent combination of strategy and character. But if you must be without one, be without the strategy.

GENERAL NORMAN SCHWARZKOPF

Values and morals, through their direct influence on our actions, are the soul of effective and ethical leadership. Without a strong internal moral compass or a sense of right and wrong, leaders cannot earn the trust of their stakeholders, nor can they take appropriate actions in challenging and changing situations. Unfortunately, in recent years we have seen a lack of trust and poor decision making manifested in for-profit firms, not-for-profit organizations, and governmental agencies. What was missing in these situations? To use the words of Bill George, authentic leaders are "people who live their values every day and who know the true north of their moral compass." In short, we were missing leaders with character and integrity who modeled appropriate behavior and infused these qualities in everything they did.

Where does this authentic character or unwavering sense of right and wrong come from? Or stated differently, if leadership is about doing the right thing, how do we know what the "right" thing is? The struggle to answer this question dates back to ancient Greek philosophy, with Socrates exploring the dilemma of moral rightness in *Euthyphro* by posing the question, "Is the pious loved by the gods because it is pious, or is it pious because it is loved by the gods?" Is moral rightness derived from some universal source, or is it simply an arbitrary determination by a particular authority? And even though a definitive, objective answer to the question of moral foundation remains elusive, most people would agree that the majority of us possess a basic, somewhat universal standard as to what constitutes appropriate and inappropriate actions. Yes, cultural differences surely come into play, but there is an overarching set of "core values," such as honesty, responsibility, fairness, and respect, that transcends individuals, organizations, and cultures. Thus, when leaders make unethical decisions, it's not simply because they are unaware of the right thing to do. Rather, it's because their actions are not aligned with the organization's and society's core beliefs. They make choices inconsistent with accepted norms and values, demonstrating a lack of integrity.

Determining the moral imperative of an organization and the corresponding responsibility of its leaders generates much debate. Most people agree that contemporary organizations, both for-profit and not-for-profit, need to satisfy a host of stakeholders and simply cannot focus on one objective, such as maximizing shareholder wealth. Leaders need to steer their organizations in a manner that generates value for multiple stakeholders. One such approach to moving in this direction is the "triple bottom line" where leaders seek to simultaneously generate economic outcomes (e.g., profits, innovation), facilitate social well-being (e.g., human rights, safety, and health), and engage in environmental stewardship (e.g., emissions reductions, resource efficiency). And although every organization emphasizes idiosyncratic outcomes based on its particular mission, the general expansion to a multiple stakeholder model forces leaders to take a broader approach, often referred to as corporate social responsibility (CSR), when leading their organizations and people.

Such a broad approach creates important challenges for today's leaders with regard to developing themselves, leading their followers, and creating an appropriate organizational culture. First and foremost, leaders need to possess a strong moral sensibility regarding their obligations to a wide array of stakeholders, and they need to spend more time strategically thinking about their organization's core values and work to build a consensus around them. From these core values organizations can develop what Michael Porter and Mark Kramer call "points of intersection" where "shared value" is created among the organization and other parts of society. Examples of this intersection include Whole Foods engaging in local sourcing and using biodiesel in its vehicles, Coke protecting and developing clean water sources throughout the world, and Marriot providing training and skill development to chronically unemployed job candidates.

Leaders cannot restrict the development of such broadened moral sensibilities to themselves. They need to foster it in their followers and create an organizational culture supporting such a philosophy. More specifically, they need to make sure there are no value ambiguities within the organization about where it stands on issues such as ethical practices, human rights, social justice, and environmental sustainability. And even though every organization will have different strategic priorities surrounding these issues, leaders need to clearly articulate their positions on them using language that gives meaning to the organization's values and operationalizes specific behaviors congruent with these values. Leaders also need to create an open and transparent culture that provides the means for followers to openly challenge any potential deviations from the leader's and the organization's prescribed positions.

LEADERSHIP PERSPECTIVES

In "Leadership Lessons from Everyday Life" (Chapter 21), Vinita Bali argues that the lessons we learn in everyday life can and should be carried into our work environments to help us become better leaders. And given that everyday life provides leadership lessons, Bali contends that there is some leadership capability within all of us. She also points out that our core values are the underpinnings of leadership, as they provide the basis for our actions, and she notes that the discipline and empathy required in our everyday lives are important ingredients in the leadership equation. And to her, great leadership boils down to aligning our thoughts and actions and simply doing the right thing. In one word, leadership is about character.

Gerhold K. Becker, in his piece "Moral Leadership in Business" (Chapter 22), draws upon ancient Confucian insights to present a view that genuine leadership is based on personal moral principles. To Becker, moral leadership plays out in the tension between the pessimistic view suggesting humans are self-centered and morally flawed and the optimistic view pointing toward our cooperation, fairness, and morality. Ultimately, leadership activities, like all human actions, are grounded in a moral dimension that can neither be ignored nor superficially attended to. And, according to Becker, leaders without a moral backbone quickly lose the trust of their followers and are seen as people who lack sincerity and honesty.

In Chapter 23, "Leadership and Advocacy: Dual Roles for Corporate Social Responsibility and Social Entrepreneurship," Manuel London explores the intertwined, complementary roles of leadership and advocacy. He points out that CSR has become a competitive necessity in most organizations and that today's leaders are becoming advocates for wide-ranging social causes, such as education, health, environmental sustainability, and fair wages, which create competitive advantages for their organizations while simultaneously benefiting society. In order to respond to multiple stakeholders and succeed in these advocacy roles, London argues, leaders need to exhibit empathy, integrity, and a willingness to take strategic risks with organizational resources—attributes that, we would argue, are required of all good leaders in all contexts.

Warren Bennis outlines his views on developing transparency within organizations in his short essay "Building a Culture of Candor: A Crucial Key to Leadership" (Chapter 24). Even though demands for transparency within our business and governmental institutions have never been higher, Bennis suggests that no amount of public demand or legislation can magically bring it about. Rather, transparency results when leaders develop what Bennis calls a culture of candor in organizations—a culture in which leaders develop thicker skin, followers can openly give direct feedback, and principled dissidents are not simply tolerated but rewarded.

We conclude this part and the book with John W. Gardner's classic essay from 1965, "The Antileadership Vaccine" (Chapter 25), in which he discusses the dispersion of power and our failure to cope with the "big questions." This is a meaningful contemporary review even though almost half a century has passed since Gardner wrote it. In his opinion, the antileadership vaccine is administered by our educational systems and by the structure of our society, causing people to lose the confidence they need to assume leadership roles. Gardner notes that in training people for leadership, we have neglected the broader moral view of shared values, thus inhibiting vision, creativity, and risk taking. He also argues we appear to be approaching a point at which everyone will value the technical expert who advises the leader or the intellectual who stands off and criticizes the leader, but no one will be concerned with the development of leadership itself.

21

∾

Leadership Lessons
from Everyday Life

Vinita Bali

A lot has been written about people who shape and change companies and other organizations and what makes them who they are and do what they do. Equally, there are larger numbers of people who lead everyday exemplary lives but who go unnoticed. What leadership lessons can we learn from such people? What makes them disciplined and empathetic, with an unwavering focus on the end goal, as they strive for excellence and perfection?

Leadership is a capability that each of us has within us. It is formed as we take on the opportunities and challenges of everyday life, and it is measured by our successes and failures. It is my belief and experience that the leadership lessons we learn in our everyday lives can and should be carried with us into our work environments, and that they can help us become better leaders of our people.

As I have reflected on leadership over the years based on my own experiences across several countries and continents, I have been inspired by people everywhere, irrespective of their country or their socioeconomic status, who exemplify the true qualities of leadership. And they do so by the strength of their character and their authenticity—by the way they live their lives every

---

Reprinted by permission of *Leader to Leader* (Spring 2011). Copyright 2011 Leader to Leader Institute.

day. I admire and respect them because their motivation is pure, and they live on the strength of their conviction.

Across all domains and disciplines, leadership is about the human spirit and human endeavor, underpinned by core values that define character. It is this spirit and endeavor that makes the difference in the form and quality of accomplishment. Howard Gardner has talked about leadership as the capacity to continually create. That capacity, infused with the relentless drive for excellence that is inspirational, creates enduring success—whether we talk about successful sports people, successful artists and composers, successful companies, or successful professionals in any field.

In the sections that follow, I explore some of the key lessons from everyday life.

CHARACTER AND AUTHENTICITY ARE CORE TO A LEADER

More than anything else, leadership is about character and authenticity. It is about taking ownership for changing something and making it better than you found it. And when that change operates with responsibility, it earns respect. Leadership is exercised every day—in schools, homes, and other institutions. In this article, I look at it from the corporate lens, though its central premise holds everywhere.

The word *character* comes from an ancient Greek verb that means "to engrave," and its related noun meaning "mark" or "distinctive quality." General Schwarzkopf said, "The main ingredient of good leadership is good character. This is because leadership involves conduct and conduct is determined by values." Simply stated, character is about doing the right thing and not letting anything get in the way. Examples of "doing the right thing" abound in the world of business, art, sports, medicine, and many other fields. The common thread of human endeavor and human spirit is what defines leaders. I believe it was Elvis Presley who said that "values are like fingerprints, nobody's are the same, but you leave them all over in everything you do."

At a time when CEO tenures are shrinking to an average of six years across the Fortune 500 companies, management educators and the corporate world must necessarily reflect on the quality of leadership, for that will determine the quality of the world we are all going to live in. Tony Hayward lost his job at BP, not just because of the Gulf of Mexico oil spill (oil spills have happened before) but because of the way he handled the situation and the lack of leadership and ownership he displayed for addressing the problem once it had occurred.

The interesting thing about leadership behavior is that it must be displayed in major moments but is created in the small ones over time. Reputation is based on the integrity and consistency of words and actions—repeatedly.

LEADERSHIP IS ABOUT HANDLING ADAPTIVE CHALLENGES

Despite the general convergence of views that technical and functional skills are essential but not enough to succeed in any field, management education continues to place great significance on precisely those aspects—analytical and conceptual abilities, critical thinking, and problem solving—and not enough on adaptive skills. What distinguishes effective leaders from others is not just their technical or functional expertise, but their ability to handle adaptive challenges, that is, those situations or circumstances that cannot be predicted but can occur at any time in the course of business.

Contrast the handling of the 2010 BP Gulf of Mexico oil spill with the dialysis filter crisis that confronted Baxter in Europe in August 2001, when approximately fifty deaths were reported in Spain and Croatia following the use of the company's dialysis filters.

Even though, at first, all investigations were inconclusive as to the cause of death of these patients, the commonality was that these filters came from the same lot and were manufactured by Althin Medical AB, a company that Baxter had acquired in March 2000. Harry Kraemer, the CEO of Baxter, immediately owned up to the situation, apologized for the malfunctioning of these filters, took full responsibility for what happened, asked the Board to reduce his bonus, and put in place standards and processes to prevent a repeat occurrence.

TRUE LEADERSHIP CALLS FOR ALIGNMENT BETWEEN MORAL COMPASS AND BEHAVIOR

One of the greatest leaders of the twentieth century, Mahatma Gandhi, changed the course of history—not just for India but for many other parts of the world as well—by the courage of his convictions and his authenticity. He epitomized what successful leaders do: he created a sense of purpose and shared vision, he challenged existing ways of thinking, and he energized purposeful action. His moral compass, purpose, and behavior were fully and always aligned.

Gandhi is perhaps the only transformational leader in recent times who held no public office and who has not been given any formal award—either in his lifetime or posthumously. Yet he is one leader who, even six decades after his death, continues to inspire people globally. He did something else that effective leaders do—he listened empathetically to people, even as he fortified his resolve to transform the reality of India. He formulated his ideas of independence, and the broad strategy for getting it, by first traveling extensively around the country to see and hear about the problems and issues faced by ordinary people. He neither delegated nor outsourced that work to anyone else. He was always there, in the midst of his people, inspiring them to action through the sheer brilliance of his strategy and the sense of purpose he instilled in what he said and did.

The story of Gandhi is multifaceted, and a key facet of the story is his indomitable will and character—the endurance to hold to his purpose without vacillation and with thought and action always aligned. In this, he carried with him everyday people, molding and shaping their thinking.

When I worked at the Coca-Cola Company in Atlanta, I had the privilege of meeting Mohammad Ali, who, in response to a question on what makes a champion, said, "Champions aren't made in gyms. Champions are made from something they have deep inside them—a desire, a dream, a vision."

BEING YOURSELF—EVERY DAY

The silent majority of people (the real champions) wake up every morning and bring their best to what they do. They don't necessarily lead companies or countries (in a conventional sense) and they can be found everywhere—from the flower seller to the schoolteacher to the farmer, to moms and dads who believe in character and authenticity and who are driven by a set of values that provide the moral compass for all their actions. We don't write about them often because they occur every day, but if we stop to listen and observe, we can see exemplary behaviors, not in search of recognition but manifesting what is right in the absolute sense and not contextually. It is this vast majority in every organization, in every nation, that can be harnessed to produce extraordinary results, as is empirically evident.

The culture and environment in an organization are influenced not just by top management but by the ability of top management to inspire and motivate people to take the right actions. According to Jim Collins, good to great organizations have three forms of discipline: disciplined people, disciplined thought, and disciplined action, thereby eliminating the need for hierarchy, bureaucracy, or controls.

Warren Bennis said, "Becoming a leader is synonymous with becoming yourself. It is precisely that simple and also that difficult." So the question is, how do we get there? Where do awareness and learning and training come from?

From a corporate perspective the demands of leadership are intense and the spotlight seldom leaves you. But the corporate world also creates a set of expectations that at times cause people to behave in ways that may not be truly desirable, either from a governance perspective or from a moral perspective. The failures have less to do with strategy and execution and more to do with the judgment of people in positions of power, where they either make the wrong choices or make convenient choices because the alternatives are hard.

MAKING BIG IDEAS REAL

In my experience, everyday people can become extraordinary leaders when they have a compelling vision to change the world around them for the better. but they don't just have big ideas, they turn them into reality.

I have selected three stories that embody the human spirit and endeavor I discussed earlier and that underscore the exceptional willingness and courage to change the rules. In each of the stories there is a profound leadership insight:

- The first story is that of Thimakka, an uneducated and poor casual worker who lives in a village in the south of India. Her story has moved several people and has been shared through prose, poetry, music, and dance. Thimakka is a true environmentalist even though she received no formal education. She and her husband started taking saplings from banyan trees that grew in the village and planting these along a road. From ten in the first year, Thimakka planted 284 banyan trees along a four kilometers stretch of highway. These saplings were planted just before the monsoon so they would get sufficient rainwater to take root and grow.

  Thimakka had no resources but she was resourceful and galvanized an entire village through a compelling sense of purpose and accomplishment. She led by example, undaunted by her poverty and not letting anything get in the way of this dream for her village.

- Aravind Eye Care Hospital began with a dream to eliminate unnecessary blindness in India. With its humble beginnings in 1976, in a small town called Madurai in the state of Tamil Nadu in southern India, Aravind

Eye Care is changing the world of blindness through an insight that led to the creation of an exceptional business model that is sustainable because it is profitable. The unique insight was that, of the nearly 24 million blind people in the world, about one-third could be treated with a medical intervention. However, in many cases this intervention requires surgery, and there weren't enough surgeons to cope with this requirement! So, Aravind Eye Care concentrated on increasing a surgeon's productivity—and it did so by a factor of ten—by perfecting the technique of assembly line surgery (the inspiration for this came to one of the founding members as a result of observing how McDonald's ran its operation!). Remarkably, Aravind Eye Care has created a business model where 30 percent of the paying patients enable the remaining 70 percent to be treated free. The business makes a 35 percent operating profit, which in turn is plowed back into expansion.

The dream of an individual changed the lives of many. What began as an eleven-bed hospital in the house of the founder (Dr. Venkataswamy, or Dr. V. as he is popularly known) is now a hospital that treats 2.4 million outpatients and performs over 285,000 cataract surgeries every year. Aravind hires paramedical staff from rural and backward areas, trains them, and gives them more responsibility than other institutions do. So it is not the education that is the differentiator—but the attitude, training, and trust that is invested in people.

- Another well-known inspirational leadership story comes from Bangladesh: the Grameen Bank, founded by an individual, Muhammad Yunus, who believed that the way out of poverty was economic freedom and that the poor have skills that are underutilized. Therefore, if credit could be given to the poor, based on potential, through access to microfinance and technology, they would work themselves out of poverty. Grameen bank has broken all stereotypes by extending micro loans to women and others who have no collateral that have consistently been repaid.

Grameen Bank's success is in a large measure due to its unique structure, which while being formal also incorporates participatory and collaborative approaches, providing effective linkages with existing community structures and the government. These are pivotal to the entire delivery of savings and credit structures. Muhammad Yunus is a leader who has translated and crafted a practical business model that addresses poverty in a fundamental way, by developing and providing an important instrument called micro-finance.

IT IS NOT WHAT WE DO BUT WHAT WE BECOME

The common thread across all these stories is that they revolve around everyday individuals who did not occupy any formal office, and yet who significantly affected the thoughts, feelings, and behavior of a large number of other people, to create something truly meaningful and profound. These leaders have not just fashioned stories but embodied these stories into their everyday life. In that sense they have demonstrated that leadership is less about what we do and more about what we become—and in the process how we influence and learn from those around us.

22

⁊⁊

Moral Leadership in Business

Gerhold K. Becker

LEADERSHIP

Two Contrasting Conceptions

Considerations about moral leadership in business and government are challenged by the hard facts of business reality and inspired by the moral vision of a good life. In anthropological terms, moral leadership stands in the tension between a pessimistic outlook that regards human nature as morally flawed and self-centered and an optimistic perspective that points to the seeds of morality, cooperation, and fairness. "The gulf between how one should live and how one does live is so wide that a man who neglects what is actually done for what should be done moves towards self-destruction rather than self-preservation. The fact is that a man who wants to act virtuously in every way necessarily comes to grief among so many who are not virtuous. Therefore if a prince wants to maintain his rule he must be prepared not to be virtuous, and to make use of this or not according to need" (Machiavelli, 1999, p. 50).

Niccolo Machiavelli's book *The Prince* is arguably one of the most astute leadership manuals ever written that lays bare the mechanism of power and its underlying psychology. Its tenets apply almost as well to a modern corporation

Reprinted by permission of *Journal of International Business Ethics* (Vol. 2, No. 1, 2009).

as to a Renaissance state. In *The Prince* Machiavelli painted for the new class of powerful individuals, who emerged during the Italian Renaissance, a leadership ideal that identifies self-interest as the overriding motivational force, and efficiency as its exclusive purpose. Ethics stands for a nice and lofty ideal that may be admired by simpletons but is ignored by the wise and manipulated for their own purposes by the hard-nosed realists who seek to make the most of the world as it is; they are the real leaders who know how to rule. Their political wisdom is grounded in the following observation: The answer to the question "whether it is better to be loved than feared" is that "one would like to be both the one and the other; but as it is difficult to combine them, it is far better to be feared than loved if you cannot be both. . . . For love is secured by a bond of gratitude which men, wretched creatures that they are, break when it is to their advantage to do so; but fear is strengthened by a dread of punishment that is always effective" (Machiavelli, 1999, p. 54). Note the pessimistic outlook on both human nature and society: human beings are utterly selfish and their destructive tendencies can be held in check only by force from outside.

Now the other view. It presents a powerful concept of leadership that takes a positive and even optimistic approach to human nature. Perhaps for that reason, it never really failed to fascinate, from the early days of Chinese history up to the present. It is the Confucian vision of virtue (de) and morality that lies at the heart of every human activity, particularly at the heart of leadership: "The Master said: Exemplary persons (junzi) understand what is appropriate (yi); petty persons understand what is of personal advantage" (Ames & Rosemont, 4:16). Or: "Wealth and honor are what people want, but if they are the consequence of deviating from the way (dao), I would not have part in them" (Ames & Rosemont, 4:5). Further: "Governing with excellence (de) can be compared to being the North Star: the North Star dwells in its place, and the multitude of stars pay it tribute" (Ames & Rosemont, 2:1). Finally: "If people are proper (zheng) in personal conduct, others will follow suit without need of command. But if they are not proper, even when they command, others will not obey" (Ames & Rosemont, 13:6).

These words of wisdom encapsulate conceptual signposts that mark out the solid ground on which a viable theory of moral leadership can be built that is neither too lofty a construction nor too easily weighed down by fears of futility or pessimism.

The Power of Leadership—A Reminder

Today, leadership has proliferated into many fields and leaders can now be found in various areas of society. While politicians and government leaders are still the most visible representatives of leadership, the enormous financial assets held by multinational corporations, which in some cases exceed the reserves of individual countries, suggest that the power of business leaders may compete with that of governments. In democratic governments, policy decisions typically represent compromises between elected members of parliament, their various factions, coalition partners, and interest groups. Business leaders, however, are accountable only to the shareholders and their board of directors. Bad decisions by government leaders may be remembered in the next elections at the ballot box and lead to the defeat of the government. While business leaders too can be dismissed for bad management or wrong decisions, they are, as various recent examples illustrate, usually handsomely compensated with a golden handshake—and always seem to fall on their feet by quickly finding another top position somewhere else.

Thus one of the questions usually asked when something went wrong is whether the checks and balances of business leaders are really adequate to their power. Business leadership is characterized by asymmetrical power-authority relationships in hierarchical organizations. It can be exercised by "coercion (the possession of, and threat to use, the means of inflicting pain), reward (the possession of, and the promise to bestow, pleasure) and legitimate authority (warrant to speak for the group)" (Newton, 1987, p. 74). Powerful CEOs can close down whole departments that no longer fit in with their favorite business strategy or seem too costly. They can move their factories to low-cost countries, they have the power to "fire or demote, they can pay bonuses and promote, and the organizational chart backs up their right to command the obedience of their subordinates" (Newton, 1987, p. 75). In addition, they are largely in charge of setting the parameters that will define their companies' corporate culture, code of conduct, or operational principles; and this is one aspect of leadership that is of greatest significance in our present context.

In most countries, most notably in the United States, the influence of business leaders even extends well beyond their own enterprises and into the heart of government. Through donations to political parties, lobbying activities, and direct pressure they seek to tip political decisions in their favor. In his farewell speech to the nation almost fifty years ago (17 January 1961), president Dwight D. Eisenhower felt the need to draw attention to one of the most powerful but shady influence groups in his country, for which he coined the term "military-industrial complex." Due to its potential for a "disastrous rise of misplaced power," he called all Americans to "guard against the acquisition of unwarranted influence . . . by the military-industrial complex" (Eisenhower, 1960). At the end of George W. Bush's presidency, it seems that his advice has been largely ignored and the influence of the military-industrial complex on government has only grown stronger.

While in public life it is ultimately the law that sets enforceable limits to business leaders and their deals, the law is neither able nor the best possible tool for the protection of the interests of companies, shareholders, employees, and consumers. This suggests that a new focus on leadership in business is needed and that, above all, it must be on its moral implications.

Semantic Connotations of Leadership

Prior to exploring this moral dimension of business leadership further, we need to reflect in passing on the very terms "leader" or "leadership" as they carry some heavy emotional and normative baggage. Their meaning is historically and socially constructed and thus does not carry everywhere the honorific connotation it seems to have in the English language. In America, the phrase 'he or she is a real leader' is a compliment and leadership the focus of numerous training courses that promise to turn (average) managers into (great) leaders by teaching them some special skills and psychological tricks. The cultural attitude toward the word leadership seems also to influence the direction of research. "In America, leadership has positive moral connotations embedded in it, which may explain why an overwhelming number of articles focus on charismatic, transformational, transforming and, most recently, authentic leadership" (Ciulla, 2005, p. 325).

In Germany and Italy, however, the words Führer and Duce sound very different and recall the dark episodes in their recent histories. This may be one of the reasons why in Germany leadership research is frequently located within an organizational and political discourse that is intertwined with and seeks justification from general ethics. Leadership ethics (Führungsethik) thus is a sub-discipline of managerial ethics, which in turn is a sub-discipline of organizational ethics (Steinmann & Löhr, 1994). The so-called Munich school of economic ethics even integrates it within the basic framework of economic activity or at the "macro" level, since on this view ethical decision making of individuals or organizations are of minor importance as their moral space is seriously limited by the economic system (Homann, 2001).

I will try to steer a middle-course by claiming a genuine moral responsibility for business leaders that is complemented by norms of corporate ethics. I will argue that leadership today would be impoverished if it were exclusively based on power or the fear of punishment. Neither would its implicit assumptions be sound, nor its strategy successful. My thesis is therefore: leadership must be equally based on moral principles and the ethical vision of a good life in the emphatic sense of the term. Its power and authority must have moral legitimacy by extending beyond individual selfishness, and its commitment to ethics must have not merely instrumental, but intrinsic value. That is to say, the moral dimension that gives leadership its authenticity transforms leaders from power-hungry individuals into persons respected by peers and subordinates alike. Moral leaders represent values that are not confined to the secrecy of boardrooms and centers of power but are universally recognized as the fundamental building blocks of a life worth living.

FOUNDATIONS OF MORAL LEADERSHIP

The Standard View of Business Leadership

Much of the skepticism about moral leadership in business is grounded in the strange but popular assumption that business operates in amoral space and any concern for ethics is either unproductive or outright detrimental. Why then would 'good' companies need moral leaders? For some, the very term 'business ethics' is little more than an oxymoron: either you do business, or you are ethical; you can't have both. It is not really surprising that such a view also affects the public perception of business leaders. Only a handful of them is seen as committed to moral principles, quite a number are regarded as outright immoral and unethical, but the vast majority is thought to be amoral as they lack moral awareness and believe that business is something like an ethics-free zone without a moral dimension. According to a recent survey, only nine percent of Germans have faith in business leaders and trust them; among all the elites, business leaders rank last—and that was even before the global economic crisis (Jörges, 2008).

If we examine the philosophical implications of this view a little more deeply, we discover a specific picture of humanity, human agency, and—in particular—of the business person. In ideal-typical overexposure, it is the picture of the lonely, highly rational individual whose sole interest is self-preservation. All actions are, ultimately, motivated by self-interest. In a world in which everyone is my potential enemy, self-preservation is always a shifting goal, since I can never know how much self-protection is enough. This explains much of the stressful dynamics of modern life, particularly in business and politics, which requires ever increasing efforts to secure (individual and collective) survival.

It is an extension of this view that sees business exclusively defined by economic factors, which are driven by the rationality of individual self-interest. This is the familiar construct of the homo economicus that still holds sway over many. While they may complain about the cold world of self-interest, they have nevertheless resigned to it as the best possible playground for doing business, since it still holds the promise of general predictability of human interaction. On the assumption of self-interest as the sole motivation in each and every market player, the specter of irrational markets gives way to the calculations of economics and its scientific models of markets and consumer behavior. To the extent that ethical values do in fact hold influence on the general public, economists of this persuasion tend to regard it as an aberration in the system that can be taken care of either by mere conformity of economic activity with ethical norms, or by instrumentalizing ethics as a means to increase profit. It is not important whether something is being done for genuine ethical reasons, all that counts is that it is seen as such by the general public. If ethics helps increase profit, all the better and it will be employed exactly as long as it delivers.

To illustrate this point, look at environmental concerns. Since the public cares about the environment and expects business to minimize ecological damage, companies around the globe all of a sudden have discovered their heart for nature and are presenting themselves as environmentally responsible actors. Not everyone, however, is sincere, and in a number of cases critics have argued that what is being claimed as environmental responsibility amounts in fact to little more than "green-washing." Companies are proud to take credit for some well publicized protective measures, but hide the fact that they still cling to their old and wasteful ways of production.

A case in point is the trading of environmental certificates under the Clean Development Mechanism (CDM), an offshoot from the Kyoto Protocol that allows the crediting of emission reductions from greenhouse gas abatement projects in developing countries. Ten years after the adoption of the Kyoto Protocol, the CDM has become an immense global market of a value of several billion Euros. Yet the CDM has also recently been heavily criticized for not delivering on its environmental and sustainable development objectives. In various instances, companies simply bought certificates without assuring the stipulated additionality of sustainable development projects in developing countries. The overall contribution of the CDM to assisting host countries to achieve sustainable development is therefore rather small.

Similar doubts have been raised about some companies' honesty in their commitment to Corporate Social Responsibility (CSR). Since good CSR seems to increase the value of companies, it is tempting to use it for the appeasement of a weary public and to avert legislation on emission standards that would decrease profit.

The philosophy of self-interest and self-preservation is thus incapable to recognize any genuine role for ethics in business transactions and instead responds to conflicts through evasion of responsibility and make-belie[ve]. The famous Kantian alternative between acting merely in conformity with moral principles and acting on moral principles is unavailable. Though this picture of the human being has been painted in rough strokes, it may explain some of the deep-seated aversion against a positive role of ethics in business. At the same time it challenges us to reconsider the question about the public relevance of ethics.

Societal Relevance of Ethics

Recently, the standard model of business activity has lost ground. In one of the most frequently cited new papers of experimental economics, Gary E. Bolton and Axel Ockenfels have argued that it is psychologically flawed by inadequate moral assumptions. While it takes for granted that people are guided solely by selfish, particularly pecuniary concerns, in reality people care about other things as well. In accordance with psychologists and sociologists, their research has identified several non-pecuniary motives as important drivers of behavior—above all concerns for fairness and reciprocity. "Social preference models assume that traders care about their own monetary payoff but that some traders may additionally be concerned with the social impact of their behavior. Reciprocity models conjecture that people tend to be kind in response to kindness and unkind in response to unkindness, while fairness models posit that some individuals may have a preference for equitably sharing the efficiency gains from trade" (Bolton & Ockenfels, 2006). On their account, economic theory underestimates the degree of fairness in business transactions. Instead of reducing business to self-interest and market forces, they see it dominated by the ERC [Ethics Resources Center] triple principle: equity, reciprocity, and competition.

What is missing in the standard view is the perspective in which we see ourselves not only as role-bearers and functionaries of economic systems but also as social beings and morally concerned citizens with a shared history of beliefs about "the good life." As social beings, we can only expect to further our self-interest when we recognize the needs of others as well. The necessary rules for effective cooperation between individual players are not only the result of rational behavior and economic prudence but derive also from the common interest in "the good."

We should remind ourselves that, as a matter of fact, business never lacks moral background institutions and internalized normative standards, and would be impossible without them. We all depend on them and usually take for granted that we can trust each other, that people normally keep their promises, and that they are not without compassion or a sense of justice. The amorality of business may therefore indeed be a myth (DeGeorge, 1993) that is still characteristic of certain types of economic theory but not of business culture in general, despite all the scandals and widespread moral shortcomings of individuals. Thus a truly amoral economic system, should it be feasible at all, would have to be parasitic on the embedded ethical norms the average citizen could normally be expected to adhere to. It is like truth-telling and lying: A lie can only do the trick when people normally tell the truth so that it can take advantage of their truthfulness as a parasite feeds on its healthy host. In conclusion, the business of business is not business but human flourishing, and this cannot be had without ethics.

Ethics and Economic Space

If all this is true, then moral leadership is based on the assumption that business is not exclusively determined by economic and social forces, as these would leave no space for moral decision-making. The economic system as well as its key players depend on, and thus benefit from, the common ethos that they did not generate on their own. Even the autonomy of the economic system is not absolute, contrary to popular perception, and its rules do not have the status of immutable laws of nature. Instead, it is the product of human culture whose further development can be directed in accordance with human needs and the moral vision of the good society.

Business leaders therefore retain sufficient space for responsible acting even within the parameters of economic imperative, i.e. profitability, and its constraining objectivity. Economic rationality is relative to cultural settings and societal preferences, and both the economic and the ethical are interrelated dimensions of human agency. What lacks economic rationality is lacking in justice as well, and what contradicts human justice cannot really be economically rational (Rich, 2006). In other words, business leaders are not simply prisoners of the economic system. They do have a choice.

Ethics as the Heart of Leadership

If ethics does in fact play an important role in society, or if human flourishing is possible only on the basis of internalized moral norms, then business actions—like all other human actions—have a moral dimension that can neither be ignored nor be merely superficially attended to. Thus business leaders must walk the talk and instead of paying lip-service and engaging in some ethical window-dressing, they must genuinely be concerned about ethics.

In the words of Confucius this reads as follows: "Exemplary persons (junzi) first accomplish what they are going to say, and only then say it" (Ames & Rosemont, 2:13). They would also feel "shame if their words were better than their deeds" (Ames & Rosemont, 14:27). This is echoed in modern companies. In the BASF statement of Vision, Values, and Principles we read: "We act in accordance with our words and Values. We comply with the laws and respect the good business practices of the countries in which we operate." Needless to say, the test case for such statements has come when profit and ethics clash, or rather seem to clash, and in the mind of the average manager and business leader, this is regarded as the standard situation. It is then tempting for ethics consultants to prove, or at least try to prove that ethics in fact pays and that this should be a sufficient reason to behave ethically even in difficult situations. While such a strategy of selling ethics as a means for greater profit may be psychologically advisable so as to persuade doubting and reluctant business leaders to do what would be morally required of them, we should be mindful that ethics is not for sale and must not be traded off against profit. We may manoeuvre as long as we like, in the end it will be decisive whether or not we believe in such a simple truth that former Bosch CEO Hans Merkle summarized in one sentence: "There are certain things an honest person simply does not do—period."

Obviously, the coincidence of ethics and good business on the one hand and the reasons for behaving ethically on the other are two quite different concerns. To argue that ethics will "enhance the bottom line" offers little more than "an easy, prudentially acceptable, attractive, and enticing reason for business to be ethical" (Cohen, 1999, p. 15). It ignores, however, the fact that every one of us, including business leaders, stands under the moral obligation. The ethical imperative demands that one does first what is good and right and just—and looks for personal gain later.

There is a long tradition in moral philosophy East and West arguing that ethics is never only a means of profit or well-being but an integral and most fundamental component of what we call the good life. When the ancient Chinese philosopher Mencius went to see King Hui of Liang and the latter expected him to "profit" his state, Mencius replied: "Your Majesty, what is the point of mentioning the word 'profit'? All that matters is that there should be benevolence and righteousness. If Your Majesty says, 'How can I profit my state?' and the Counselors say, 'How can I profit my family?' and the Gentlemen and

Commoners say, 'How can I profit my person?' then those above and below will be trying to profit at the expense of one another and the state will be imperiled. . . . If profit is put before righteousness, there is no satisfaction short of total usurpation" (Mencius, 1984, 1A:1).

Again, this typical statement from the Confucian tradition is not as "ancient" as it may at first appear: Leadership consultant Peter Koestenbaum recalls a business leader who came across his true self: "I am the top executive in a very large organization and I live with a deep conflict. There is a fundamental 'bad' in business, a pervasive cancer. Business lives in a cutthroat, ruthless, dishonest atmosphere. You do what it takes and care nothing about morality. You are not true to your word. In the end, you cheat, deceive, and lie. Eventually, even the most determined among us must contract this disease. This presents me with a fundamental dilemma: Can you win being 'good'?" And he states in his own words what I call the priority of ethics: "I do not want to take on the characteristics that disturb me in some of my colleagues" (Koestenbaum, 2002, p. 127).

Obviously, the moral imperative cannot be ignored indefinitely. There is a moral self in each of us, which proves that ethics defines our very humanity. The vision we hold of the "good" life in the emphatic sense of the term gives priority to moral principles and values that certainly include reciprocal relationships of justice, trust, sympathy, compassion, and care. If we need another warning about the unpleasant alternatives, Thomas Hobbes is a good witness. He reminds us very clearly that the options we have for individual and social life outside moral norms are either the severe restriction of human freedom through an overpowering government that alone can secure collective survival, or—the war of all against all in which life will be "solitary, poor, nasty, brutish, and short" (Hobbes, 1981, p. 186).

TWO MAJOR FACTORS OF MORAL LEADERSHIP

Moral Leadership, Character, and Authenticity

If we now look a little more closely at the most important characteristics and practical requirements of moral leadership, we will quickly notice that they have an individual and an organizational dimension. For Bill George, former chairman and CEO of Medtronic, the world's leading medical technology company, the various qualities of a moral leader can be summarized in one word: authenticity. It is the "most important characteristic one has to have to be a leader." It stands for moral commitment to a purpose or a mission: Authentic leaders "are people who live by their values every day and who know the true north of their moral compass." "Without a moral compass, any leader can wind up like the executives who are facing possible prison sentences today because they lacked a sense of right and wrong" (George, 2003, p. 20).

Not everyone, however, agrees. Rainer Niermeyer, a psychologist and Kienbaum Management Consultant, has argued that in today's business environment of lean management, shareholder value, and fierce competition, authenticity is the best recipe for self-destruction. In his view, it is not the quality of authenticity that is required of business leaders, but the ability to convincingly play any role, including the role of the authentic leader. Authentic leaders are simply incapable of responding to ever changing business environments with the appropriate role. His prudential imperative is therefore: grasp the expectations of your business environment and perform the role in which you can answer them best.

I submit to disagree. If it is true that amoral business is a myth, business leadership has an indispensable moral dimension that must not be ignored in daily operations and strategic decisions. Leaders without a moral backbone who change roles as fast as they change their clothes will quickly lose trust and will be seen as people who lack sincerity and honesty. When business consultants James M. Kouzes and Barry Z. Posner asked in a survey of thousands of managers what they wanted in their leaders, honesty came out on top (87%). The authors concluded: "Honesty is absolutely essential to leadership. After all, if we are willing to follow someone, whether it be into battle or into the boardroom, we first want to assure ourselves that the person is worthy of our trust. We want to know that he or she is being truthful, ethical, and principled. We want to be fully confident in the integrity of our leaders" (Kouzes & Posner, 1993, p. 255).

It is universally agreed that a good reputation is one of the most important business assets. Good reputation, however, must be earned through a proven commitment to honesty and sincerity—and that is what gives a leader his or her authenticity. Unfortunately, the authentic commitment to moral values is one of the earliest casualties when the going gets rough and the morally tough are no longer going. This has as much to do with human psychology as with the basic function of business: business is no charity, but looks for profit as the well-deserved reward for all the troubles that come with it in the first place. In Milton Friedman's memorable phrase: "there is one and only one social responsibility of business—to use its resources and engage in activities designed to increase its profits." Yet he adds a phrase that is frequently ignored: "to increase its profits—so long as it stays within the rules of the game, which is to say, engages in open and free competition, without deception or fraud" (Friedman, 1962, p.133). As we have seen, those rules of the game are not and cannot be exclusively defined by business. Most obviously, they are derived from the law and grounded in common morality.

The line that separates the genuine desire for profit from greed is, however, rather thin. From the perspective of self-interest as sole motivation in business, the temptation is nearly overwhelming to do whatever it takes to increase profit. Critics have argued that the current financial crisis has one of its major causes in instruments of remuneration for top executives that link salaries to short-term increases in company value and encourage risky or even irresponsible business operations through attractive bonuses and share options. It is the carrot-approach without the stick that fuels greed and ignores accountability. Economist and Nobel laureate Myron Scholes has therefore suggested a radical change in the remuneration system, which should exclusively be tied to long-term business success.

While this may prevent some irresponsible operations motivated by greed, moral leadership requires more. Most fundamental is what may be called moral sensibility, a sense for right and wrong, and a competence of signaling morally relevant elements in business situations. Moral leaders will also need to develop a competence for moral reasoning and the ability to argue convincingly on moral grounds. This competence is of particular importance in today's media society and communication age where various groups challenge not only individual business operations but the capitalist free-market society as a whole. Business leaders should not shy away from taking part in the debate about social values and market systems and be capable of persuasively explaining strategic decisions to an ethically doubtful public.

Moral Leadership and Organizational Structure

Moral leadership, however, is not restricted to individuals only, but includes business organizations and corporations as well. The best qualities of moral leadership are useless unless they are embedded in a supportive company structure. That is to say, moral leadership not only interacts with internal environments, corporate cultures, and hierarchical structures, it also influences their development.

While leaders may be the most visible representatives of an enterprise, companies, particularly corporations, are themselves moral agents with their own sets of values and objectives. CEOs come and go, while companies are usually there for the long term. Corporations are moral persons on equal footing with natural persons with all the privileges, rights, and duties moral persons normally have. In France and the UK, companies and not only individuals can be sued and brought before the courts. In Germany, in the wake of recent scandals, calls for a criminal law for corporations have become louder. The head of the European Anti-Fraud Office (OLAF), Franz-Hermann Brüner, proposed to blacklist corrupt companies and to temporarily exclude them from applying for new contracts.

The public too expects companies to be committed to moral standards so as to earn the moral license to operate. Organizational ethics of leadership must therefore be seen as an operational factor and not merely as an expense or cost factor. Internally, a variety of company-wide mechanisms have become available that seek to bring moral leadership to bear. They include codes of ethics, mission or core value statements, ethical training programs and reporting channels for ethical grievances (ethics office).

Thus ethical principles help define the corporate mission, determine obligations to various constituencies, and set guidelines for the organization's policies and practices. While in some cases unethical behavior of managers may have its root causes in character flaws, most often in greed and selfishness, in other instances it is facilitated by a lack of guidelines or by conflicting guidelines. Surveys indicate that many ethics violations by mid-level managers signal in fact conflicts of loyalty resulting from their leaders' inconclusive, ambiguous, or outright misleading value statements and personal behavior. Harvard business ethicist Lynn Sharp Paine recalls how she once met a businessman on a plane who told her frankly that his job was to be "a liar": After his company had been bought by a large global enterprise his first truthful report as regional manager was received with such hostile response "that he never again dared to tell the truth." Since then he regularly fabricated reports for headquarters (Sharp Paine, 2003, p. 40).

It is easy to condemn this manager for false reporting and dishonesty. Yet, the company's leadership failed even more severely by encouraging a climate of untruthfulness and not defining clear and unambiguous values. Its insensitivity to the humiliating treatment of its employees produced an unethical environment that would undermine not only its reputation but also its profitability.

Morally committed leaders will therefore not only define their companies' values and principles, they will also pay close attention to value ambiguities. They will take measures to assure the development of moral sensibility and morally sound judgment in their subordinates and throughout the company. Through exemplary behavior, compliance standards, and ethics training of employees, they will see to it that the moral point of view becomes an integral part of company performance and strategy.

A written code enables an organization to clarify standards that may otherwise be vague expectations left to individual interpretation. Where there is disagreement, codes can achieve a certain degree of consensus. Codes are also effective means to disseminate easily understandable rules and principles to all employees, including top-down from leaders and management to front-line employees. A code that is enforceable and enforced in an organization provides employees with a tool for resisting pressures to perform unethical or illegal actions. Thus it will encourage as well as protect employees to do what is right.

BASF's statement of their Vision, Values, and Principles is just one such example; it stands in glaring contrast to companies that pressure their employees to report only what the top wants to hear. Among the key values, BASF lists mutual respect and integrity. The principles that translate the values into action-guiding statements include: "We involve our employees in work and decision processes in a timely manner through open communication and information sharing not hindered by hierarchical and organizational boundaries." "Every executive is expected to be a role model and to set an appropriate example in accordance with our Vision and Values. We abstain

- from any practice that is illegal
- from any practice that violates fair trade" (BASF, 2004).

There are many ways how moral leaders can tie the strategic interests of their companies to common morality. Yet above all, they must recognize the fundamental importance of issues of human rights, global justice, and environmental sustainability. One possibility is the adoption of global codes that apply the moral point of view to all areas of business activities. They include codes of corporate responsibility as well as international standards concerning labor practices, corruption, and the environment. Examples are: The UN Global Compact (which since its official launch on 26 July 2000 has grown to more than 5600 participants, including over 4300 businesses in 120 countries around the world); the Global Reporting Initiative (GRI); the UN Convention Against Corruption (UNCAC); and Transparency International.

Corporate Ethics and Compliance

The best codes, however, are not worth the paper on which they are printed if business leaders do not ensure that they are adhered to, especially when times are rough—and that means: always. In the final analysis, it is individuals who will determine the ethical quality of business conduct. Many companies still seem to regard their codes as what business ethicist Daryl Koehn has called "good times" codes of ethics that presuppose "that everything is going well with the core business, but doesn't address what happens when the core business is under attack"(Millman, 2002, p. 17).

Once upon a time there was a famous accounting firm by the name of Anderson, whose biggest client was Enron. Both had codes of ethics, and their executives presented them at every occasion. They even gave public talks on their companies' mission and values and talked as if they did indeed believe in them. But as it turned out, they never cared to bother about values or codes. When Enron's voluminous code of ethics got in the way of doing what management wanted done, its board was easily persuaded to lay aside certain provisions—most notoriously, the conflict-of-interest provision. And when everything collapsed, Anderson shredded all its accounting documents, and the large numbers of unused ethics codes were eventually auctioned off at Ebay. This final act was in fact the last in a long series of continuous betrayals of company values. Over a number of years, Anderson sold its soul and with it its reputation to its clients. The firm gradually compromised their values more and more, just to make money. As one observer noticed, what looks at first glance as a giant step in destroying documents was to them just another step in sacrificing values for greed (George, 2003, p. 75).

What we can learn from this is that no code can ever work unless its operation is embedded in a company's culture, and accepted by all concerned, particularly the leaders at the top. Yet the development of a corporate culture takes time as it involves habits of mind and action that are only produced through the continued, sincere upholding of company values and principles and the encouragement to abide by them. Eventually, this will set parameters of good practice the individual employee and manager can hardly ignore. Codes of ethics can only be useful when they are clearly linked to the daily operations, and this can be achieved most effectively by building adherence to standards into management systems, into performance evaluation, compensation, audit, and control.

Siemens: The Costs of Neglecting Moral Leadership

What is at stake when business leaders ignore good ethical practice and companies lose their ethical reputation can be illustrated by one of the latest scandals. Siemens was recently embroiled in a huge corruption scandal that has severely shaken the confidence of a once proud and self-conscious Siemens "community," tarnished its reputation, and caused substantial financial losses. Like most large corporations, Siemens had a code of ethics and a code of business conduct, was an early subscriber (2003) to the ten principles of the UN Global Compact, and proudly proclaimed to place high priority on principles of corporate responsibility. Its Code of Ethics for Financial Matters required of every employee, among others, to:

(1) act with honesty and integrity and avoid actual and apparent conflicts of interest in personal and professional relationships;
(6) promote proactively ethical behavior as a responsible partner among colleagues and subordinates;
(7) comply with all applicable laws, guidelines and regulations.

Its Business Conduct Guidelines stated unambiguously:

A3. We are open and honest and stand by our responsibility. We are reliable partners who make no promises we cannot keep.
A4. Every manager must earn their respect by exemplary personal behavior, performance, openness, and social competence. He/she shall set clear, ambitious, and realistic goals, lead by trust and confidence and leave the employees as much individual responsibility and leeway as possible.

In section B2 Offering and Granting Advantages, the guidelines read: "Client gifts to business partner employees must be selected so as to avoid any appearance of bad faith or impropriety in the mind of the recipient. No employee may directly or indirectly offer or grant unjustified advantages to others in connection with business dealings, neither in monetary form nor as some other advantage. Gifts must not be made to public officials or other civil servants." Its value statement listed responsibility above all else and defined it as being committed to ethical actions.

In spite of all this, in his Foreword to the company's 2007 Corporate Responsibility Report the new Siemens President and CEO, Peter Löscher, had to admit: "Siemens—as a global enterprise—also has an impact on social developments, the single most important expectation is that our conduct be flawless from an ethical standpoint. The fact that our company made mistakes here in the past is a painful realization" (Siemens, 2008). What went wrong in the company that was once considered a role model for corporate Germany?

In May 2007, two former mid-level managers—Andreas Kley, a former finance chief at Siemens's power-generation unit, and Horst Vigener, a consultant—were convicted of paying about 6 million Euros in bribes from 1999 to 2002 to help Siemens win gas-turbine supply contracts with Enel, a state-owned Italian energy company. The contracts were valued at approximately 450 million Euros ($609 million). The managers explained their actions, which they knew were illegal, with last-minute demands from their Italian contractor. They believed they acted "in the interest of the company," since only by paying the money could Siemens secure the contract and enter the Italian market. They did not benefit personally from the deal. The court convicted them of bribery and ordered the company to pay a fine of 38 million Euros ($51.4 million).

The Darmstadt trial was the first verdict in a widening corruption scandal that engulfed the engineering and electronics giant with more than 400,000 employees worldwide and revenue of 72.4 billion Euros in the fiscal year 2007. In the meantime, prosecutors around the world formally launched bribery investigations against Siemens. They include the US Justice Department and the US Securities and Exchange Commission as well as prosecutors in Hungary, Indonesia, Norway, Israel, Italy, and Russia. In China, Siemens is (or was) under investigation in a number of jurisdictions including Guangdong, Jilin, Xian, Wuxi, Shanghai, Ting Hu, Shandong, Hunan, and Guiyang.

The case against a former Siemens manager who was recently convicted by a court in Munich of several counts of breach of trust revealed not only the massive scale of corruption in the company but also a lack of moral leadership at the top. On 27 July 2008 and after a two-month trial, Reinhard Siekaczek, a former manager at the ICN fixed-line telephone network division, received a two-year suspended sentence and a 108,000 Euros fine. He got off relatively lightly, since his comprehensive cooperation with the prosecution helped reveal the complex and highly sophisticated corruption and bribery mechanisms that had gradually developed in Siemens for at least a period of six years, from 2000 to 2006. The prosecution could prove that a system of bribery was installed, and that Siekaczek had set up slush funds and "used an impenetrable system of sham contracts, which didn't allow any control once Siemens money was paid out" (Matussek, 2008). Siemens has acknowledged that a total of 1.3 billion Euros of "unclear payments" were made during the period.

Yet the most damaging allegations were leveled against the Siemens leadership. The defendant claimed that the complex network of shell corporations he used to siphon off company money was installed with full knowledge of the whole sectoral management. Everyone knew that "commissions" were to secure orders, although this matter was handled "very discreetly" with only a very small circle of people in the know. Siekaczek testified that his superiors had even told him to create a new payment system after paying bribes abroad became a criminal offense in Germany in 1998. He said at a meeting with four managers in 2002 he was given the job of organizing the payments. "It was naturally clear to all that this does not correspond to the law," he said, adding that their attitude was: "We're not doing it for ourselves, but for the firm" (Marquart, 2008).

Once the scandal broke, all that Siemens could do to minimize the disastrous fallout was to admit its wrongdoings, replace its tarnished top leadership, and aggressively attack the cancer of corruption top-down through a variety of measures. One of the first steps taken by the new CEO, who came from outside the company, was the declaration that anti-corruption measures are now a priority for the senior management. This was backed up by the appointment of a Chief Compliance Officer (19 September 2007) and by the institution of a new directorate "Law and Compliance" on the Siemens Managing Board. In fiscal 2007, Siemens imposed personnel sanctions on a total of around 500 employees for violation of external regulations or internal policies. The contracts of thirty percent of those employees were terminated and eight percent were punished with salary deductions. The rest received either a reprimand or a warning.

Furthermore, Siemens consolidated all its internal anti-corruption regulations within a single, easy-to-use source, the Siemens Compliance Guide Anti-Corruption, and distributed it to every employee throughout the company. It set up a Compliance Help Desk with an "Ask us" function as central contact point for employees with questions related to matters of compliance and corruption. The second function of the Compliance Help Desk is a "Tell us" function that gives employees and all external stakeholders the opportunity to report any indications of possible violations of the Business Conduct Guidelines, on the assurance that reports are neither traced nor registered. Siemens also stepped up its anti-corruption and ethics training program and claims that between February and October 2007, 1,400 managerial employees enrolled and a total of 36,000 employees completed a web-based training program on the specific rules and regulations to be observed in money transfers, accounting, and the handling of gifts; it expects that up to 100,000 employees will complete this training program. Siemens appointed an independent compliance consultant who will advise the Board of Directors and regularly report to the Chief Compliance Officer. In the first two quarters of 2008, Siemens paid 302 million Euros for external compliance consultants and cleaning-up measures. In the meantime, Siemens has confirmed to press charges against and seek damages from eleven former top managers, including former chairman of the supervisory board, Heinrich von Pierer, and former CEO Klaus Kleinfeld.

CONCLUSION

Andreas Pohlmann, the new Siemens Chief Compliance Officer, summarized the task ahead as follows: "Integrity management requires the acceptance of responsibility at all levels of the company. This is not just a matter of being aware of and complying with rules and guidelines. Effective integrity management goes much further: it involves a credible dialogue based on trust, with corresponding communication across all hierarchical levels. Only then can the necessary change process be initiated and acceptance established among the workforce" (Pohlmann, 2008).

In the end, it is ethics that counts and it is ethics that sets the benchmark for true excellence and success in business as in personal life. Only when it has been understood and accepted that moral leadership is a business asset and a fundamental company value, the market economy can be sustainable and financial systems of benefit to all.

References
Ames, R. T., & Rosemont, H., Jr. (1998). *The analects of Confucius: A philosophical translation*. New York: The Ballantine Publishing Group.

BASF (2004). Vision, values, principles. Retrieved from http://www.basf.com/group/corporate/en/function/conversions:/publish/content/about-basf/vision-values-principles/images/Vision_Values_Principles_BASF.pdf.

Bolton, G. E., & Ockenfels, A. (2006). The limits of trust in economic transactions: Investigations of perfect reputation systems. Retrieved February 5, 2009, from http://ockenfels.uni-koeln.de/uploads/tx_ockmedia/Bolton_Ockenfels_Limits_of_Trust.pdf.

Ciulla, J. B. (2005). The state of leadership ethics and the work that lies before us. *Business Ethics: A European Review,* 14(4), 323–335.

Cohen, S. (1999). Good ethics is good business—revisited. *Ethics and Society,* 7(1), 10–16.

DeGeorge, R. (1993). *Competing with integrity in international business.* New York: Oxford University Press.

Eisenhower, D. D. (1960). Military-industrial complex speech. In Public Papers of the Presidents, Dwight D. Eisenhower: 1035–1040. http://coursesa.matrix .msu.edu/~hst306/documents/indust.html.

Friedman, M. (1962). *Capitalism and freedom.* Chicago: University of Chicago Press.

George, B. (2003). *Authentic leadership: Rediscovering the secrets to creating lasting value.* San Francisco: Jossey-Bass.

Hobbes, T. (1981). *Leviathan.* C. B. Macpherson (Ed.). Harmondsworth: Penguin Books.

Homann, K. (2001). Ökonomik: Fortsetzung der Ethik mit anderen Mitteln. In G. Siebeck (Ed.), *Artibus ingenuis* (pp. 85–110). Tübingen: Mohr-Siebeck.

Jörges, H.-U. (2008). Die Knute der Rendite. *Stern,* 36, 56.

Koestenbaum, P. (2002). *Leadership: The inner side of greatness: A philosophy for leaders.* San Francisco: Jossey-Bass.

Kouzes, J. M. & Posner, B. Z. (1993). *Credibility: How leaders gain and lose it, why people demand it.* San Francisco: Jossey-Bass.

Machiavelli, N. (1999). *The prince.* London: Penguin Books.

Marquart, M. (2008, May 26). Reinhard Siekaczek, former Siemens AG manager, testifies at corruption trial: bribery and slush funds. The Huffington Post. Retrieved from http://www.huffingtonpost.com/.

Matussek, K. (2008, July 28). Ex-Siemens manager is convicted at corruption trial. Bloomberg.com. Retrieved from http://www.bloomberg.com/.

Millman, G. J. (2002). New scandals, old lessons: financial ethics after Enron. *Financial Executive,* 18(5), 16–19.

Newton, L. (1987). Moral leadership in business: The role of structure. *Business and Professional Ethics Journal,* 5(3–4), 74–90.

Pohlmann, A. A new direction for Siemens. Improving preventive systems. *Compact Quarterly.* Retrieved July 14, 2008, from http://www.enewsbuilder.net/globalcompact /e_article001149152.cfm?x=bd2Hd2m,b2QLrDD5.

Rich, A. (2006). *Business and economic ethics: The ethics of economic systems.* Leuven: Peeters Publishers.

Schneider, L. (2007). Is the CDM fulfilling its environmental and sustainable development objectives? An evaluation of the CDM and options for improvement. *Re-*

port prepared for WWF. Berlin: Institute for Applied Ecology. Retrieved from http://assets.panda.org/downloads/oeko_institut2007 is_the_cdm_fulfilling_its _environmental_and_sustainable_developme.pdf.

Sharp Paine, L. (2003). *Value shift: Why companies must merge social and financial imperatives to achieve superior performance.* New York: McGraw-Hill.

Siemens. (2008). Corporate Responsibility. Report 2007. Retrieved from http://w1 .siemens.com/responsibility/report/07/en/statement.htm.

Steinmann H. & Löhr, A. (1994). *Grundlagen der Unternehmensethik.* Stuttgart: Schäffer-Poeschel.

23

&

Leadership and Advocacy

Dual Roles for Corporate Social Responsibility and Social Entrepreneurship

Manuel London

When we think about corporate leadership, we generally don't think about the role of social advocate. Yet advocacy has become increasingly important as organizations recognize their social obligations to stockholders and the communities in which they operate. In for-profit organizations, corporate social responsibility has become a competitive advantage and, sometimes, a way to generate new revenue streams. Corporate leaders become advocates for social causes such as environmental sustainability, education, health, and economic conditions that generate employment opportunities, pay fair wages, and reduce poverty. Corporate social action takes place locally and globally. In addition, corporate advocacy addresses issues that affect employees and the organization's bottom line, such as policies for health benefits, work-family balance, and working conditions. Corporate officers spearhead solutions to these issues within their own organization and in the corporate community at large. In not-for-profit organizations that have social advocacy as their principal aim, the founder/advocate is an entrepreneur, generating organization structures that respond to situational conditions, including beneficiaries' needs,

Reprinted by permission of *Organizational Dynamics* (Vol. 37, No. 4, 2008). Copyright 2008 Elsevier Inc.

availability of financial and non-financial support, and existence of adversaries and those who stand to lose if the organization's goals are met. These advocates must become effective leaders.

The roles of leader and advocate are complementary. Leaders need to understand and develop their role as advocate and recognize how it fits with other roles and requirements of organizational leadership. Advocates need to understand and develop their role as leader as they garner support and create organizations to accomplish their advocacy goals. This article describes advocacy processes, examines conditions that encourage and discourage advocacy, and recommends ways for corporate leaders to be more effective advocates and for social entrepreneurs to be more effective leaders.

DEFINING ADVOCACY

Advocacy is the act of supporting an idea, need, person, or group. Social advocates take public action to engender fair treatment or further the cause of people in need who can't speak for themselves (or do so effectively). The goal may be to promote social welfare in general (e.g., protect the environment) and/or improve the conditions of individuals or groups (e.g., bring aid to a village in Africa that is desperate for food, clothing, health care, and education). The benefits may be direct, visible, and immediate, such as sheltering the homeless, or they may be indirect and long-term, such as raising money for medical research that will cure cancer some day. Advocates speak out and take action to effect change, often overcoming resistance. They increase awareness of an issue and generate positive attitudes. They recruit and retain volunteers who become advocates themselves. They influence government policies. They deliver services, raise money, and build organizations to sustain their advocacy goals.

Advocacy as a general process happens all the time within corporations. Leaders advocate for ideas and issues that promote organizational profitability, quality, and performance. They advocate for corporate social responsibility in a variety of ways linked to the organization's contribution to the community, for instance, donating to the arts or other charities, promoting ethical decisions, or being sensitive to the environment. These initiatives may affect the bottom line directly through product improvement or increased sales or indirectly through good publicity and recruitment of talented employees.

Corporate social responsibility is more than demonstrating concern for the environment, fair business practices, and socially responsible business decisions. It can entail making extra efforts to improve social welfare. Fortunately, we have many examples of corporate leaders who extended themselves and their organizations to donate efforts and profits.

SOME EXAMPLES

Jonathan Schwartz, President and Chief Executive Officer, Sun Microsystems, wrote in the Sun's 2007 CSR Report that the company is "100% committed to developing and adhering to principles that guide our actions in business and social conduct . . . to enable the sharing of knowledge and technologies for positive social and environmental impact." Raytheon's chairman, William H. Swanson, stated in the company's 2006 annual report that Raytheon is "committed to creating dramatic and lasting change through strategic charitable giving." He cited the company's focus on supporting math and science education with MathMovesU, an online system designed to inspire middle school students to study math. Businesses mesh charity with profit-making missions. Ben and Jerry's and Newman's Own come to mind. John Sage established a Fair Trade coffee business, Pura Vida, to fund programs for the poor. Lee Zimmerman's Evergreen Lodge outside of Yosemite National Park hires promising young people from low-income areas.

There are numerous examples of advocates becoming social entrepreneurs, founding and leading organizations to promote their advocacy goals. Some are common household names, such as Al Gore, whose Nobel Prize winning initiatives focused attention on global environmental issues, Bill Gates, whose foundation is working to eradicate illness and poverty, and Jimmy Carter, whose support of Habitat for Humanity helped the organization gain worldwide attention. Others are unsung, local heroes. For instance, Pattye Pece and her associates, Jonathan and Vanessa Langer, founded a totally volunteer-operated, not-for-profit Fair Trade store in Hampton Bays, New York, to provide funds for AIDS-orphaned children in Kenya and Zambia. Mary Ann Bell founded a soup kitchen for the homeless in Port Jefferson, New York. David Krause, a paleontologist, started a school and health clinic in a remote area of Madagascar, the location of his discovery of predatory dinosaur remains. Patricia Wright, another anthropologist working in Madagascar, founded the national Ranomafana rain forest to protect the environment and rare species of the area.

Now consider two role models who demonstrate leadership for social advocacy: an executive who spearheads corporate social responsibility initiatives and an emerging successful social entrepreneur. They are father and son.

Stanley M. Bergman has been Chairman and CEO of Henry Schein, Inc. since 1989. A CPA educated in South Africa, he is responsible for the firm's substantial growth and financial success and the continuation of a cutting edge social mission that has been a hallmark of the firm since its founding in 1932. The company distributes healthcare products and services to office-based clinicians (dentists, dental labs, physicians, veterinarians, and government and other institutions) throughout North America, Europe, Australia and New Zealand. Stanley Bergman started with the firm in the early 1980s and worked closely with its founder, Henry Schein, to grow the business, and with it, the company's tradition of social action. They forged a commitment to understand community problems and ways their resources could be used effectively to respond to current needs and prepare for emergencies. The company structures its social mission into categories that allow tracking and reporting contributions and results. Bergman communicates his personal and corporate values through a history of action and social justice that is a legacy for the firm's future. The company has a global social responsibility program to support health care advocacy and education, increase access to care for underserved populations, prepare and respond to disasters, and generally strengthen community wellness programs. The company has donated millions of dollars in products, services, and cash. The firm's philosophy is to help people and groups at the grassroots level through a variety of local programs that often involve company personnel raising money and delivering services.

Edward J. Bergman co-founded Miracle Corners of the World, Inc. (MCW), a non-profit organization, which serves young people worldwide, primarily through programs of leadership training, community center and housing development, and healthcare outreach. The organization's motto is "Local Change Through Global Exchange." MCW focuses on Africa but has projects in the U.S. and China as well. Eddie traveled to Africa on missions when he was a high school student in the late 1990s. He continued his volunteer work as an undergraduate student in hotel and tourism management at New York University and a graduate student at NYU, where he created an individualized study program in social entrepreneurship. Now in his mid 20s, Eddie is director of the Africa Travel Association in addition to his leadership of MCW. He has a passion for service and creating initiatives that do good. Influenced by his father, Stan Bergman and Team Schein as role models and sources of encouragement, Eddie is a passionate social entrepreneur with innovative ideas and a can-do attitude. MCW has helped develop community centers in Arusha and Songea, Tanzania, and Kissey, Sierra Leone. In Addis

Ababa, Ethiopia, the MCW-built community center supports orphans and teaches community members about organic gardening, environmentalism, and health. MCW's annual Youth Leadership Retreat brings teens and young adults from underdeveloped countries to Burlington, Vermont, to learn about advocacy and social entrepreneurship. Eddie understands networking and fund raising. MCW's third annual gala in New York City in 2007 honored tennis legend Billie Jean King, World Team Tennis CEO and Commissioner Ilana Kloss, Cal Ramsey of the New York Knicks, and Baltimore Ravens linebacker and Super Bowl MVP Ray Lewis.

As advocates, both Stanley and Eddie Bergman create a compelling vision of problems and how to address them. Their strategy is to act locally by garnering support globally. They travel extensively, identify local needs, spearhead partnerships with local groups, and find supporters in the U.S. and elsewhere. They recognize political realities locally, and have an active network of board members, educators, health care professionals, and philanthropists who participate in many ways, including fund raising and volunteering. They listen closely and provide a voice and avenues for action. They report results as they grow their respective initiatives for corporate social responsibility and social entrepreneurship.

INDIVIDUAL CHARACTERISTICS AFFECTING ADVOCACY

Individual dispositions affect a person's motivation to get involved in social advocacy, whether the individual is a corporate leader or independent social entrepreneur. Think of advocacy motivation as a combination of three categories of individual characteristics:

1. Conviction about caring for others: Advocates want to help. They don't ignore or avoid issues. When they see a homeless person in the street, they take action. They seek solutions and implement them.
2. Self-confidence to overcome barriers: Successful advocates and leaders are high in self-efficacy; they have a sense that they can make a difference.
3. Transformational skills: Advocates and leaders convey a compelling vision and inspire others through their values.

Overall, advocates are altruistic, committed to social justice and fairness, extroverted, not hesitant to express a strong opinion on a controversial subject, open to new ideas, creators of change, conscientious, empathic, and the type to go out of their way to do more than is expected of them (pro-social behavior). They create a vision of what could be and identify paths for accomplishing their goals. Advocates need to be strong communicators, insightful and influential politicians, entrepreneurs, and change agents. They need to have resilient personality characteristics such as self-confidence, internal control, self-efficacy, insight into their own and others' strengths and weaknesses, and flexibility to adapt as conditions change.

CONDITIONS THAT STIMULATE ACTION

Leaders are more likely to get involved in advocacy efforts the more the need is local and personal. Examples are social or health problems that involve employees, their families, and/or community members, such as a child suffering from a disease. Of course, people feel empathy and are stimulated to help distant groups or individuals who are anonymous and not related to the organization or its community when information demonstrates the need. Videos, site visits, and/or testimonials from those who were firsthand witnesses make the need personal. (Think about corporate and community responses to Hurricane Katrina and the Thailand tsunami.) Another condition that promotes advocacy is an initiative that allows participants to have direct, visible impact—for instance, building (or raising money to build) a community center or homeless shelter. The physical structure itself is evidence of success. Other success measures may be the number of programs started, the amount of dollars raised, and the number of people served.

So, for instance, Mary Ann Bell's local food pantry was the direct response of one individual who saw the need of the poor and homeless, recruited volunteers, and developed an ongoing program for soliciting donations and providing food. Pattye Pece worked with other local Long Islanders to found a small Fair Trade gift store operated and staffed entirely by volunteers. The product sales benefit craftsman and coffee and tea growers around the world. The profits are sent to orphanages in Africa. David Krauss's Madagaskar Ankizy (meaning children) Fund built a school in the remote village close to his anthropological digs. He and his colleagues were so touched by the welcome and acceptance they felt during several years of their research that they wanted to help by building a two room school house and raising money to hire a teacher and purchase books.

Generally, people are likely to become advocates when they believe they can be effective. Stanley Bergman's corporate initiatives at Henry Schein Inc. and Eddie Bergman's initiatives with Miracle Corners of the World are focused on local communities. They and their teams identify needs, get to know the people involved, establish local initiatives that put a personal face on the recipients and volunteers, and communicate the need to others who have resources to help. Social advocacy efforts tend to have high costs to get underway and sustain, at least relative to available resources. Moreover, they often have a low, or at least uncertain, probability of success. The larger the effort, the more challenging it is to tackle and achieve.

ADVOCACY AND LEADERSHIP

Advocates become leaders as they communicate a vision, garner support, set strategies, and organize tasks to accomplish their goals. Similarly, leaders of organizations become advocates when they identify issues and promulgate solutions for the benefit of their stockholders, employees, customers, suppliers, and community members. This raises several questions: What makes an advocate a good leader, and what makes a leader a good advocate? Does advocacy require special leadership skills in addition to skills needed by all leaders? Do leaders who become advocates need to do something different than other advocates?

Table 23.1 (left column) lists advocacy behaviors. Advocates identify one or more problems that need to be addressed. They recognize situational conditions that are likely to support or thwart their efforts. Their behaviors demonstrate their personal characteristics that underlie and motivate their social concern. They set goals, formulate strategies, take actions, and then evaluate their progress and learn from their successes and failures. In the process, they develop leadership and advocacy skills.

LEADERS AS ADVOCATES

Table 23.1 (middle column) describes advocating for corporate social responsibility. Leaders articulate problems and recognize their company's role to help solve them. The issue or situation may stimulate their involvement, particularly if they have direct exposure to the issue. For instance, a corporate executive may establish a manufacturing plant in an impoverished area and recognize

TABLE 23.1—EXAMPLES OF LEADERSHIP AND SOCIAL ADVOCACY ROLES

ADVOCACY BEHAVIORS	THE LEADER AS ADVOCATE FOR CORPORATE SOCIAL RESPONSIBILITY	THE ADVOCATE AS LEADER FOR SOCIAL ENTREPRENEURSHIP
Identify the problem(s)	Step up to the plate to address problems, recognize organization's role in corporate social responsibility, be ready to use leadership skills to address the issue	Focus on ways to create a compelling vision of the problem and potential solutions to attract others' attention and commitment
Recognize situational conditions	Have direct experience with the problem, seeing an issue close-up and personal	Generate sources of support, recognizing stakeholders
Demonstrate personal characteristics that motivate advocacy	Integrity, honest, altruism, willingness to take risks and speak up, knowledge of organizational change	Ability to communicate, understanding others' situation and vested interests, political skills
Set goals	Meet organization's and personal goals while also addressing advocacy issues	Focus on meeting the needs of beneficiaries
Formulate strategies	Use power of position and own leadership skills, draw on idiosyncrasy credits and call in favors	Develop and coordinate support structures, recognize adversaries
Take action	Make decisions, allocate resources, form coalitions, constrain others' behaviors	Use commitment building and influence tactics, such as listening closely and giving others public voice to confirm their support
Evaluate and learn from outcomes	Collect bottom line measures, show that this is a win-win situation (positive outcomes for beneficiaries, supporters, and the organization)	Report and celebrate results, acknowledge losses, learn and improve
Develop advocacy and leadership skills	Take risks, identify and communicate values, link corporate social responsibility to organizational goals, don't tolerate—and certainly don't contribute to—social injustice, indeed redress social injustices and promote fair treatment	Develop skills (communications, transformational and transactional leadership, openness to new ideas, teambuilding, continuous learning)

how the company can train unskilled young people in the community to give them employable skills. In taking social action, corporate leaders demonstrate their integrity, honesty, altruism, and willingness to take risks with organizational resources. These leaders attempt to mesh corporate and social goals. These goals may conflict. Also, social goals may not have an immediate benefit to the corporation of the people they intend to help. Of course, they may increase the company's good will with its customers and employees. CEOs' motives are complex with uncertain relationships between social welfare and stakeholder perceptions, cost control, and profit maximization. A classic example is the case of P. Roy Vagelos, the Merck CEO, who, in the 1980s, gave away the drug that cured river blindness, recognizing that it would benefit only poor people who could not afford to pay for the drug and finding that governments and private nonprofits were unwilling to pay. The decision demonstrated the company's underlying value that medicine is for people, and profits will follow . . . sometimes.

Being a leader in social responsibility is not necessarily enough to ensure social welfare. Mattel recalled millions of toys with lead paint in the summer of 2007 despite having spent $10 million for ten years to monitor its 13 Asian factories and many more contract suppliers for employee safety and product quality. CEO Robert A. Eckert apologized to Congress and to Chinese officials for the lead-paint failures. Some companies appear to act responsibly in some respects, but not in others. Wal-Mart, for example, has been called to task for its treatment of employees. Lee Scott, CEO of Wal-Mart, went to its Battle Creek, Michigan, store in December 2007, to announce a $1 million national donation to the Salvation Army.

Leaders as advocates have an advantage over social entrepreneurs. Corporate leaders have resources, position power, control, idiosyncrasy credits (freedom to do what they like up to a point), and time before they are held accountable. Corporate leaders are likely to have an infrastructure at their disposal including the technology for data collection, storage, retrieval, evaluation of outcomes, and communication about need and accomplishments. Their social advocacy is evident in their business decisions, allocation of resources, coalitions they form, and constraints they impose of employees' and contractors' behaviors. Corporate leaders use the power of their positions as well as their leadership skills to demonstrate the value of social advocacy for beneficiaries, supporters, and the organization.

Leaders as advocates seek social justice, accept social responsibility, and link doing good with doing well. The organization gains value by producing socially beneficial outcomes and learning in the process. For instance, employees and customers who contribute to environmental sustainability through recycling (e.g., Toshiba's and Best Buy's jointly-sponsored electronics recycling events around the U.S.) learn how to establish and track the success of a program across functional and geographic areas. They celebrate their success together, enhancing their sense of belonging, teamwork, and loyalty to the organization. The leader and the organization gain credibility, which may have spin-off benefits in increasing revenue and reducing costs. Small successes in one area can lead to new initiatives (e.g., first recycling paper, later saving energy in a host of ways). Leaders and their companies teach others, including their competitors. Mattel acted affirmatively when lead paint was discovered. Companies such as Evergreen Lodge and Pura Vida are role models for win-win situations for beneficiaries and investors.

CEOs may not be natural advocates. They reach beyond traditional corporate goals to attack problems that may be unpopular and do not have immediate benefit. The corporate leader as advocate learns to take risks, identify and communicate personal and corporate values, and relate corporate social responsibility to organizational goals. Corporate leaders are likely to become successful advocates when they identify and understand different stakeholders, recognize intended and unintended costs (who benefits and who loses), and have realistic expectations and accurate perceptions of others' behavior and attitudes.

COMMUNITY ADVOCATES AS LEADERS

Table 23.1 (right column) describes how social entrepreneurs use leadership. The social entrepreneur creates a compelling vision of the problem and potential solutions in order to attract and sustain others' attention and support. Garnering resources and building a set of committed stakeholders are critical early steps in the advocacy process. The advocate must communicate clearly and forcefully, take into account competition for tight recourses, and possibly face adversaries—those who stand to lose if the advocacy initiative is successful. The advocate must be skillful at commitment building and influence tactics, such as listening closely and giving others public voice to confirm their support.

Advocacy has leadership challenges. Advocates elicit the support of people who don't have a clear stake in contributing to the advocacy effort. The effort may depend on people committing to a set of distinct values or beliefs that may not be held by others or that are not usually what motivates behavior—for instance, an initiative that is not well known and beneficiaries who are anonymous. Advocates often start with limited or no resources. They may be rebuffed frequently as people turn down their requests for action, given the competition among other good causes. The goal may seem insurmountable or only making a small dent in a large problem. Within organizations, advocacy for an issue may seem risky, especially if the effort is unpopular, unusual, or complex, even if the organization stands to benefit. People in the organization may not see the value or be willing to commit resources to social responsibility goals that do not have an immediate positive impact on the bottom line. Advocates need tact (political skills), resilience, and an understanding of human behavior that goes beyond the usual demands of a leader.

Social entrepreneurs as leaders are passionate and focused on the needs of their beneficiaries as their primary goals. They engage in transactional management. They organize, plan, delegate, monitor, and reward. They also engage in transformational leadership, showing passion, inspiring others, and building relationships. Social entrepreneurs have advantages over corporate leaders. Although corporate leaders have resources and a power base, community advocates have flexibility. They are not constrained by corporate responsibilities. They are not locked in by stockholders and potentially conflicting goals. They don't have a fixed base of operation. If one potential source of support doesn't materialize, they can turn elsewhere. They seek resources from like-minded individuals and groups, developing and coordinating support structures when necessary. They are not accountable, at least, not until they form an organization with a board of directors and other structures. They take less risk because they don't face competing goals. Still, they may face adversaries. For example, Ralph Nader promoted automobile safety in the face of massive industry lobbying. Sometimes advocates need to acknowledge losses as they encounter barriers that are not easily overcome. In the process, they develop skills that are vital for successful advocacy, such as communications, transformational and transactional leadership, teambuilding and openness to new ideas and continuous learning.

THE ADVOCACY PROCESS

Advocacy begins with the kernel of an idea prompted by evidence of a need. Advocates as entrepreneurs test the waters by talking with others about their idea and how to respond. Does the idea make sense to others? Are people interested and concerned? Will they help? In this early stage, advocates conceptualize and define the problem. They discuss and agree to general goals and methods of accomplishing them. They determine needed resources and possible sources. They identify the decision makers who need to be influenced and other stakeholders whose opinions need to be shaped. They also identify groups and individuals who are likely to be antagonistic, and they consider ways to react, for example, by focusing on common interests, convincing them of the need, demonstrating threats or benefits, etc. The advocacy initiative evolves as it gains public awareness, vocal support, financial resources, and partners or allies. Eventually, it begins to affect attitudes, behaviors, and/or policy decisions, and ultimately affects the intended beneficiaries without harming others. This is an evolutionary process. The effort may progress in fits and starts. It may falter and dissolve altogether. It may take new directions that were initially unanticipated, perhaps because the problem was resolved and the resources and organizational structures could be devoted to other challenging problems (e.g., the Jimmy Fund shifting from raising money to eradicate polio to raising funds for muscular dystrophy). Advocates who are open to continuous feedback throughout the process are likely to adapt to situational conditions and changes, sometimes altering methods and other times altering goals.

STAGES OF ADVOCACY

Generally speaking, there are four stages of advocacy that are repeated as the effort develops.

1. Defining the goal: This includes conceptualizing the problem (e.g., the need to change awareness, attitudes, behaviors, and/or decisions), its scope (whether local and/or global), and time line.
2. Mapping the territory: This includes recognizing stakeholders; forming partnerships, alliances, and networks; setting targets; identifying resources; and distinguishing roles. Also, it may entail competing for resources and attention and is influenced by advocates' values, drive/passion, and underlying beliefs about people (e.g., that indeed they are generous or that they can change their attitudes).
3. Call to action: This is selecting and implementing strategies to accomplish advocacy goals while maintaining control. It includes developing strategies and actions focused on specific, realistic, time-bound goals

(e.g., specifying how much money needs to be raised during the next six months).

4. Evaluation: This is determining the effectiveness of the advocacy effort and making adjustments in strategy and tactics to improve outcomes.

ADVOCACY STRATEGIES

Advocacy uses political and social influence to alter attitudes, behaviors, and/or decisions. Cognitive advocacy strategies are giving information to generate awareness for an issue and encourage action. Emotional strategies include warnings or threats, inducements of guilt or fear, or promises of satisfaction or delight. Behavioral strategies include modeling the desired behavior (as when the advocate contributes financially and volunteers) and rewarding desired behaviors (the ubiquitous recognition award dinners, for instance).

Advocates' beliefs about others are likely to affect their advocacy behaviors. For instance, if advocates believe that people don't change their attitudes and behaviors, or at least don't change them easily, the advocates may be likely to take forceful action or not get involved altogether. If advocates believe people do change, they may focus on cognitive strategies that simply provide people with information or data, assuming that once they are informed, they will see the light and do what is needed. If advocates believe that people are more sensitive to losses than gains, they are likely to use threats, highlighting the bad things that will occur if the decision or behaviors do not change. If advocates believe that people will act affirmatively when they understand how their behavior can help, advocates will highlight behavior-outcome relationships and the value of the outcomes.

CONDITIONS THAT FACILITATE AND DISCOURAGE ADVOCACY

Table 23.2 (left column) lists situational conditions that influence advocacy. The situation includes contact with the beneficiary, time frame for action, the clarity of goals and actions, the degree of difficulty of goals and actions, and the cost of action relative to the gain. Advocacy goals differ in the extent to which trying to do something positive has a direct, visible, and immediate impact. Another condition is the extent of support available, including alliances, social support, and, conversely, the extent to which there are adversaries, naysayers, and doubters, and extent of support.

Conditions That Facilitate Advocacy

Conditions that facilitate advocacy are described in Table 23.2 (middle column). These include being personally acquainted with one or more people who have a visible need and having a short time frame to deliver services or make a decision. Having clear goals and high agreement about what to do helps. So does having a sense that the outcomes can, indeed, be produced. Support is also important, of course. Support may be from alliances and volunteers who are readily available and happy to participate. Pattye Pece's Fair Trade initiative was a partnership with a small group of other religiously-committed people with similar beliefs, values, and goals. David Krause was able to elicit the imagination of contributors, never tiring of the chance to generate excitement with his emotionally moving slide presentation and dynamic talk. The relationship between effort and outcomes needs to be strong. That is, there is a high relationship between effort, action, and goal accomplishment. David Krause showed that small amounts of money went a long way in Madagascar. Naturally it helps to be encouraged by others and have few if any adversaries to block the way.

Conditions That Discourage Advocacy

Conditions that discourage advocacy (Table 23.2, right column) include having an impersonal and/or ambiguous goal, long-term outcomes, low agreement about what to do, the need for considerable effort and resources to accomplish the goal, little support from other organizations (low shared interests), low social support, many adversaries, low impact objectives, and a high cost of action with low immediate value. There may be too many competing interests for the same resources. Potential volunteers and donors may be put off by warnings. The costs may be viewed as too high relative to the benefits. For instance, people are reluctant to give up energy-consuming luxuries for small, long-term, or imperceptible gains. Another factor that weakens advocacy is not bothering to evaluate the outcomes and communicate change as success.

We don't hear much about failed advocacy initiatives. Many individuals would like to make a difference but don't even try. Others make an attempt and then burn out. They work too hard with little result and the effort fizzles. This could happen when the problem and sources of support are not being clear. Outcomes take ages to achieve if anything positive happens at all. Goals are unclear, the problem seems too big, and there is little agreement about what to do to help. Efforts that seem easy at first may become difficult, for instance,

TABLE 23.2—CONDITIONS THAT FACILITATE AND DISCOURAGE SOCIAL ADVOCACY

SITUATIONAL CONDITIONS	CONDITIONS THAT FACILITATE ADVOCACY	CONDITIONS THAT DISCOURAGE ADVOCACY
Contact with the beneficiary	Personal beneficiary (the advocate or someone close: identifiable by name), visible need	Impersonal (e.g., a village in Africa) or general common good (e.g., global warming)
Time frame for action	Short-term, immediate outcomes; help needed now—e.g., to assist flood victims	Long-term outcomes, outcomes will occur sometime in the future—e.g., save energy, promote green construction
Clarity of goals and action	Clear goals and high agreement about what to do	Ambiguous goals and low agreement about what to do
Goal and action difficulty	Low—desired outcomes require minimal effort and resources	High—desired outcomes require considerable effort and resources
Cost and value	Action is low cost, high value	Action is high cost and low immediate value (but presumably high long-term value)
Relationship between effort and effect	High—direct impact; high relationship between effort, action, and goal accomplishment (e.g., seeking volunteers to drive cancer patients to chemotherapy appointments)	Low—low impact; low relationship between effort, action, and goal accomplishment (e.g., raising money for cancer research, which eventually affects medical treatment and outcomes)
Support	Clear alliances and coalitions with shared goals, volunteers readily available	Few shared interests
Social encouragement (peer pressure and reinforcement)	High	Low
Adversaries, naysayers, and doubters (controversy and potential polarization)	Low	High

when bureaucratic red tape intervenes. Most advocacy efforts impose some barriers. These may be rules and regulations that have to be overcome or just convincing people who control the resources that this is something that is important to do. Alliances may be present one day, and gone the next. People may not share the interest, and the advocate may not help them visualize the problem or what they can do to make a difference. Naysayers may abound—people who doubt the value of the effort, fail to see its relationship to the mission of a company, or are not ready to stick out their necks until others are on board.

RECOMMENDATIONS FOR ACTION

Corporate leaders as advocates can go wrong, for instance, by acting without a clear purpose or following others' ideas without linking the effort to organizational goals. They can be criticized for taking time and resources away from bottom-line business objectives. Social entrepreneurs can go wrong in many ways, too, for instance, by assuming others will share their goals, taking up the gauntlet for an issue few people are willing to support, not learning from failed attempts, ignoring feedback, not delegating for fear of losing control, or not changing course when strategies have failed and other methods should be tried. Here are some recommendations to promote effective leadership and advocacy within organizations:

- Get the word out: Educate employees about corporate social responsibility, how the organization is contributing, and how they can help. Provide education and opportunities for participation about specific issues and initiatives, whether they are corporate-wide donation campaigns and team efforts (the United Way, Habitat for Humanity), individual employees' volunteering in the community (one employee starting a soup kitchen for the homeless in a local community), or corporate investments in environmental sustainability in the community (a recycling initiative).
- Link to bottom line objectives: Clarify the tie between social advocacy and the corporation's success. Don't assume that stakeholders will see the relationship. Explain how the effort helps to attract more customers or talented employees, for instance.
- Recognize accomplishments: Celebrate (reinforce) achievements to build organizational commitment and loyalty and honor those who contributed most.

- Highlight spin-off benefits: Show how corporate social responsibility can increase employee pride and loyalty, enhance team-building, improve communication between departments, and generate goodwill that benefits sales and attracts and retains valued employees.
- Invest corporate resources: Provide support for individuals who want to be involved in corporate advocacy efforts or start their own. Consider starting a community service support center that would offer materials, advice from fellow employees who are social entrepreneurs, and money (for instance, small grants, micro-loans, or contributions from company-wide fund raising efforts with employees determining how to distribute the proceeds).
- Encourage employee participation: Identify people who have a proclivity to work on and lead advocacy efforts. Ask for volunteers. Assess their skills and development needs (e.g., design an assessment center or on-line, self-administered assessment tools) to evaluate advocacy skills such as communication ability, political sensitivity, and knowledge of change management. Involve executives in corporate social responsibility projects to increase the projects' visibility and importance. These can become developmental assignments for high potential managers. Don't make these assignments for soon-to-be downsized executives or people who are being forced to retire.

Here are some ways to overcome these barriers and respond to naysayers and doubters:

- Provide convincing data or other information: This may be information about the numbers of people affected; the costs to the individual, the company, or society; testimonies from those affected or helped; or other demonstrations of the seriousness of the problem or issue and the positive impact that is possible.
- Join forces with others who have like minds or shared interests: There is power in numbers, especially if others are opinion leaders, people who are respected and have resources.
- Negotiate with opposing forces: People who object strongly may be amenable to small trial efforts or experiments to demonstrate the value of the initiative. If the goal is seeking volunteers for a community initiative, the advocate may start in one department or business unit to see how people react. In general, small, local efforts may be more palatable

to the organization than grandiose ambitions. Small efforts can get employees involved and demonstrate impact. Note that Henry Schein Inc.'s social programs are targeted initiatives. Over the years, specific efforts have become part of a corporate strategy for social advocacy in relation to the health care mission of the business.

- Use behavioral tactics (e.g., demonstrations, ad campaigns, petitions): Today, there are many methods to gain attention including on-line blogs, YouTube, and television sound bites. Corporate leaders can use such technology within their organizations to build momentum and enthusiasm for a social issue.

- Learn advocacy skills: Leaders can learn and practice advocacy skills. One step in that direction is understanding the advocacy process. Here are some steps that can be taken to educate leaders in advocacy. Leaders can observe successful advocates, such as Stanley and Eddie Bergman and the others I described here. Consider examples of advocates for local and global initiatives. Also, look for examples of advocates who have a personal objective (i.e., to help specific individuals) and those who benefit others in general or in communities far removed. Examples might reflect a variety of topics and goals, areas such as social welfare (poverty, education, wellness, health care), the environment, politics, and religion. Include goals such as raising money, delivering services, building awareness, preventing negative outcomes, and influencing others' votes and resource allocation decisions. Understand how these advocates carried out the basic elements of advocacy including issue identification, solution formulation, taking action, and evaluating and refining the effort. Think about the problems these advocates faced, how what could have been done (or still could be done) differently. Consider the skills and knowledge that advocates need to be effective. These include communication skills (e.g., ways to formulate a clear message and how to use media effectively), how to elicit support (e.g., recruiting volunteers and raising money), political and cultural sensitivity, knowledge of change management (unfreezing seemingly intransigent attitudes), forming alliances and coalitions and seeking compromise, and resolving conflicts and negotiating agreements.

- Practice advocacy: Leaders can practice and fine tune their advocacy efforts. Try the following: Write a mission statement. Are your goals clear? Collect to determine the nature and scope of the problem(s). Set short-term goals that target specific outcomes (e.g., increase recycling in the organization by 5% within the next year). What actions will you take? Determine who controls policies and brainstorm ways to approach policy makers (e.g., a letter writing campaign, forums for speaking, anticipating questions and practicing answers). What transformational and transactional leadership steps will you take to recruit, motivate, and direct volunteers? Consider how you can evaluate and report outcomes, celebrate your successes, and learn from failures.

CONCLUSION

Advocacy and leadership skills are important for corporate social responsibility and social entrepreneurship initiatives. Corporate leaders need to be effective advocates, and advocates need to be effective leaders. Advocates lead by communicating their vision, securing support and resources, and organizing goal-centered tasks. Corporate leaders seek ways to benefit the organization in a socially responsible manner. Corporate and independent advocacy requires transactional and transformational leadership, showing passion and conveying inspiration. Leaders are motivated by strength of conviction for doing good, self-confidence in the face of difficult goals, and their transformational abilities. They are more likely to initiate social action when there is a local and personal need, volunteers can work directly with the people who benefit, and the value of the initiative is clear; in short, they believe they can make a difference.

Successful advocates define their goals clearly, recognize the scope of their goals and efforts including the range of stakeholders involved, and initiate a clear call to action—that is, indicate just what needs to be done by whom and by when. In addition, they incorporate evaluation in the process, tracking, reporting, and celebrating their accomplishments. Advocacy strategies depend on the leader's beliefs about how people will react to their initiatives. For instance, advocates inform people, warn them, and/or constrain or reward their behaviors. Also, they recognize conditions that discourage and encourage advocacy. Advocacy is more difficult when goals are impersonal, positive outcomes are years away, and there is little agreement about what to do.

Generally, leaders know that corporate social responsibility is not an easy sell. Critics abound and resource expenditures must be justified. Effective leadership and advocacy requires education about corporate responsibility and advocacy processes, tying social action to the company's bottom line when possible, celebrating and reinforcing achievements, and encouraging employee participation. Barriers to advocacy can be overcome by providing convincing information, joining forces with allies, negotiating with opponents, and actions that demonstrate beliefs (e.g., "putting your money where your mouth is").

Selected Bibliography

For arguments about the importance of corporate social responsibility, see Philip Kotler and Nancy Lee, *Corporate Social Responsibility: Doing the Most Good for Your Company and Your Cause* (New York, Wiley, 2004). Joanne B. Ciulla described the case of P. Roy Vagelos of Merck in "The importance of leadership in shaping business values," *Long Range Planning*, 1999, 32, 166–172. For reasons why corporate officials get involved in social advocacy, see Adam M. Grant, "Relational job design and the motivation to make a pro-social difference," *Academy of Management Review*, 2007, 32, 393–417. For examples of advocates who have become successful social entrepreneurs, I recommend David Bornstein, *How to Change the World: Social Entrepreneurs and the Power of New Ideas* (New York: Oxford University Press, 2004); and Paul R. Loeb, *Soul of a Citizen: Living with Conviction in a Cynical Time* (New York: St. Martin's Press, 1999). Ideas for educating corporate managers and leaders in social entrepreneurship can be found in J. Gregory Dees, Jed Emerson, and Peter Economy, *Enterprising Nonprofits: A Toolkit for Social Entrepreneurs* (New York: Wiley, 2001); and Paul Tracey and Nelson Phillips, "The distinctive challenge of educating social entrepreneurs," *Academy of Management Learning & Education*, 2007, 6, 264–271. For a training program on the elements of advocacy, see Ritu R. Sharma, *An Introduction to Advocacy: Training Guide* (Support for Analysis and Research in Africa [SARA] Project Advocacy, Washington, DC: Academy for Educational Development, 1996), available online at http://www. aed.org. For more details about Stanley Bergman and Henry Schein Inc.'s social advocacy efforts, see http://www.henry schein.com. For more information about Edward Bergman and his social advocacy foundation, Miracle Corners of the World, see http:// www.miraclecorners.org. For a study of how managers sell issues to top executives as a form of internal corporate advocacy, see Jane E. Dutton, Susan J. Ashford, Regina M. O'Neill, and Katherine A. Lawrence, "Moves that matter: Issue selling and organizational change," *Academy of Management Journal*, 2001, 44, 716–736.

24

⍥

Building a Culture of Candor
A Crucial Key to Leadership

Warren Bennis

The word transparency crops up more and more in public statements by politicians and corporate officials—as if simply saying it were enough to guarantee it. Understandably. Now more than ever, we know that keeping secrets is dangerous for organizations and the people affected by them. But no amount of incantation or legislation can make an organization transparent. That happens only when an organization creates a culture of candor, one in which followers feel free to speak truth to power and leaders are willing to hear it.

Unfortunately, while many organizations pay lip service to those values, few organizations are genuinely committed to openness and candor. Instead, when it comes to sharing secrets, most organizations hold onto inside information with obsessive zeal. And even within the family, as it were, far too many organizations have traditions and structures that keep essential information from reaching decision makers. History tells us that lack of transparency too often has tragic results. The 9/11 Commission Report is only the most recent evidence of how devastating the consequences can be when vital information does not flow freely within and between organizations.

Reprinted by permission of *The Conference Board Annual Report* (2004). Copyright 2004 Conference Board, Inc.

And yet, in recent years candor and transparency seem to have all but disappeared from our organizations. Accounting fraud, insider trading, and just plain lying have destroyed one promising enterprise after another. Top executives who were once as celebrated as rock stars are now in prison or bound for it. Trillions of dollars of investor wealth vanished overnight. The restating of corporate earnings, once rare, has become commonplace, and every such announcement reinforces many people's jaded belief that business has lied to them before and is likely to do so again.

No wonder that only 15 percent of respondents to a November 2002 CBS/New York Times poll expressed much faith in American business, and that two-thirds of those CBS canvassed at around the same time believed most corporate leaders are dishonest. It would be hard to overstate just how low the reputations of business leaders and business itself have sunk in recent years. This pervasive lack of public trust threatens the economy far more than the direction of interest rates or even the outcome of any single presidential election.

LESSONS FROM LOS ALAMOS

Of course, there are rare instances—national security is the most obvious—when information must be limited to a few people who are demonstrably trustworthy. And businesses have the right, even the obligation, to protect intellectual property and other assets. But even in wartime, a compelling case can often be made for prudent transparency. One of J. Robert Oppenheimer's acts of genius as the scientific leader of the Manhattan Project was to persuade the project's Armed Forces head, General Leslie Groves, that the atomic scientists recruited for the project should be able to speak freely among themselves, even about top-secret matters. Yes, increasing the number of people who knew that the United States was trying to build an atomic weapon increased the likelihood that the enemy would learn of the effort, Oppenheimer conceded. But he argued persuasively that the enemy could already guess that the effort was underway—after all, the names of most Allied scientists doing bomb-relevant research had vanished from the pages of the scientific journals. Groves reluctantly, and courageously, acquiesced. As a result, although the scientists' letters left Los Alamos only after being censored, the scientists themselves could speak freely to each other as long as they were on the secret base. The scientists' ability to share vital information helped them accomplish their goal in a remarkable two years.

In addition to speeding up the discovery process at Los Alamos, information sharing within the group had a potent morale-building effect. Physics *wunderkind* Richard Feynman was put in charge of a group of engineers doing tedious but essential calculations for the project. The engineers were told nothing about the nature of the bomb project or how their own work fit into it. Their performance was slow and lackluster. Then, Feynman persuaded Oppenheimer to extend the culture of candor enjoyed by the scientists to the engineers. Oppenheimer spoke openly to the engineers about the project and their critical contribution to it. The lecture was transforming. Afterwards, the engineers worked tirelessly, without prompting and without complaint. Feynman estimated that knowing the nature and importance of their work made the engineers work almost ten times as fast and with fierce commitment.

How effectively information flows through an organization is directly related to its culture. Many institutional cultures make transparency all but impossible. In an epic confessional essay in the May 2004 issue of *The Atlantic Monthly,* former *New York Times* Executive Editor Howell Raines accuses the paper of what he terms "management by mendacity." He writes that *Times* publisher Arthur Sulzberger Jr. chose him for the job for the express purpose of shaking up the paper's corporate culture, including the unacknowledged practice of letting the mediocre and unproductive remain once they were admitted to the club.

According to Raines, when Sulzberger introduced Raines' successor, Bill Keller, to the *Times* staff, the publisher said: "There's no complacency here— never has been, never will be." But Raines insists: "I can guarantee that no one in the newsroom, including Arthur himself, believed what he said. It was a ritual incantation meant to confirm the faith of everyone present in the *Times'* defining myth of effortless superiority. Arthur's politic words were a declaration that although *Times* people may talk and sometimes even joke among themselves about the paper's deeply rooted complacency, that characteristic must be vehemently denied when mentioned outside the tribal circle."

Many of us have been in organizations that have been harmed by their defining myths. Such myths are always Janus-like: On one hand, they help create cohesion, and that spirit of being part of a grand, exclusive club often facilitates the best kind of collaboration. On the other hand, these same myths make it harder for the organization to criticize itself in any meaningful way, no matter how illuminating and useful such self-analysis would be.

ARE YOU WORKING IN A TOXIC CASTE SYSTEM?

I am convinced that an essential first step in making any organization more transparent is to examine its culture. The first question to ask: Who talks to whom? In many organizations, information flows down but not up. Observers of the recent scandals at both *The New York Times* and *USA Today* claim that editors had allowed a toxic caste system to develop. Editors interacted only with a handful of anointed reporters, whose work was dangerously exempt from the kind of critical, even cynical, scrutiny that was standard for everyone else. Both newsrooms had buzzed for months about the suspect quality of work by rogue reporters Jayson Blair and Jack Kelley that eventually embarrassed both papers.

A more egalitarian newsroom would have served both papers better. A more collegial organization would have allowed information to flow more freely. If the editors had spent more time with more people, they would not have been blindsided by dishonest reporters who ruthlessly manipulated them as well as the truth. Some critics said the editors had succumbed to the Golden Boy syndrome. In fact, what the editors had succumbed to was the all-too-human tendency to limit their interactions to a coterie of charming, ego-massaging individuals who told them only what they wanted to hear.

When leading a large organization, it is not enough to say, as so many leaders do, "My door is always open." Employees with an ounce of emotional intelligence know not to drop in to the boss's office on a whim. People in power have to insist that those who report to them tell the truth, however unpleasant. That isn't as easy as it seems. Power is intimidating, and those who have it often make their own importance known in myriad ways, some explicit (bespoke suits), some not. Leaders routinely send out signals that make it clear they want to hear only confirming information. The stated policy may be: "You need to take responsibility" or "No whining." But the real message, never voiced but understood organization-wide, is often that the only way to succeed here is to tell the leader what he or she has already decided.

It is not surprising that people at the bottom of the rarely acknowledged organizational pyramid are loathe to put their jobs—and their family's health insurance—on the line by telling the boss his or her idea is faulty, wrong, or dangerous. What is more surprising is that the so-called "shimmer effect" that surrounds most leaders dazzles even their ostensible peers. A case in point is the alacrity with which the trustees of Hollinger International approved then CEO Conrad Black's $8 million purchase of a collection of Franklin Delano Roosevelt's papers. Black wanted the documents for a Roosevelt biography he was writing. Fine. But why didn't a single trustee question the inflated valuation of the papers, to which only the seller—hardly a disinterested party—

had attested? The answer, according to *The New York Times*, "was not negligence [on the part of the trustees], but something more like awe."

GREAT LEADERS ASK NOT TO BE SPARED

Ordinary mortals like having their egos massaged. Great leaders ask not to be spared. They want to know everything, not just the good news, because they understand that the more they know the better their decisions will be. Decision making rises and falls on the quality of information at hand. And listening isn't easy. Active listening, intelligent listening, is a demanding task, which is why too many leaders develop what they call in the Middle East "tired ears." Wise leaders become skeptical when what they hear simply validates their current position. Universal assent makes strong leaders nervous. When everybody in the room says, "Great idea, boss," the authentic leader quickly asks for a second opinion.

I was fascinated to discover recently, in reading David Hackett Fischer's *Washington's Crossing,* that our first president never relied on his own gut or the counsel of his closest advisors when going into battle. Instead, he would consult widely, even asking civilians what they thought. Most remarkably, according to Fischer: "It was typical of Washington's leadership to present a promising proposal as someone else's idea, rather than his own. It was his way of encouraging open discussion and debate." Still a good strategy more than 200 years later.

In order to get the information and the knowledge he or she needs, a leader must have the ego-strength to say "I don't know. What do you think?" Princely executive compensation should make that easier, but it is amazing how few CEOs are capable of that kind of modesty, despite the huge payoff that can result. You can hear how great you are from a paid subordinate or you can hear it from history. You choose.

One way to make sure that the cons as well as the pros of any strategy are probed is to listen to your contrarians. If you don't have any, hire some immediately. That too is harder than it sounds. People like being surrounded by people who agree with them and tell them how brilliant they are. It's human nature. But the person who is willing to look his or her boss in the eye and say "Nonsense" is worth a thousand yes men. As a leader, you already know what you think. What you need to know is what the smartest person who is least enamored of your idea sees as its weakness. That is your best hope of polishing your idea so that it really shines or, just as important, dumping the idea before it makes you look like a fool or, more important, harms the organization.

The contrarian is the one person in the organization who really earns his or her salary—and should earn the leader's gratitude as well. Bonuses should routinely be given to employees who save their leaders from making stupid decisions. Instead, such people tend to be shunned because "they are not with the program" and are more likely to be fired than rewarded.

The fact is, our leaders need to develop thicker skins. They do our companies no service when they react to principled feedback like the princess with the pea under her royal mattress. The kind of toughness we should value in our leaders is not their rigidity but a willingness to profit from the thoughtful criticism of those brave enough to speak up, even when they may not have courtly manners. Followers need to remember that some things are worth getting fired for. That is always easier to say than to do. The courage of the follower is always more laudable than that of the leader, because the follower's losses cut so much closer to the bone.

REWARDING PRINCIPLED DISSIDENTS

Principled dissidents should not simply be tolerated. They should be rewarded. And those who are close to the top and don't speak out should be punished. That alone sends a powerful message to the rest of the organization that speaking truth to power is not some odd and embarrassing happening but an obligation. When we start reading in the company newsletter about individuals who have loyally revealed weaknesses in the operation, we will know that the organization is finally committed to the kind of openness it may already have boasted of in its mission statement.

The Sarbanes-Oxley Act of 2002 helped make corporate governance more transparent, but no amount of legislation will make our organizations truly transparent. Only courageous leaders, and followers who are even more courageous, can do that.

As a leader, the most important action you can take is to seek out and embrace dissent. Whistle-blowers are made, not born—made by leaders with "tired ears" who prefer sycophancy to candor.

Recently, the media have reported on several employees of the FBI—one a translator of Farsi and other Middle Eastern languages, another an agent who had successfully infiltrated terrorist groups—who put their careers on the line to expose weaknesses in the bureau's procedures. The result? One was dismissed, the other sentenced to career death. If history tells us nothing else, it tells us this: Angry individuals who know where an organization's bodies are buried will eventually become so frustrated at being ignored, so indignant at being treated unfairly, that they will call a reporter and tell all. How brilliant does a leader have to be to realize that the wiser strategy is to hear what the potential whistle-blower has to say and correct the problem, if humanly possible? How many shuttles does NASA have to lose before it realizes that all pre-launch rumblings about potential problems should be taken seriously?

There is a great irony about the growing lack of transparency in our organizations. Even as organizations try more and more desperately to keep the lid on their secrets, information is becoming harder and harder to control. The Internet has democratized the spread of information in ways that could not have been imagined 20 years ago. Your disgruntled former employees, your angry ex-wife, all have access to computers. They can reveal your most intimate secrets to millions of people around the globe by pressing a single computer key. No matter what safeguards you think are in place, it is harder than ever to keep secrets in this wired world. Just ask the judge in the Kobe Bryant case who recently—for the second time—had to apologize for the release of the name of the alleged rape victim by a court employee.

As a leader, what can you do to encourage a culture of candor and the greater transparency that will predictably follow? One way is to do what the Roman Catholic Church has done for centuries when vetting candidates for sainthood: Appoint a Devil's Advocate. Choose the most persuasive person you know, or a panel of the brightest people in the organization, and ask them to shoot holes in your latest project. Insist that they research the weaknesses of the project with the same fervor they would bring to advocating it. If they succeed in demolishing your idea, reward them. People know that whistle-blowers tend to lose their jobs, and often never work again. It will take years of organizations embracing their whistle-blowers before the average person overcomes his or her understandable reluctance to speak out. Not until candor is truly reflexive will organizations be truly transparent.

Another approach is to hold so-called qualming sessions whenever an important decision is about to be made. Invite everyone who is party to the decision to some pleasant site away from the office and insist that they try to imagine every possible way the plan could fail and why. Once again, it must be made clear that no idea is unacceptable and that no one will be punished for speaking out. The rules should be those of brainstorming sessions—the more ideas, the better. There are no bad ideas, at least in the early rounds of conversation. Nobody's head will roll for saying something an executive doesn't want to hear. It won't solve all your organization's problems, but it will be a promising and potentially powerful start.

At the least, employees may feel empowered to speak up the next time they see a flaw in an idea that is about to be put into action. If such a culture of candor had been in place when decisions were being made at Enron, it might still be a name that would evoke pride.

25

The Antileadership Vaccine

John W. Gardner

It is generally believed that we need enlightened and responsible leaders—at every level and in every phase of our national life. Everyone says so. But the nature of leadership in our society is very imperfectly understood, and many of the public statements about it are utter nonsense.

This is unfortunate because there are serious issues of leadership facing this society, and we had better understand them.

THE DISPERSION OF POWER

The most fundamental thing to be said about leadership in the United States is also the most obvious. We have gone as far as any known society in creating a leadership system that is not based on caste or class, nor even on wealth. There is not yet equal access to leadership (witness the remaining barriers facing women and Negroes), but we have come a long, long way from the family- or class-based leadership group. Even with its present defects, ours is a relatively open system.

The next important thing to be said is that leadership is dispersed among a great many groups in our society. The president, of course, has a unique, and uniquely important, leadership role, but beneath him, fragmentation is the rule. This idea is directly at odds with the notion that the society is run by

President's essay reprinted from the 1965 *Carnegie Corporation of New York Annual Report*.

a coherent power group—the Power Elite, as C. Wright Mills called it, or the Establishment, as later writers have named it. It is hard not to believe that such a group exists. Foreigners find it particularly difficult to believe in the reality of the fluid, scattered, shifting leadership that is visible to the naked eye. The real leadership, they imagine, must be behind the scenes. But at a national level this simply isn't so.

In many local communities and even in some states there is a coherent power group, sometimes behind the scenes, sometimes out in the open. In communities where such an "establishment," that is, a coherent ruling group, exists, the leading citizen can be thought of as having power in a generalized sense: He can bring about a change in zoning ordinances, influence the location of a new factory, and determine whether the local museum will buy contemporary paintings. But in the dispersed and fragmented power system that prevails in the nation as a whole one cannot say "So-and-so is powerful," without further elaboration. Those who know how our system works always want to know, "Powerful in what way? Powerful to accomplish what?" We have leaders in business and leaders in government, military leaders and educational leaders, leaders in labor and in agriculture, leaders in science, in the world of art, and in many other special fields. As a rule, leaders in any one of these fields do not recognize the authority of leaders from a neighboring field. Often they don't even know one another, nor do they particularly want to. Mutual suspicion is just about as common as mutual respect—and a lot more common than mutual cooperation in manipulating society's levers.

Most of the significant issues in our society are settled by a balancing of forces. A lot of people and groups are involved and the most powerful do not always win. Sometimes a coalition of the less powerful wins. Sometimes an individual of very limited power gets himself into the position of casting the deciding ballot.

Not only are there apt to be many groups involved in any critical issue, but their relative strength varies with each issue that comes up. A group that is powerful today may not be powerful next year. A group that can cast a decisive vote on question A may not even be listened to when question B comes up.

THE NATURE OF LEADERSHIP

People who have never exercised power have all kinds of curious ideas about it. The popular notion of top leadership is a fantasy of capricious power: The top man presses a button and something remarkable happens; he gives an order as the whim strikes him, and it is obeyed.

Actually, the capricious use of power is relatively rare except in some large dictatorships and some small family firms. Most leaders are hedged around by constraints—tradition, constitutional limitations, the realities of the external situation, rights and privileges of followers, the requirements of teamwork, and most of all the inexorable demands of large-scale organizations, which do not operate on capriciousness. In short, most power is wielded circumspectly.

There are many different ways of leading, many kinds of leaders. Consider, for example, the marked contrasts between the politician and the intellectual leader, the large-scale manager and the spiritual leader. One sees solemn descriptions of the qualities needed for leadership without any reference at all to the fact that the necessary attributes depend on the kind of leadership under discussion. Even in a single field there may be different kinds of leadership with different required attributes. Think of the difference between the military hero and the military manager.

If social action is to occur, certain functions must be performed. The problems facing the group or organization must be clarified, and ideas necessary to their solution formulated. Objectives must be defined. There must be widespread awareness of those objectives, and the will to achieve them. Often those on whom action depends must develop new attitudes and habits. Social machinery must be set in motion. The consequences of social effort must be evaluated and criticized, and new goals set.

A particular leader may contribute at only one point to this process. He may be gifted in analysis of the problem, but limited in his capacity to communicate. He may be superb in communicating, but incapable of managing. He may, in short, be an outstanding leader without being good at every aspect of leadership.

If anything significant is to be accomplished, leaders must understand the social institutions and processes through which action is carried out. And in a society as complex as ours, that is no mean achievement. A leader, whether corporation president, university dean, or labor official, knows his organization, understands what makes it move, comprehends its limitations. Every social system or institution has a logic and dynamic of its own that cannot be ignored.

We have all seen men with lots of bright ideas but no patience with the machinery by which ideas are translated into action. As a rule, the machinery defeats them. It is a pity, because the professional and academic man can play a useful role in practical affairs. But too often he is a dilettante. He dips in here or there; he gives bits of advice on a dozen fronts; he never gets his hands dirty working with one piece of the social machinery until he knows it well. He will not take the time to understand the social institutions and processes by which change is accomplished.

Although our decentralized system of leadership has served us well, we must not be so complacent as to imagine that it has no weaknesses, that it faces no new challenges, or that we have nothing to learn. There are grave questions to be answered concerning the leadership of our society. Are we living up to standards of leadership that we have achieved in our own past? Do the conditions of modern life introduce new complications into the task of leadership? Are we failing to prepare leaders for tomorrow?

Here are some of our salient difficulties.

FAILURE TO COPE WITH THE BIG QUESTIONS

Nothing should be allowed to impair the effectiveness and independence of our specialized leadership groups. But such fragmented leadership does create certain problems. One of them is that it isn't anybody's business to think about the big questions that cut across specialties—the largest questions facing our society. Where are we headed? Where do we want to head? What are the major trends determining our future? Should we do anything about them? Our fragmented leadership fails to deal effectively with these transcendent questions.

Very few of our most prominent people take a really large view of the leadership assignment. Most of them are simply tending the machinery of that part of society to which they belong. The machinery may be a great corporation or a great government agency or a great law practice or a great university. These people may tend it very well indeed, but they are not pursuing a vision of what the total society needs. They have not developed a strategy as to how it can be achieved, and they are not moving to accomplish it.

One does not blame them, of course. They do not see themselves as leaders of the society at large, and they have plenty to do handling their own specialized role.

Yet it is doubtful that we can any longer afford such widespread inattention to the largest questions facing us. We achieved greatness in an era when changes came more slowly than now. The problems facing the society took shape at a stately pace. We could afford to be slow in recognizing them, slow in coping with them. Today, problems of enormous import hit us swiftly. Great social changes emerge with frightening speed. We can no longer afford to respond in a leisurely fashion.

Our inability to cope with the largest questions tends to weaken the private sector. Any question that cannot be dealt with by one of the special leadership groups—that is, any question that cuts across special fields—tends to end up being dealt with by government. Most Americans value the role played by nongovernmental leadership in this country and would wish it to continue. In my judgment it will not continue under the present conditions.

The cure is not to work against the fragmentation of leadership, which is a vital element in our pluralism, but to create better channels of communication among significant leadership groups, especially in connection with the great issues that transcend any particular group.

FAILURE OF CONFIDENCE

Another of the maladies of leadership today is a failure of confidence. Anyone who accomplishes anything of significance has more confidence than the facts would justify. It is something that outstanding executives have in common with gifted military commanders, brilliant political leaders, and great artists. It is true of societies as well as of individuals. Every great civilization has been characterized by confidence in itself.

Lacking such confidence, too many leaders add ingenious new twists to the modern art that I call "How to reach a decision without really deciding." They require that the question be put through a series of clearances within the organization and let the clearance process settle it. Or take a public opinion poll and let the poll settle it. Or devise elaborate statistical systems, cost-accounting systems, information-processing systems, hoping that out of them will come unassailable support for one course of action rather than another.

This is not to say that leadership cannot profit enormously from good information. If the modern leader doesn't know the facts he is in grave trouble, but rarely do the facts provide unqualified guidance. After the facts are in, the leader must in some measure emulate the little girl who told the teacher she was going to draw a picture of God. The teacher said, "But, Mary, no one knows what God looks like," and Mary said, "They will when I get through."

The confidence required of leaders poses a delicate problem for a free society. We don't want to be led by Men of Destiny who think they know all the answers. Neither do we wish to be led by Nervous Nellies. It is a matter of balance. We are no longer in much danger, in this society, from Men of Destiny. But we are in danger of falling under the leadership of men who lack the confidence to lead. And we are in danger of destroying the effectiveness of those who have a natural gift for leadership.

Of all our deficiencies with respect to leadership, one of the gravest is that we are not doing what we should to encourage potential leaders. In the late eighteenth century we produced out of a small population a truly extraordinary group of leaders: Washington, Adams, Jefferson, Franklin, Madison, Monroe, and others. Why is it so difficult today, out of a vastly greater population, to produce men of that caliber? It is a question that most reflective people ask themselves sooner or later. There is no reason to doubt that the human material is still there, but there is excellent reason to believe that we are failing to develop it—or that we are diverting it into nonleadership activities.

THE ANTILEADERSHIP VACCINE

Indeed, it is my belief that we are immunizing a high proportion of our most gifted young people against any tendencies to leadership. It will be worth our time to examine how the antileadership vaccine is administered.

The process is initiated by the society itself. The conditions of life in a modern, complex society are not conducive to the emergence of leaders. The young person today is acutely aware of the fact that he is an anonymous member of a mass society, an individual lost among millions of others. The processes by which leadership is exercised are not visible to him, and he is bound to believe that they are exceedingly intricate. Very little in his experience encourages him to think that he might someday exercise a role of leadership.

This unfocused discouragement is of little consequence compared with the expert dissuasion the young person will encounter if he is sufficiently bright to attend a college or university. In those institutions today, the best students are carefully schooled to avoid leadership responsibilities.

Most of our intellectually gifted young people go from college directly into graduate school or into one of the older and more prestigious professional schools. There they are introduced to—or, more correctly, powerfully indoctrinated in—a set of attitudes appropriate to scholars, scientists, and professional men. This is all to the good. The students learn to identify themselves strongly with their calling and its ideals. They acquire a conception of what a good scholar, scientist, or professional man is like.

As things stand now, however, that conception leaves little room for leadership in the normal sense; the only kind of leadership encouraged is that which follows from the performing of purely professional tasks in a superior manner. Entry into what most of us would regard as the leadership roles in the society at large is discouraged.

In the early stages of a career, there is a good reason for this: Becoming a first-class scholar, scientist, or professional requires single-minded dedication. Unfortunately, by the time the individual is sufficiently far along in his career to afford a broadening of interests, he often finds himself irrevocably set in a narrow mold.

The antileadership vaccine has other more subtle and powerful ingredients. The image of the corporation president, politician, or college president that is current among most intellectuals and professionals today has some decidedly unattractive features. It is said that such men compromise their convictions almost daily, if not hourly. It is said that they have tasted the corrupting experience of power. They must be status seekers, the argument goes, or they would not be where they are.

Needless to say, the student picks up such attitudes. It is not that professors propound these views and students learn them. Rather, they are in the air and students absorb them. The resulting unfavorable image contrasts dramatically with the image these young people are given of the professional who is almost by definition dedicated to his field, pure in his motives, and unencumbered by worldly ambition.

My own extensive acquaintance with scholars and professionals on the one hand and administrators and managers on the other does not confirm this contrast in character. In my experience, each category has its share of opportunists. Nevertheless, the negative attitudes persist.

As a result the academic world appears to be approaching a point at which everyone will want to educate the technical expert who advises the leader, or the intellectual who stands off and criticizes the leader, but no one will want to educate the leader himself.

ARE LEADERS NECESSARY?

For a good many academic and other professional people, negative attitudes toward leadership go deeper than skepticism concerning the leader's integrity. Many have real doubts, not always explicitly formulated, about the necessity for leadership.

The doubts are of two kinds. First, many scientific and professional people are accustomed to the kinds of problems that can be solved by expert technical advice or action. It is easy for them to imagine that any social enterprise could be managed in the same way. They envisage a world that does not need leaders, only experts. The notion is based, of course, upon a false conception of the leader's function. The supplying of technically correct solutions is the least of his responsibilities.

There is another kind of question that some academic or professional people raise concerning leadership: Is the very notion of leadership somehow at odds with the ideals of a free society? Is it a throwback to earlier notions of social organization?

These are not foolish questions. We have in fact outgrown or rejected several varieties of leadership that have loomed large in the history of mankind. We do not want autocratic leaders who treat us like inferior beings. We do not want leaders, no matter how wise or kind, who treat us like children.

But at the same time that we were rejecting those forms of leadership we were evolving forms more suitable to our values. As a result our best leaders today are not out of place in a free society—on the contrary, they strengthen our free society.

We can have the kinds of leaders we want, but we cannot choose to do without them. It is in the nature of social organization that we must have them at all levels of our national life, in and out of government—in business, labor, politics, education, science, the arts, and every other field. Since we must have them, it helps considerably if they are gifted in the performance of their appointed task. The sad truth is that a great many of our organizations are badly managed or badly led. And because of that, people within those organizations are frustrated when they need not be frustrated. They are not helped when they could be helped. They are not given the opportunities to fulfill themselves that are clearly possible.

In the minds of some, leadership is associated with goals that are distasteful—power, profit, efficiency, and the like. But leadership, properly conceived, also serves the individual human goals that our society values so highly, and we shall not achieve those goals without it.

Leaders worthy of the name, whether they are university presidents or senators, corporation executives or newspaper editors, school superintendents or governors, contribute to the continuing definition and articulation of the most cherished values of our society. They offer, in short, moral leadership. So much of our energy has been devoted to tending the machinery of our complex society that we have neglected this element in leadership. I am using the word *moral* to refer to the shared values that must undergird any functioning society. The thing that makes a number of individuals a society rather than a population or a crowd is the presence of shared attitudes, habits, and values, a shared conception of the enterprise of which they are all a part, shared views of why it is worthwhile for the enterprise to continue and to flourish. Leaders can help in bringing that about. In fact, it is required that they do so. When leaders lose their credibility or their moral authority, then the society begins to disintegrate.

Leaders have a significant role in creating the state of mind that is the society. They can serve as symbols of the moral unity of the society. They can express the values that hold the society together. Most important, they can conceive and articulate goals that lift people out of their petty preoccupations, carry them above the conflicts that tear a society apart, and unite them in the pursuit of objectives worthy of their best efforts.

About the Editors and Contributors

Editors

William E. Rosenbach is the Evans Professor of Eisenhower Leadership Studies and professor of management, emeritus at Gettysburg College. Formerly professor and head of the Department of Behavioral Sciences and Leadership at the U.S. Air Force Academy, he is the author or coauthor of numerous articles, papers, and books on leadership topics. He is especially interested in the elements of effective followership, and he is an active consultant to private and public organizations in North America, the Middle East, Europe, New Zealand, and Australia on executive leadership development. He is a founding partner of the Gettysburg Leadership Experiences, an innovative executive leadership development program in historic Gettysburg, Pennsylvania. He may be reached at rosenbach@leadingandfollowing.com.

Robert L. Taylor is professor of management and dean emeritus of the College of Business at the University of Louisville. Formerly professor and acting head of the Department of Management at the U.S. Air Force Academy and the Carl N. Jacobs Professor of Business at the University of Wisconsin at Stevens Point, he has been a student of leadership for nearly forty years. In 1999–2000, Dr. Taylor served as board chair of AACSB: The International Association for Management Education. He has taught in MBA programs in Asia, Europe, and Latin America. His interests in teaching and scholarship have resulted in undergraduate and graduate seminars, presentations, and consultancies with a primary focus on the elements of effective leadership. Serving on the board of several companies and organizations, Dr. Taylor has enjoyed being a student and practitioner of leadership in countries throughout the world. He may be reached at rltaylo1@gmail.com.

Mark A. Youndt is an associate professor of management and strategy at Skidmore College. Formerly a professor at the University of Connecticut and the University of Vermont, he has published articles on a wide range of strategy and leadership issues in leading journals such as *Academy of Management Journal, Strategic Management Journal,* and *Journal of Management* and is currently an editorial board member at *Journal of Management Studies.* He is especially interested in how organizational leaders develop and manage their organizations' human and intellectual capital in today's knowledge-intensive environments. In addition to his teaching and research activities, Dr. Youndt consults and leads executive education programs focused on strategy and leadership development in both for-profit and not-for-profit organizations. He may be reached at myoundt@skidmore.edu.

Contributors

Robert J. Allio is a veteran strategic management consultant who has held senior corporate and academic leadership positions; he has authored a number of books on strategy and leadership. His academic credentials include positions as Dean of the School of Management at Rensselaer and professor of management at Babson College. He has designed leadership education programs for numerous organizations, including the Conference Board, *Business Week*, the American Management Association, and the Young Presidents' Organization. Allio was the founding editor of *Planning Review* (now *Strategy & Leadership*) and was president of the North American Society of Corporate Planning.

Vinita Bali is the CEO and managing director of Britannia Industries Limited, a leading food company in India. Prior to this, she held marketing and general management roles in preeminent multinationals such as the Coca-Cola Company and Cadbury Schweppes PLC and has lived and worked in six countries and five continents. She has won several awards and accolades for her marketing acumen and business leadership: She was named "Businesswoman of the Year—2009" by the *Economic Times* and was ranked twenty-first among the world's top fifty businesswomen by the *Financial Times*.

Eoin Banahan is associate professor of human resources management at the Audencia School of Management, France Managing Director, RoundRose Associates Ltd., Aylesford, Kent.

Gerhold K. Becker is regular visiting professor in the Graduate School of Religion and Philosophy, Assumption University of Thailand, Bangkok. He is the founding director of the Center for Applied Ethics and a retired Chair, as well as professor of philosophy and religion at Hong Kong Baptist University.

Warren Bennis is an American scholar, organizational consultant, and author who is widely regarded as the pioneer of the contemporary field of leadership. Bennis is university professor and distinguished professor of business administration and founding chairman of the Leadership Institute at USC. In 2007, *BusinessWeek* called him one of ten business school professors who have had the greatest influence on business thinking. The *Financial Times* recently named his classic book *Leaders* one of the top fifty books of all time.

Linda L. Carli is an associate professor of psychology at Wellesley College; her current research focus is on gender discrimination and other challenges faced by professional women. She has conducted extensive research on the effects of gender on women's leadership, group interaction, communication, and influence, as well as reactions to adversity, resulting in more than seventy-five scholarly articles, chapters, and presentations. She holds a PhD in social psychology from the University of Massachusetts at Amherst.

Pierre Casse is professor of leadership at the Moscow School of Management. Professor Casse is the academic dean emeritus of the Berlin School of Creative Leadership. Formerly a senior World Bank staff development officer, he brings a wealth of knowledge through his work on understanding cultural differences and leadership in a turnaround world. In addition to his role as academic dean, he holds the Suez Chair of Leadership at the Solvay Business School and is adjunct professor for leadership at the Kellogg School of Management and professor and associate dean for international affairs at the IAE (Institut d'Administration des Entreprises).

Ira Chaleff is the author and coauthor of two books on followership, including *The Courageous Follower: Standing Up to and for Our Leaders,* 3rd edition, www.courageous follower.net. He is the founder of International Leadership Association Followership Learning Community (www.followership2.pbworks.com) and chairman of the Congressional Management Foundation, which has given him an inside perspective on power relationships between elected officials and their staffs, both in Washington and third world legislatures.

Dawn E. Chandler is an assistant professor of management at California Polytechnic State University, San Luis Obispo.

Mary Crossan is a professor of strategic management at the Richard Ivey School of Business. Prior to joining the school, Crossan worked for such organizations as Bell Canada, the RCMP, Finance Canada, and the Canadian Centre for Justice Statistics. She earned a BA, MBA, and PhD from the University of Western Ontario.

Richard L. Daft is the author of "The Executive and the Elephant: A Leader's Guide for Building Inner Excellence." As the Brownlee O. Currey, Jr. Professor of Management at Vanderbilt University's Owen Graduate School of Management, he teaches and coaches executives and MBA students on leadership and self-management. He has written thirteen books, including his best-selling textbooks on management and leadership, and is listed as one of the most highly cited professors in the fields of business and economics.

Alice H. Eagly is a professor of psychology and holds the James Padilla Chair of Arts and Sciences at Northwestern University; she is also a faculty fellow at Northwestern's Institute for Policy Research. Dr. Eagly is particularly known for her research on the psychology of gender and the psychology of attitudes. She has received the Distinguished Scientist Award from the Society of Experimental Social Psychology and the

Donald Campbell Award for Distinguished Contribution to Social Psychology from the Society for Social and Personality Psychology.

Lillian Eby is a professor of psychology at the University of Georgia.

Robin J. Ely is the Warren Alpert Professor of Business Administration at Harvard Business School.

Frances X. Frei is the UPS Foundation Professor of Service Management at Harvard Business School.

John W. Gardner served six presidents of the United States in various leadership capacities. He was secretary of Health, Education, and Welfare; founding chairman of Common Cause; cofounder of Independent Sector; and president of the Carnegie Corporation and the Carnegie Foundation for the Advancement of Teaching. The author of *On Leadership,* he served as Miriam and Peter Haas Centennial Professor at Stanford Business School.

Bill George is a professor of management practice at Harvard Business School, where he has taught leadership since 2004. He is the former chairman and chief executive officer of Medtronic. He joined Medtronic in 1989 as president and chief operating officer, was chief executive officer from 1991–2001, and chairman of the board from 1996 to 2002. Earlier in his career, he was an executive with Honeywell and Litton Industries and served in the U.S. Department of Defense. He is also currently a trustee of Carnegie Endowment for International Peace, World Economic Forum USA, and the Guthrie Theater. He has served as chair of the board of Allina Health System, Abbott-Northwestern Hospital, United Way of the Greater Twin Cities, and Advamed.

Daniel Goleman is founder of Emotional Intelligence Services, an affiliate of the Hay Group in Boston. A psychologist who for many years reported on the brain and behavioral sciences for the *New York Times,* Dr. Goleman previously was a visiting faculty member at Harvard. He has received many journalistic awards for his writing, including two nominations for the Pulitzer Prize for his articles in the *Times* and a Career Achievement Award for Journalism from the American Psychological Association. In recognition of his efforts to communicate the behavioral sciences to the public, he was elected a Fellow of the American Association for the Advancement of Science. Dr. Goleman attended Amherst College, where he was an Alfred P. Sloan Scholar and graduated magna cum laude. His graduate education was at Harvard, where he was a Ford Fellow and he received his MA and PhD in clinical psychology and personality development.

Barbara Kellerman is research director at the Center for Public Research and lecturer in public policy at Harvard University's John F. Kennedy School of Government.

James M. Kouzes is the Dean's Executive Professor of Leadership at the Leavey School of Business Administration, Santa Clara University. He is the 2010 recipient of the Thought Leadership Award from the Instructional Systems Association and was named one of *HR Magazine's* 2010 Most Influential International Thinkers.

Manuel London is professor of management and director of the Undergraduate College of Leadership and Service and the Center for Human Resource Management at the State University of New York at Stony Brook. He received his PhD in organizational psychology from the Ohio State University. His areas of research are leadership and work group development, 360-degree feedback, and advocacy processes.

Michael Maccoby, author of *The Gamesman and the Leader,* is a consultant on issues of leadership, strategy, and organization to business, government, and unions. He is president of the Maccoby Group in Washington, DC, where he lives.

Daina Mazutis is at the Richard Ivey School of Business, and her research investigates how business leaders manage the tension between their personal values and the behavior expected of them under the "rational actor model" of the firm, which places the individual pursuit of maximizing profits above all other strategic goals. She is particularly interested in business executives who have been able to steer their firms in the simultaneous pursuit of both financial and social objectives. She is fluently trilingual and proud to call Latvian her mother tongue.

Bill McCabe is a partner with the McLane Group.

Andrew McLean is an independent consultant, an adjunct faculty member at Bentley College, and a former research assistant at Harvard Business School.

Stacy E. McManus is a principal at Park Spencer Group, an executive and leadership development consultancy in Cambridge, Massachusetts.

Anne Morriss is the managing director of the Concire Leadership Institute, a consulting firm that helps leaders surface and remove performance barriers.

David Parmenter is recognized for the development of winning KPIs, replacing the annual planning process with quarterly rolling planning, management and leadership practices that improve organizational performance, and corporate accounting best practice. He has delivered workshops to thousands of attendees in many cities around the world.

Craig L. Pearce is associate professor of management at the Peter F. Drucker and Masatoshi Ito Graduate School of Management in Claremont, California, and is a principal of CLP Associates LLC, a management consulting firm.

Thane S. Pittman is a social psychologist who is professor of psychology and recent chair of the Department of Psychology at Colby College; a visiting professor of law at the Brooklyn Law School, where he teaches negotiation; and an associate in the Gettysburg Leadership Experience.

Barry Z. Posner is professor of leadership at Santa Clara University, where he served as dean of the Leavey School of Business for twelve years. He is the recipient of the 2011 Outstanding Scholar Award from the *Journal of Management Inquiry.* Together with James Kouzes, they are the best-selling authors of a variety of books on leadership.

Earl H. Potter III is president of St. Cloud State University, former provost of Southern Oregon University, and former dean of the College of Business Administration at Eastern Michigan University. He has a doctorate in organizational psychology from the University of Washington and over thirty years of experience in research and consulting on issues of leadership, team effectiveness, and organizational change. As a leader, he has led polar diving explorations, sailed a square-rigged ship with a crew of two hundred as executive officer, and chaired countless faculty meetings.

Deborah L. Rhode is Ernest W. McFarland Professor of Law and director of the Stanford Center on Ethics at Stanford University.

Marshall Sashkin is professor emeritus of human resource development of the Graduate School of Education and Human Development at the George Washington University. More than fifty of his research papers on leadership, participation, and organizational change have been published in academic journals, and he is the author or coauthor of more than a dozen books and monographs.

Lois J. Zachary is president of Leadership Development Services, LLC, a consulting firm in Phoenix, Arizona. She coaches leaders and their organizations in designing, implementing, and evaluating learner-centered mentoring programs.

Lightning Source UK Ltd.
Milton Keynes UK
UKHW040204170123
415471UK00001B/2